730

D0806127

An admirable statement of the aims of the Library of Philosophy was provided by the first editor, the late Professor J. H. Muirhead, in his description of the original programme printed in Erdmann's *History of Philosophy* under the date 1890. This was slightly modified in subsequent volumes to take the form of the following statement:

'The Muirhead Library of Philosophy was designed as a contribution to the History of Modern Philosophy under the heads: first of Different Schools of Thought—Sensationalist, Realist, Idealist, Intuitivist; secondly of different Subjects—Psychology, Ethics, Political Philosophy, Theology. While much had been done in England in tracing the course of evolution in nature, history, economics, morals and religion, little had been done in tracing the development of thought on these subjects. Yet "the evolution of opinion is part of the whole evolution".

'By the co-operation of different writers in carrying out this plan it was hoped that a thoroughness and completeness of treatment, otherwise unattainable, might be secured. It was believed also that from writers mainly British and American fuller consideration of English Philosophy than it had hitherto received might be looked for. In the earlier series of books containing, among others, Bosanquet's *History of Aesthetic*, Pfleiderer's *Rational Theology since Kant*, Albee's *History of English Utilitarianism*, Bonar's *Philosophy and Political Economy*, Brett's *History of Psychology*, Ritchie's *Natural Rights*, these objects were to a large extent effected.

'In the meantime original work of a high order was being produced both in England and America by such writers as Bradley, Stout, Bertrand Russell, Baldwin, Urban, Montague, and others, and a new interest in foreign works, German, French and Italian, which had either become classical or were attracting public attention, had developed. The scope of the Library thus became extended into something more international, and it is entering on the fifth decade of its existence in the hope that it may contribute to that mutual understanding between countries which is so pressing a need of the present time.'

The need which Professor Muirhead stressed is no less pressing today, and few will deny that philosophy has much to do with enabling us to meet it, although no one, least of all Muirhead himself, would regard that as the sole, or even the main, object of philosophy. As Professor Muirhead continues to lend the distinction of his name to the Library of Philosophy it seemed not inappropriate to allow him to recall us to these aims in his own words. The emphasis on the history of thought also seemed to me very timely; and the number of important works promised for the Library in the very near future augur well for the continued fulfilment, in this and other ways, of the expectations of the original editor.

H. D. LEWIS

MUIRHEAD LIBRARY OF PHILOSOPHY

General Editor: H. D. Lewis

Professor of History and Philosophy of Religion in the University of London

Action by SIR MALCOLM KNOX
The Analysis of Mind BERTRAND RUSSELL 8th impression
Clarity is Not Enough by H. D. LEWIS
Coleridge as Philosopher by J. H. MUIRHEAD 3rd impression
The Commonplace Book of G. E. Moore edited by C. LEWY
Contemporary American Philosophy edited by G. P. ADAMS and W. P. MONTAGUE 2nd impression
Contemporary British Philosophy First and second series edited by J. H. MUIRHEAD 2nd impression
Contemporary British Philosophy third series edited by H. D. LEWIS 2nd impression
Contemporary Indian Philosophy edited by RADHAKRISHNAN and J. H. MUIRHEAD 2nd edition
The Discipline of the Cave by J. N. FINDLAY
Doctrine and Argument in Indian Philosophy by NINIAN SMART
Essays in Analysis by ALICE AMBROSE
Ethics by NICOLAI HARTMANN translated by STANTON COIT 3 vols
The Foundations of Metaphysics in Science by ERROL E. HARRIS
Freedom and History by H. D. LEWIS
The Good Will: A Study in the Coherence Theory of Goodness by H. J. PATON
Hegel: A Re-Examination by J. N. FINDLAY
Hegel's Science of Logic translated by W. H. JOHNSTON and L. G. STRUTHERS 2 vols 3rd impression
History of Æsthetic by B. BOSANQUET 2nd edition 5th impression
History of English Utilitarianism by E. ALBEE 2nd impression
History of Psychology by G. S. BRETT edited by R. S. PETERS abridged one-volume edition 2nd edition
Human Knowledge by BERTRAND RUSSELL 4th impression
A Hundred Years of British Philosophy by RUDOLF METZ translated by J. H. HARVEY, T. E. JESSOP, HENRY STURT 2nd impression
Ideas: A General Introduction to Pure Phenomenology by EDMUND HUSSERL translated by W. R. BOYCE GIBSON 3rd impression
Imagination by E. J. FURLONG
Indian Philosophy by RADHAKRISHNAN 2 vols revised 2nd edition

Muirhead Library of Philosophy

EDITED BY H. D. LEWIS

NON-LINGUISTIC PHILOSOPHY

NON-LINGUISTIC PHILOSOPHY

BY

A. C. EWING

LITT.D., F.B.A.
Honorary Fellow of
Jesus College, Cambridge

LONDON · GEORGE ALLEN & UNWIN LTD
NEW YORK · HUMANITIES PRESS

PRINTED IN GREAT BRITAIN
in 11 on 12 Imprint
BY UNWIN BROTHERS LTD
WOKING AND LONDON

CONTENTS

INTRODUCTION

It is always difficult to select a quite suitable title for a book consisting of a collection of articles written at very different times on very different subjects, but the one I have chosen does, I think, express the thread of unity which runs through them. They are all either criticisms of various aspects of the thought of the leading school of philosophy in Britain today (or at least of prominent members of it) or attempts at doing the sort of philosophy which that school forbids, and the adjective now most commonly applied to distinguish that school is 'linguistic'. What I have just said applies even to the article on the syllogism since it tries to work out a logic of the syllogism on intensional and not, as is now the almost universal practice, on extensional lines, a practice which is very characteristic of the school to which I have referred with its tendency to refuse to admit connections of content except those of mere inclusion in reasoning. It is perhaps least true of the article on the Correspondence Theory of Truth, but this article is relevant to the characteristic approach of the school to ethics and to the 'semantic' theory of truth.

The articles are printed in their chronological order except that I thought it best to put together the three articles on philosophy of religion, which however all fall in the later part of the period. Two articles of mine which, I venture to think, expose fundamental mistakes in the school I criticise have not been included by me because they had already been published in another recent book of the Muirhead Library, *Clarity is not Enough*.[1] The titles of these articles are *The Linguistic Theory of A Priori Propositions* and *Professor Ryle's Attack on Dualism*. They are needed to give full point to my attack on the most influential (or at any rate best known, school of philosophy today.

Only one of the articles has been amended except by way of correcting minor verbal mistakes, namely art V, and even here the amendments relate not to substance but rather to mode of expression. Though the articles cover a period of some thirty years I find that, while my philosophical views have changed in some respects, these changes little affect the views I have put forward in these articles except in two respects, which I shall mention, that would however leave my main arguments intact. (1) In art. 1 I use the argument that the verification principle is on its own showing

[1] Edited H. D. Lewis, 1963.

meaningless since it cannot be verified by sense-experience.[1] The reply has been made that the verification principle is not itself a factual statement and the conditions as to meaningfulness laid down by it were intended to apply only to factual statements. I accept this reply but almost all the argument of the article still stands, for even non-factual statements cannot be asserted without justification and the verification principle excludes any possibility of its own justification. It cannot even be justified by its results in solving philosophical problems, for we can never tell whether a solution of a philosophical problem (or a scientific problem for that matter) is right or wrong simply by sense-experience. The verification principle has not now the prestige it had at the time I wrote the article (1937), and it has for long been put forward even by its supporters rather as a methodological assumption than as a dogmatic statement; but I think the article is still worth reprinting because the principle still lingers on as an implicit assumption in much that is said about philosophy, e.g. in the attitude of those who exclude the very possibility of what are put forward as religious statements being objectively true because they cannot be verified empirically and in the paradigm argument, which I attack in art. IX, and which seems to me to owe its plausibility to the assumption that, since philosophers are not disputing about what can be settled empirically, they must be disputing about language.[2] Those who say they are using the verification principle only as a methodological assumption must remember that, unless a proposition can be put forward not merely as an assumption but as true, one is not entitled to infer anything from it.

Secondly, I while still emphasizing the importance of the coherence test am now inclined to regard coherence or even ability to make a coherent system of our experience as not only not the sole criterion of truth but not an ultimate criterion at all. That is, I now think that it can only be used as a criterion because there are grounds other than itself for thinking that with a given subject-matter a set of propositions are more likely to be true if they form a relatively coherent system than if they do not. But I do not think that this change of view obliges me to contradict anything I actually said in art. II, the only one which deals with the coherence criterion, though the emphasis might be somewhat different if I were writing it again.

My thanks are due to the editors of *Mind, Philosophy, Analysis,*

[1] Below at I p. 17.　　　　[2] At IX p. 177.

Philosophy and Phenomenological Research, the *Revue Internationale de Philosophie, The Personalist,* and *Religious Studies,* and the British Academy and Aristotelian Society for permitting me to have reprinted here articles originally published by them.

A. C. EWING
Jesus College
Cambridge

I

MEANINGLESSNESS

In this article I intend to examine the conditions under which a sentence may be said to be meaningless. I have been stimulated to do so by a belief that present-day thinkers are often far too ready to dismiss a philosophical statement as meaningless, and particularly by my opposition to the theory that the meaning of all statements is to be analysed solely in terms of verification by sense-experience. (Note that only sentences can be properly said to have meaning, not propositions. A proposition is what certain sorts of sentences mean and cannot again itself have meaning except in a quite different sense of the word, such as that in which the 'meaning' of something is equivalent to its implications. A meaningful sentence[1] is a sentence which expresses a proposition, a meaningless sentence is a sentence which expresses no proposition. 'Statement', on the other hand, is used both to stand for a proposition and for a sentence expressing a proposition. I shall use it in the latter sense. I am not hereby intending to imply that propositions are separate subsistent entities; this is not a theory which I hold, but I have no time to discuss the question here.) In this article I shall use the term *positivist* for short to mean simply 'upholder of any of the verification theories which I shall consider'. I shall use 'meaning' in the same sense in which it would be used, say, in the *Strand Magazine*.[2]

I shall first take the extremer form of the theory, according to which a statement is said to be verifiable, and therefore to have meaning, if and only if its truth could be conclusively established by sense-experience. 'Sense-experience' is used to include (*a*) sense-perception, (*b*) introspection of images and emotions. Positivists would not usually admit that the occurrence of 'mental acts' could be verified by experience, and would presumably have either to regard these as logical constructions out of sense-data and images, or deny their existence altogether. Still less would the term cover apprehension of 'non-natural' properties or relations. Now I should have thought the first duty of any advocate of a

---

[1] Of this kind   [2] This sentence is taken from *Wisdom*.

verification theory of meaning would be to inquire how his theory itself was to be verified, and I propose to be a good positivist in this one case at least and put the question myself. How could we verify the statement that all meaningful statements are verifiable?

The first difficulty is that it is a universal proposition and therefore can never be conclusively established merely by experience; but we shall relax the condition, as probably most positivists themselves would, so far as to allow of progressive and incomplete verification, and count the verification theory of meaning as verified for all practical purposes if an adequate number of samples of all the different kinds of meaningful statements we can think of are found on examination to be verifiable and we are unable to think of any which are not verifiable. I doubt the consistency of this but I will be as charitable as possible and let it pass. How could the theory then be verified in this sense? It would no doubt be verified if we could take examples of all the different kinds of statements which have ever been made, find by direct inspection what was meant by them, and then discover that they were all verifiable. But I do not think the positivist would or could admit that we can always detect the meanings of statements by direct inspection. If we always can, why all the difficulties about analysis? And it is not by any means sufficient for the purpose that we should *sometimes* be able to do so, for what has to be verified is a proposition about all, not about some, meaningful statements. I doubt in fact whether the positivist would even admit that meaning is the sort of thing that could ever be detected by direct inspection. Further, if we relied on the meaning that statements seem to have when we try to inspect their meaning directly, I do not see how we could ever become positivists. It is surely not by direct inspection of the propositions in question that a positivist learns that propositions about other people's toothache are really propositions about his own sense-data, or that so-called propositions about the past are merely rules for the prediction of those experiences in the future which would verify them. Surely they only come to such conclusions because they first assume the general principle that all meaningful statements are verifiable and then deduce that, since statements about other people can be verifiable only if they are analysed as statements about one's own sense-data, they must be thus analysed. No doubt they can find examples of meaningful statements which are directly verifiable. Perhaps even all meaningful statements on certain kinds of topics are thus verifiable, *e.g.* all singular propositions about one's present sense-data; but to argue that, because this is true of all of one kind of propositions, it is true of other kinds is as dangerous as to argue that because cats always live on the land, and cats and whales are both mammals, whales must also live on the land. Finally, I do not see how the positivists could establish the truth of their view even in a single case merely by sense-experience. For how can we ever know by sense-experience that there is not a part of the meaning of a statement that we cannot verify? The fact that we do not have any sense-experience of such a part proves nothing, since the point at issue is whether there is something in what we mean beyond sense-experience; and how can we know by sense-experience that there is not?

It therefore seems impossible that the verification theory could be verified in the way suggested, and I cannot conceive what other way there could be of verifying it. For according to the fundamental principles of those who hold the theory it could not be established by any sort of *a priori* argument, and therefore it must presumably be established, if at all, by the empirical examination of particular cases. Now, not merely is it the case that it has not in fact been verified in that way; we have just seen that it is logically impossible that it could be so verified. The statement that all meaningful statements are verifiable is therefore not itself verifiable. It follows that if it is true it is meaningless. But a sentence cannot possibly be both true and meaningless. Therefore the sentence in question cannot be true, but must be either meaningless or false. According to my view it is the latter.

Perhaps it will be said that, although the verification theory is nonsense, it is important and useful nonsense, while the kind of nonsense I talk is unimportant and useless nonsense. But if the statement that it is important and useful nonsense is to be accepted this statement in turn ought to be verified by sense-experience, and how that could possibly be done puzzles me. It might be held that it is useful because it helps to solve philosophical problems; but how can we tell by sense-experience whether a philosophical problem is solved or not? The mere fact that we do not feel an emotion of puzzlement does not prove that we have reached a solution. Otherwise unlettered peasants would have solved all philosophical problems far better than philosophers, and persistent neglect to think would be the golden method for attaining success in philosophy. Also the method prescribed might easily remove the emotion of puzzlement in some men but not in others, and be useful for some philosophical problems but misleading for others.

It might be suggested that the statement of the verification theory should be regarded as a tautology and therefore as meaningless only in the comparatively innocuous sense in which all correct *a priori* statements are meaningless according to the theory. But, if this line were taken, it would be necessary to show that some formal contradiction was committed by denying the theory; and this is not claimed. The only *a priori* propositions that the theory admits are analytic tautologies, if these indeed can be called propositions, but the statement of the theory itself is essentially synthetic. It gives new information, and information not capable of formal proof. The theory therefore cannot, if it is true, be known *a priori*. No *a priori* arguments for it are possible on its own showing since it is synthetic, and it therefore cannot be meaningful even in the modified sense in which a positivist might admit analytic *a priori* statements to be so. It can be meaningful only in the sense in which synthetic statements are supposed to be, i.e. in the sense of being verifiable by sense-experience, and this I claim to have shown it can never be. It is true that it might be deduced analytically from some definition of meaning, but the definition itself must, like all definitions, be synthetic. A proposition giving an analysis must be distinguished from an analytic proposition, or, to put the same thing in different language, a proposition true by definition is not the same as a definition. There can be no self-contradiction in denying a given analysis of the meaning of a term unless some definition is already presupposed, thus begging the question; for there certainly is no analytic logically necessary connection between a word and the analysis of its meaning, and this undoubtedly applies to the word, meaning, itself. That certain marks or noises express propositions and others do not is surely a synthetic proposition if any is. No doubt a positivist can decide to use 'meaning' in any way he chooses, but then he will not be giving an analysis of the ordinary sense of 'meaning', but inventing an arbitrary usage of his own. However this can hardly be what he is doing, for he certainly claims that those who use meaning in a sense in which unverifiable statements are meaningful are committing an error, attributing to certain statements a property they do not possess.

The positivist is thus debarred from giving *a priori* reasons for his theory because it is synthetic, and also from giving empirical reasons because it cannot be based on an empirical inspection of meaning. His only refuge is to make his theory a purely arbitrary convention which therefore requires no justification. But, if this is allowed, a philosopher may assert anything whatever he pleases. The positivist is excused from having to prove his theory, but only at the expense of admitting that there is no more ground for accepting it than there is for accepting any theory whatever. Even such an argument as that it is simpler than other accounts or more useful for establishing deductive systems would be an appeal to a criterion conformity with which certainly cannot be discovered by sense-experience. And it remains true that his theory could mean nothing on its own showing, being neither an *a priori* analytic proposition nor one verifiable by sense-experience.

Now if a theory means nothing I really cannot be expected to refute it. Perhaps it is a very good lyrical expression of the positivist's emotions, but while not wishing to show any lack of sympathy towards his emotions I cannot see that this of itself could make it a useful contribution to philosophy. I add the autobiographical detail that I have never had any emotion myself of which it seemed to me at all a suitable expression. Or perhaps it is a command to treat only those propositions as meaningful which are verifiable; but with all due respect to the positivists I do not see why I should obey their commands unless they can show me that I (or the world) will gain by my doing so.

Let us now turn to the milder form of the theory which was sponsored by Mr Ayer.[1] According to this a statement is meaningful if and only if it is logically possible that observations might be made which would be relevant to its truth or falsehood, i.e. make its truth more or less probable. (He does not use the word probable here, but since he thinks no conclusive verification of anything is possible this must be what he means.) Now this formulation of the theory does not give Mr Ayer nearly as much as he wants. For, with the possible exception of the ontological proof, which I do not wish to defend, it is doubtful whether any philosophers have ever asserted a proposition to the truth of which they did not think some experience or other was relevant. What I mean may be made clear by taking a few examples from among the most abstract of metaphysical arguments. The cosmological proof, for instance, starts with the premise that something or other exists,

---

[1] *Language, Truth and Logic*, p. 26. It must not be assumed that this expresses the present view of Mr Ayer, who, I gather, has become less positivistic.

this being regarded as given in experience; the argument for an Absolute Mind including all human minds professes to start from the incomplete and incoherent character of our experience, which is held therefore to point to a more complete experience, and to be supported by citing the empirical facts of co-operation and love; the realist view of physical objects claims to be based on the experience of perception either as in itself a proof of their existence (the direct theory of perception) or as a premise from which causal inferences can be made showing that they probably exist. No doubt in some of the cases I have mentioned the metaphysician may be wrong in thinking that experience renders his conclusion probable, but we can only decide whether this is so after we have examined and refuted his argument. Since he claims that experience is relevant we cannot dismiss his theory as meaningless without examination, as the positivist would like to do, merely on the ground that its probability cannot be affected by any experience. Most metaphysical arguments may be hopelessly wrong, but I do not see how we can tell whether they are except by examining them separately on their own merits, to see whether they can really be supported by experience. We cannot nonsuit all of them *en masse* by the positivist criterion without begging the whole question.

The statement that the world of sense-experience is altogether unreal, which is taken by Mr Ayer as a good example of a nonsensical utterance, is certainly a statement to the truth or falsity of which experience is relevant, and it should therefore by his criterion have a meaning. For it is contradicted by all our sense-experience and therefore ought to be rejected as false (not meaningless), unless the man who makes it is speaking in metaphors. And, even if he is speaking in metaphors and does not mean 'altogether unreal', but e.g. 'incoherent when taken by itself' or 'relatively unimportant', his statement certainly claims to be based on the alleged self-contradictory or otherwise defective character of our sense-experience, and therefore the specific empirical character of our sense-experience is certainly relevant to it. Again take the statement that the whole universe was created by a morally perfect God. This would be held by Mr Ayer to be meaningless, and would be generally admitted to be a metaphysical doctrine if anything is. Yet it is quite clear that empirical facts regarding the amount and distribution of suffering in the world will affect its probability. If we came to the conclusion that there was much more suffering in the world than we had thought and that there were hardly any empirical cases of suffering producing any good result, it would obviously make the truth of the belief in some degree less probable. Further the truth of the belief would increase the probability of some propositions about the future being true. For it would certainly at least increase the probability of the proposition that I shall survive bodily death being true. Now the latter is a proposition which clearly could be verified and presumably will in fact be verified, if it is true. For if it is true I shall verify it by having experiences after bodily death. The metaphysical proposition about God is therefore one which is relevant to experiential propositions and to which experiential propositions are relevant.

Incidentally the question of survival seems to create a first-class puzzle for the positivists. That I shall survive bodily death is a proposition capable of future verification, if it is true, through my having experiences after death, but the contradictory proposition that I shall not survive bodily death could never by any possible chance be verified because I cannot experience myself as having no experiences. It seems then the positivist ought to conclude that the proposition that I shall survive death is logically necessary because the only alternative is meaningless. But that such a proposition should be logically necessary is obviously inconsistent with his theories; it is clearly synthetic. Therefore I fear he will not be as grateful to me as he ought to be for having shown that his theory has proved that we can never die.

Mr Ayer has, therefore, not succeeded in giving a criterion which rules out metaphysics any more or less than the propositions he wishes to admit. Further in its second, as in its first, form it remains highly doubtful whether the verification theory can itself be verified. For we could only verify it by examining all the different kinds of meaningful statements and seeing whether sense-experience was relevant to their truth, i.e. whether they could be proved or refuted by sense-experience or rendered more or less probable. But once a positivist has admitted, as Mr Ayer has now done, that a statement may have meaning, even if it asserts something which cannot be directly experienced, provided only there could be experiences from which we might make legitimate inferences to the effect that its probability is increased or diminished, he is open to the objection that we cannot possibly learn from sense-experience alone whether an inference is legitimate or not. That B follows from A is not anything that can be sensed, and mere sense-experience cannot justify us even in thinking it probable that it will follow from A unless the sense-experience is accompanied by some principles of probable inference which are not themselves objects of the senses.

If I am right the verification theory is completely suicidal, because, if it succeeds, it shows itself to be meaningless, and therefore not true. But, even if you are not willing to go as far as this with me, you must remember that philosophers have no right to assert a theory without reasons, at least unless they seem to themselves to see quite clearly that it is self-evident; and this cannot be so in the present case, for the positivist would certainly reject self-evidence as a criterion of truth and therefore cannot use it in defence of its own doctrine. Further you must remember that, unless a theory is proved with complete certainty, part of its criterion lies in the consequences which can be deduced from it, and if these are very unplausible they will cast doubt on the theory itself. To refuse to reconsider a theory of yours because it leads to absurd consequences is, unless the theory has been proved with certainty, not to deserve praise for being logical but to deserve blame for being prejudiced.

Now so far I have discovered no positive reason at all for accepting the theory in either form. It is not, as we have seen, established by direct inspection of the meaning of statements. Certainly nobody could learn by direct inspection of the meaning of statements about other people that these really only express propositions about his own sense-data, or that statements purporting to be about the past are really only statements about possible future events which might verify them. These doctrines are not data empirically reached and then used to establish the theory, but conclusions from the theory, which is already held to be established. But if so, what reason can be given for the theory? Mr Ayer refers the reader for proof to the chapter where he deals with the *a priori*. There indeed he claims to show that we can never know synthetic propositions *a priori*. I do not agree with him in this and do not see that he has offered any real ground for his conclusion, but even if his argument here were right it would not have shown that the alleged synthetic *a priori* propositions were really only meaningless statements. The statements may be meaningful for anything he has proved to the contrary, even if false or ungrounded. And again he has not proved that there might not be meaningful statements which, while not *a priori*, were unverifiable. The statement that you are having

toothache, understood in the same way as the statement that I am
having toothache, is certainly not *a priori*. Yet Mr Ayer declares
it to be nonsense on the ground that it is unverifiable, without
having done anything at all, as far as I can see, to show that it
could not be both meaningful and yet unverifiable. I do not agree
with him that the statement in question is, according to his own
criterion, unverifiable, for the probability of its truth is increased
by observations which I certainly can make; but then it seems to
me, as I have said, that there are many genuinely metaphysical
propositions which would according to the *ipsissima verba* of his
definition be verifiable.

It is sometimes asserted that the verification theory ought to be
accepted because it is the only theory which provides a definition
of meaning. But how do the positivists know that meaning is not
indefinable? Some terms must be indefinable, and such a fundamental term as meaning is surely one of the most likely terms to be
so. Further, can the mere absence of an alternative definition of
meaning be any possible justification for giving a definition of
meaning which would make meaningless many statements that
prior to the definition were held by everybody to have meaning?
If a definition does this it is, *prima facie* at any rate, not an account
of the way in which the word defined is usually used by people.
The definition has not made the *definiens* co-extensive with the
definiendum, and can only be justified if an *independent argument*
is given to show that in the cases where meaning is attributed to
statements which cannot be verified the term 'meaning' does not
mean anything. If we are content to give definitions that cover only
part of the extension of the term defined and then deny that the
term as applied to the remainder of its extension has any meaning
merely because otherwise it will not fit our definition, as the people
who use this argument for the verification theory propose to do, we
need never have any difficulty in finding definitions of anything;
but surely it is a more philosophic course to suppose that either
the term is indefinable or a right definition has not been found yet
than to be content with definitions of this kind.

Further this reminds me that I have not stated the verification
doctrine in its most common form, simply because this form
seemed to me even less plausible than the others and I wished to
give my opponents a fair run for their money. As most usually
stated, however, the theory asserts not only that no meaningful
statements are unverifiable but that the meaning of a statement just

is its verification (or its method of verification). And if we use the argument that we must have a definition of meaning and the verification theory is the only definition that has ever been suggested, we must conclude not merely that all meaningful statements are verifiable but that their verification (or method of verification) is identical with their meaning. Otherwise the theory would not be giving a *definition* of meaning. To this extremer form of the theory there seem to me to be two objections that are not applicable to the milder forms which do not actually equate verification with meaning but only use it as a test of meaning. The first objection is that verification presupposes something which is verified, and this cannot itself be the verification but must be a proposition which cannot be reduced without residuum to its own verification. To say that what I mean in asserting a proposition is its verification seems to me parallel to saying 'I lie' when what is said to be a lie is not a previous proposition but the proposition 'I lie' itself. There is nothing to which the 'it' in 'its verification' refers unless there is a proposition to be verified over and above the verification of it. For what has to be verified is never the sentence but what it means. The sentence is a mere set of noises or black marks which occur and are experienced whether it is true or false, meaningful or meaningless.

Secondly, the belief in the occurrence of an event is very often verified by observing not it but its effects and concluding from them to the event as cause. It will follow that in these cases, if the meaning is identical with its verification, the event will be its own effects. Positivists abominate the entailment view of causation, but, if they were consistent with this definition of meaning, they would have to hold not only that the cause entails but that it analytically entails its effect. I think that an entailment view of causation is true, but even if I am right in this it is quite certain that the entailment, if present, must be synthetic not analytic.

Finally, even if there were reasons for a verification theory, I submit that, if it leads to such consequences as that propositions about other human beings are really only propositions about one's own sense-data, or that all propositions supposed to be about the past are really only about the possible future events which, if they occurred, would verify the propositions, this constitutes an objection to the theory which should outweigh even very strong arguments on its behalf. To me the conclusions in question seem absolutely incredible. Another objection to the theory is that the

truth of some statements about metaphysics may be seen logically
to entail the truth of others, but how could anything be entailed
by a sentence which meant nothing?

I do not believe in saying 'Peace' when there is no peace, and
so I have attacked the verification theory mercilessly, but I am not
blind to its merits, which I shall now briefly mention. In order to
understand a statement fully, it is, I agree, essential that we should
have some idea as to the general kind of way in which it would be
justified if it were true, and I am prepared to admit that it is often
very useful to ask about a philosophical statement both: How
could it be established if it were true? and: What difference, if any,
would it make to experience if it were true? Sometimes to ask
these questions may even lead us to the conclusion that the statement does not really express a proposition. For, I admit, it does
sometimes happen that philosophers are led through verbal
confusions into making statements which are meaningless. What
I do refuse to admit is that *all* statements which cannot be established or refuted by sense-experience are meaningless. The asking
of these questions may help us to get rid of some metaphysics, but
not of all metaphysics. The great majority of metaphysical statements that have been made by philosophers in the past are, I think,
false or ungrounded, but not meaningless. A few are true or near
the truth.

This rejection of metaphysics comes from the unwarranted
narrowing down of 'justification' to 'justification by sense-
experience.' If we want a criterion to determine when a statement
has meaning, it is arguable that 'verifiability' will do if we mean
by this that a statement to have a meaning must be such that we
can think of some conceivable method by which it might be
supported (I think it is too strong to say 'proved') or refuted. But,
even so, we are not justified in assuming that the only way of
supporting a proposition must be by sense-experience or by
inductive argument from sense-experience. Take the proposition
that there is a necessary being. That would be proved by the so-
called first cause argument if the latter were valid, and the verification of it in my wider sense would consist in going through the
argument and seeing whether it was valid. The verification of its
contradictory—There is no necessary being—would consist in
seeing, as many people think they can see, that there are no
existential *a priori* propositions. Suppose, however, we do not find
either the argument for or the argument against the existence of a

necessary being conclusive. The proposition will still be verifiable potentially if we can see what sort of argument would establish it if it were valid, or what sort of additional premises would be required to make the argument valid. Thus I might see that if we assumed that there was a reason for everything there must be a necessary being, i.e. a being which is its own reason, but I might be uncertain whether we were justified in holding that there was a reason for everything. Again I might see that no a priori proposition I knew was existential, and yet be doubtful whether I could see positively that a priori existential propositions were impossible. In that case the proposition could still be said to be verifiable in my extended sense of verifiability because I could see what would make it true, just as a proposition about the other side of the moon which we cannot practically verify is still said to be verifiable in the narrower sense of verifiability because we know the experience which, if it could occur, would verify it. I am not sure whether we need or can expect to have a criterion (still less a single criterion) for determining whether statements have a meaning, but if people *must* have a criterion I make them a present of this one. But why beg the whole question of epistemology by identifying verifiability with verifiability by sense-experience at the start?

The positivist has no doubt also done philosophy a good service by carrying out the empiricist principle more consistently than even Hume. For a philosopher should try to investigate the consequences of any possible hypothesis and in particular should try to be an empiricist if he can and as long as he can, because we must not lightly assume the presence of an *a priori* synthetic element in knowledge where an empirical explanation will serve. But I should add that in working out the logical consequences of empiricism the positivist has provided its *reductio ad absurdum*.

Finally I am prepared to grant that we cannot form any idea of anything unless we have either immediately experienced it or it is a logical construction from what we have immediately experienced. Only I use 'experience' in a wide sense according to which seeing that one proposition entails another or that something possesses the non-natural property, good, or being in immediate relation with God, will, if they occur, all be experiences. We can have no right to rule out such experiences in advance as impossible unless we know *a priori* that there cannot be any experiences which are not reducible to sense-experience; and how the positivist could know this, especially on his theory of *a priori* knowledge, is quite beyond my power to conceive. Further, even if I were willing to narrow down experience to suit him, I should still maintain that he had gone too far. For even if we could not meaningfully talk about anything except qualities or relations given in experience in his narrower sense, and logical constructions from these, it would not follow that it was impossible to make significant statements which could yet not be verified by experience, since it is perfectly possible, for anything we can see, that the same quality actually experienced by us should also qualify existents which no human being, perhaps no being at all, could ever experience. And it is likewise possible that complex characteristics which we never experience may be constructed out of simpler characteristics which we do experience, and that these characteristics may qualify existents which can never be experienced, at any rate by human beings, perhaps not at all. It may be very hard to justify any such assertions, but they are surely significant. If the positivist wishes to dispute this he must disclose some formal contradiction in the supposition.

Having rejected the verification theory of meaning, it is perhaps incumbent on me to give some account of the conditions under which verbal expressions could be said to be meaningless. This I shall now proceed to do. It seems clear that the following classes of expressions, at least, are meaningless.

1. There are sentences which express exclamations, wishes, commands, exhortations. These do not assert propositions, and therefore there is a sense in which they have no meaning, though no doubt in another sense they have a meaning since they can certainly be understood (or misunderstood). It is possible that a philosopher might confuse such a sentence with a sentence expressing a proposition and so utter a sentence which had no objective meaning, thinking it had one, though I doubt whether this occurs at all frequently.

2. There are expressions such as 'the table is beside' or 'Cambridge is between York' which are meaningless because incomplete, i.e. the form of the expression is such as to require an additional term to give it meaning and the additional term is absent. In the first example there is a dyadic relation with only one term, in the second a triadic relation with only two terms. There are, I think, cases where philosophers have uttered meaningless expressions of this type thinking they had a meaning. Thus no doubt some philosophers have thought that probability was a

quality, so that you could say *A* was probable significantly without either asserting or understanding any data to which the probability of *A* was relative, while probability is really a relative term. (The statement, *A* is probable, made in ordinary conversation is not meaningless, because another term, i.e. one's present data, to which the probability is relative, is understood if not expressed.)

3. An expression may be said to be meaningless if it includes some word or words which do not stand for anything. If the meaning of the word in question is complex, it might be said to be meaningless on the ground that it was self-contradictory, in which case it will come under a later heading; but apart from this we might conceivably have a sentence containing indefinable or undefined words which stood, not for something self-contradictory, but for absolutely nothing at all. I do not mean merely 'for nothing existent' but for nothing of which we have any idea at all. I do not know any clear instances of sentences containing such words in any philosopher except Lewis Carroll, but it would no doubt be alleged by some philosophers that, e.g. 'subsist' as opposed to exist or 'good' as used in *Principia Ethica* are examples.

4. An expression (we should hardly call it a sentence) might consist of words all of which had a meaning and yet be itself meaningless because the words were combined in a way contrary to the rules of syntax, e.g. are of fond not dogs cats. The term 'syntax' is used here in its strictly grammatical sense, not in the extended sense in which 'grammar' is used by certain positivists. I do not know whether there are instances of such expressions in philosophical works excepting those due to momentary slips or misprints.

There no doubt are these four classes of meaningless expressions, but I come now to two other alleged classes of meaningless sentences, about which I feel a good deal of doubt. In fact I shall contend against most philosophers that they are not meaningless at all.

5. It is usually held that a sentence which ascribes to something a relatively determinate value of a determinable which does not qualify it is meaningless, whether the determinate value is asserted or denied of it. The most usual example of this cited lately at Cambridge is: Quadratic equations go to race-meetings, the example in my days at Oxford was: Virtue is a fire-shovel. It is generally held that such statements are not false but meaningless.

It is further held that their contradictories: Quadratic equations
do not go to race-meetings, and: Virtue is not a fire-shovel are
not true but likewise meaningless. This, however, I am prepared
to dispute. For after all: Quadratic equations do not go to race-
meetings is entailed by: Quadratic equations do not move in
space, and entails: Quadratic equations do not watch the New-
market horse-races: but, if it is capable of entailing and being
entailed, surely it must be a proposition and not a mere meaningless set of words. Again, surely you do really know that quadratic
equations do not go to race meetings? But how could you possibly
know it if the words did not express a proposition, did not mean
anything? There would be nothing to know.

No doubt if I frequently made assertions such as: Virtue is not
a fireshovel, or: Quadratic equations do not go to race-meetings,
I should be in danger of being consigned to an aslyum, and it may
be asked why I should be regarded as a lunatic because I say
what is true. The answer is that to qualify as a lunatic it is not
necessary to say what is false or meaningless; it is sufficient
persistently to say what is true in an unsuitable context. The
proposition—2 *plus* 2=4—is impeccably and indisputably true,
but if I frequently asserted this proposition in unsuitable contexts,
c.g. whenever anybody asked me a question about something
totally different, I should soon be regarded as a lunatic. Now the
proposition that quadratic equations do not go to race-meetings
is a proposition of such a kind that there is hardly any context in
which its assertion is suitable. It is, I hope, suitable in this article,
but this is certainly the first occasion in my life on which I have
found it suitable to assert it, and most people go through their
whole lives without finding such an occasion at all. Consequently
the assertion of it outside philosophical gatherings would generally
be regarded as a mark of insanity. The reason why the context is
never suitable is because the proposition is so obviously true that
it can never enter into anybody's mind to think of questioning it,
and because, unlike 2 *plus* 2=4, it also happens to be of such a
kind that it can never, as far as I know, be used as a means of
making inferences that are practically or theoretically useful.

The proposition that quadratic equations do not go to race-
meetings belongs to a large class of propositions that may best
be characterised as true but misleading. I shall give you another
proposition that belongs to this class. The proposition is this: I
did not commit more than six murders last week. This proposition,

I assert, is true. I did not commit any murders last week, and therefore I did not commit more than six. But it is misleading because nobody would in fact ask whether I had committed more than six murders unless he assumed that I had probably committed some. Similarly, nobody would ask whether quadratic equations went to race-meetings unless he assumed that quadratic equations were at any rate the sort of things that could move in space. Other instances of true but misleading propositions are: I worked an hour yesterday (when I really worked eight), he has not stopped beating his wife (when he never started). No doubt there is an important difference between a proposition such as: Quadratic equations do not attend race-meetings—and the other examples I have mentioned in that it is logically impossible that quadratic equations should attend race-meetings while it is not logically impossible that, e.g. I should have committed six murders last week. All I am suggesting is that the propositions are similar in being both true and misleading, not that they are similar in other respects.

To go a step further in absurdity, I might be asked whether I thought it true that purple quadratic equations do not attend race-meetings, this statement differing from the other one about quadratic equations in that not only the statement as a whole but the grammatical subject of it is self-contradictory. My answer would be that, if the statement is equivalent to: It is not a fact that purple quadratic equations attend race-meetings, it is true, if it is equivalent to: There are purple quadratic equations and they do not attend race-meetings, it is false. In either case it is meaningful.

Not only should I say that the proposition: Quadratic equations do not attend race-meetings, is meaningful, I should say that its contradictory: Quadratic equations sometimes attend race-meetings, is meaningful though false. Certainly the reason which positivists sometimes give to explain why such statements are absurd seems to me untenable. They say that they are absurd simply because they recommend a usage of language different from the one which exists. I find it exceedingly difficult to understand this. It is surely just because the different words in the sentence are used in their usual senses that the assertion is absurd: if I chose to use 'quadratic equations' to mean a certain breed of race-horses or 'attend race-meetings' to mean 'occur in examination papers', the sentence: Quadratic equations attend race-meetings, would not be absurd but express a true proposition. If I were told that the person who uttered the sentence was using the words in an unusual sense I should indeed have to say that I did not know whether what he said was absurd or not till I knew in what sense he was using them. (No doubt the way in which he expressed what he meant might be absurd, but that is a different matter.) It is only if I am sure that he is not employing, and therefore presumably *not* recommending, a usage of language different from the ordinary one that I can deny off-hand the truth of his statement.

But, however that may be, the statement: Quadratic equations attend race-meetings, is self-contradictory, and most philosophers have held all self-contradictory statements to be meaningless. What about this sixth class of supposed meaningless expressions? In this connection it seems to me significant that, while perhaps few people would hesitate to say that all talk about round squares or purple equations was meaningless, they would look on statements such as 'an equilateral triangle is sometimes not equiangular' as false rather than meaningless. Yet if the first two are meaningless because they are self-contradictory, the third ought to be meaningless also; for it is self-contradictory, though the discovery that it is so requires mediation.

Now no doubt there is a sense in which it seems reasonable to say that all self-contradictory sentences are meaningless. If we try to think out what they mean we find we cannot combine the subject and predicate in thought. We cannot think what it would be like for quadratic equations to go to race-meetings or for squares to be round, nor can we really think an equilateral triangle as anything else than equiangular if the meaning of the word triangle as used by us is fixed by Euclid's postulates and we consider its implications. It may therefore be contended that we cannot think the meaning of a self-contradictory statement as a whole, though we know the meaning of the separate words.

But a self-contradictory statement does not say *how* the contradictory notions are to be combined, it merely says that they are combined somehow, and is that statement meaningless? If I know the meaning of 'quadratic equations' and the meaning of 'attending race-meetings', I may surely understand the meaning of the (false) statement that these two characteristics are sometimes combined, without having to achieve the impossible feat of combining them in thought myself. Do you understand the statement that 2547 plus 2691=5248? Surely. Yet on going through the sum you will find that the numbers have been added up wrongly and that therefore the statement is really self-contradictory. A mathematician who lived before a particular theorem had been proved could understand what was meant and view it not as a mere set of words but as a proposition even prior to finding the proof. Indeed if he did not first view it as a proposition he would not look for a proof. And, if so, he must equally be able to understand a statement which is later proved to be false but, at the time he contemplates it, has not yet been proved to be false. Now suppose later it is proved to be false. Surely this will not lead to his ceasing to understand it. If he understood it before he will continue to understand it while seeing it to be false. What could before be entertained as a proposition does not cease to be a proposition by being proved false. In fact if he did not understand it he could not see it to be false. The same will apply to propositions which are not only materially but formally self-contradictory, such as the proposition that the conclusion of a valid second figure syllogism can be affirmative.

These considerations seem to lead to the conclusion that even self-contradictory sentences are not therefore meaningless. I think that: Quadratic equations attend race meetings, is a statement which we understand perfectly well and that it is only because we can understand it so well that we see it to be so obviously false. To see that it is true that equations do not attend race-meetings is surely to see that it is false that they do. Some people would no doubt say that this sentence is meaningless while some self-contradictory statements, e.g. the false statement about triangles mentioned above, are meaningful; but if any self-contradictory statements are meaningful I do not see where to draw the line. And after all you surely can understand the statement: It is self-contradictory to say that quadratic equations attend race-meetings, but, if so, must not you equally understand its negative? It therefore seems to me that even self-contradictory statements are meaningful, at least in the most important sense of the term.

But it is time to bring this paper to a close. The subject discussed is an extremely important one. The positivists claim to settle once for all by a consistent use of their verification doctrine all the great philosophical issues of the past—the issues between empiricism and rationalism, realism and idealism, pluralism and monism, naturalism and theism, but before they have the least right to do this the verification doctrine must itself be justified. My aim in this paper has been to show both that it cannot be true, because if it were true, it would be meaningless, which is self-contradictory, and that even if *per impossibile* it could be true there is no more ground for believing it than there is for believing the damnatory clauses of the Athanasian creed. If even only the second contention is right, it follows that the verification theory as a universal principle ought to be sternly dismissed from service in philosophical controversy and never used as the major premiss of an argument to show that various sentences uttered by opponents of the positivists are meaningless. For, even if it may be true, a 'may be' without grounds is not enough for a philosopher. We have no right to assume principles which are not self-evident and for which there are no reasons. If a verification theory is to be made the basis of your philosophy there must be reasons for it, and I want to know what the positivist thinks these reasons to be.

II

REASON AND INTUITION

If there is one thing more characteristic of the intellectual climate of the world as a whole during the last ten years than any other it is the widespread distrust of *reason*.[1] This is shown not only in political movements but also in science, which seems to have largely abandoned the belief in a rational order of the physical world that was so potent an inspiration during its early stages of advance, and in very much of modern philosophy which tends to reduce the function of reason from that of being key to the whole nature of reality to that of a mere manipulator of symbols, capable indeed of ordering our experience and thought, but incapable of giving fresh information. Yet how are we to solve our problems if reason cannot solve them? 'Intuition' might possibly be an adequate ground if everybody agreed in their intuitions, but if men do not agree and the dispute cannot be settled by reason, is there anything for the disputants to do but to fight it out? Surely we should be able to deal with disputes more rationally than that. And how can we judge whose intuitions are the better? These are problems that must perplex almost every thinking man, however sure he may feel in practice of his own judgement, and they will be liable to perplex us more after the emergency of war is over, and there begins the task of repairing the damage and building up a better world order, perhaps the most vitally important task that has ever fallen to the lot of man and one for which all the available reason of the world should be mobilized if reason can be of any advantage. It therefore seems to me not a mere academic question but one of great practical importance what place we are to assign to reason in life and thought. But, whatever the ultimate practical implications of these topics, our discussion of them, if it is to be thorough and adequate, must be academic in the sense of dealing abstractly with the concepts involved and apparently moving far away from the issues which confront practical life today, because that is the only way of going to the foundations. I am convinced

[1] 'Reason', I realize, is a very ambiguous word, but I shall try to clear up the ambiguities later.

that the topic which I am discussing has much more relevance to
the present crisis than will seem obvious at first sight. What I
think it is of great theoretical and practical importance to attain is
a middle course which will do justice to intuition and yet enable
us to deal with intuitions rationally, avoiding the extremes both
of an irrationalism which spurns cold reason as useless and
hampering and an arid and narrow rationalism which seeks to
deny everything that cannot be logically or scientifically proved.

The motives behind the present widespread disparagement of
'reason' would require the ability of an expert psycho-analyst
fully to unravel, but there are various obvious causes in the recent
development of civilization which help to explain it. The first and
most obvious is the relative decline of Christian orthodoxy, which
professed to have a ready-made system of the universe, and the
consequent spread of distrust in beliefs not founded on ordinary
experience. It is indeed no ground for wonder that, when such a
large part of the thinking world rejected or gravely doubted the
system of metaphysics (for Christian orthodoxy is of course not
only a religion but a popular metaphysics) which had dominated
almost everybody and everything in the greater part of Europe for
a millennium, it was altogether beyond the capacity of a few pro-
fessional metaphysicians, generally hopelessly disunited in their
main views, to stem the tide so far as to produce widespread
respect for any metaphysical system. It is true that in the nine-
teenth century the assailants of Christianity commonly attacked it
in the name of reason, and it was in the name of reason that
science, the mightiest intellectual phenomenon of the last centuries, made its advances. But in more recent years science has
itself tended, it appears, to support irrationalism. The scientist
used to believe—and I think the belief commonly provided one
of the main motives for his untiring efforts—that he was increasing
human knowledge of the fundamental nature of reality as opposed
to the appearances which present themselves to the senses in
everyday life and that in finding the causes he was at least coming
somewhat nearer to finding the reasons, the 'why', the grounds of
phenomena. But all this is altered now. The usual view of the
scientist, when he tries to philosophize, now is that he is not in
his science dealing with reality but is merely correlating human
experiences, is not attaining truth but practical utility, and is
discovering not in any degree the why but only the how of
phenomena. I do not say that this is what scientists really believe

when they are engaged in scientific research, but it is what the philosophers and would-be philosophers among them commonly say when they philosophize, and it is highly significant of the intellectual climate in which civilization at present lives. Now if it is thought that human reason can by other means attain the knowledge of reality which it cannot attain by science, well and good. But if, as is common now, the above belief about science is not combined with a belief that reason can attain cognition of reality by methods of quite a different kind from those of physical science, it is a much more serious matter. The conclusion suggested then is that reason is indeed an instrument of practical utility, but one totally and on principle incapable of discerning the nature of the real or even of justifying the presuppositions on which science itself depends. For the scientific philosophers of the present day have not only been unable to justify metaphysics, a failure of which they would be proud, but they have been unable even to justify science. All science outside mathematics depends on inductive arguments from the observed to the unobserved, and most logicians admit that no one has yet succeeded in giving a satisfactory philosophical justification of induction. No doubt earlier logicians had not succeeded either, but they generally did not realize that they had failed, and therefore their failure did not lead to the sceptical attitude of the present day. But now the conclusion strongly suggested to very many minds is that, while we may use reason as a reliable instrument to argue from given ultimate premisses to conclusions based on them, these premisses are themselves merely instinctive beliefs with no possible rational justification, the mere product of evolution or of feeling. A contributory cause of the occurrence of the situation described has no doubt been the complete failure of philosophers to arrive at any agreed solution of metaphysical problems and the apparent refutation of all or almost all the metaphysical arguments of the past. This has provided fertile soil for the growth of epistemological theories such as logical positivism which lead necessarily to the severe disparagement of reason.

The tendency I have mentioned is further strengthened by the influence of the psycho-analyst with his stress on 'rationalization' or the use of reason to prove by sophistical arguments to ourselves or to others what we want to believe. Psychology does undoubtedly provide evidence that we are by no means as much guided by reason as we are apt to suppose. But it does not require the psycho-analyst, it only requires the daily newspaper to make clear to us how small in fact is the extent to which reason regulates large-scale political and economic life. The failure of the vaunted intelligence of man to avert 'total' war and economic disaster and the consequent bitter disillusionment have been extremely powerful factors, perhaps the most powerful factors, in leading to a 'revolt against reason'. It cannot, however, be admitted that this attitude is very logical if it amounts to a revolt against reason and not merely a suspicion as to whether people who pretend to be reasonable or think themselves reasonable are so in fact. For it is of vital importance here to make a distinction between what is and what ought to be. Even if reason in fact only plays a minor part in human life, it does not by any means follow that reason must of necessity be confined to such a humble role, any more than it follows that because there is war now there must always be wars, nor that we ought not to be guided by reason, at least as much as we can. The 'rationalization' which the psycho-analyst condemns is not good reasoning but bad reasoning, since it bolsters up false views, and it is surely only by the help of his reason that he discovers it to be bad and therefore rejects it as mere rationalization. And surely war and economic disorders only prove human irrationality if it is assumed that they could be avoided if we were reasonable. The defender of reason may reply that we are not in fact governed by reason but can and ought to be so governed, and it is quite certain that, in any sense in which it may legitimately be said that a person could act differently from the way in which he does act, it is true that people could be governed by reason, not indeed entirely, but at least more than they are governed.

I have met some of the difficulties of the rationalist by a distinction between what is and what ought to be, but the questions raised by the word 'ought' themselves raise difficulties which seem to help the irrationalist in his attack on reason. For 'ought' brings one to the realm of ethics. Now in this field men may no doubt debate effectively and usefully as to means, but, if they differ in their conception of ultimate ends, there seems to be a deadlock in which either side just appeals to intuition and cannot be refuted or refute its opponent by reasoning. This point has been specially noted in recent times because there is less agreement as to ends than there used to be, or at least the disagreement is clear, while in earlier ages it was more or less concealed, and it provides a serious philosophical difficulty to be met by the defender of

rationalism and an important part-cause of the present irrationalism, but it is a difficulty which we shall have to consider later in
this lecture and must leave for the present.

However it is time for me now to ask what is meant when a
philosopher insists on the power and importance of reason and
claims that we must obey reason in all things and only accept what
is told us by reason. This question raises considerable difficulties.
It would be plain perhaps if 'reason' could be identified with
reasoning. But this can hardly be done. Reasoning, roughly speaking, falls into two very different classes: (1) deductive *a priori*
reasoning, in which the conclusion follows with logical necessity
from the premisses; (2) inductive problematic reasoning,[1] which
consists of generalizations and analogies based on observed
empirical facts and extended to what is unobserved.

Now it is plain that neither kind of reasoning can be adequate
of itself to determine what is true. In order to prove the truth of a
conclusion reason requires true premisses, and how can we maintain that they too are to be established by reasoning without
committing ourselves to a vicious infinite regress? In order to
establish conclusions of any sort by reasoning we need premisses
which are supplied either by experience or by immediate insight as
opposed to reasoning. It might indeed be objected that, as far as
this argument is concerned, we could still establish by pure
reasoning hypothetical propositions, propositions of the form if p
then q, though not categorical propositions which claim unconditional truth. But there is a further point of still greater importance. In order to conduct a valid deductive argument we must
see that each step in the argument follows logically from the
preceding one. To argue—a, therefore b; b, therefore c; c, therefore d, we must see that b follows from a, c from b, and d from c.
But how can the fact that b follows from a be itself established by
reasoning if we understand by that mediate reasoning? Only by
interpolating another stage, e. But then the same difficulty would
obviously arise about the connexion between a and e, so we must
admit that any valid argument must ultimately be based on
connexions which we see immediately without further reasoning
and such that, if anybody denies them, he cannot be refuted by

[1] It seems to me that the kinds of 'induction' admitted in Johnson's *Logic*
other than problematic induction are either, in the case of intuitive induction,
not reasoning at all but intuition or immediate insight helped by examples, or,
in the case of demonstrative and summary induction, deductive inference from
premisses reached by observation or problematic induction.

the interpolation of any third term whatever. We could not start at all in any reasoning without assuming that we immediately perceive a connexion between certain premises and their conclusion. To argue at all we must see the connexion between the propositions which constitute the different stages of the argument not by mediate reasoning but intuitively. We can no doubt call this not 'intuition' but 'immediate', as opposed to mediate, reasoning, and this would hardly be a misuse of the term 'reasoning'. If believing p we see immediately that q follows from p and therefore believe q, we certainly may be said to be 'reasoning' from p to q, but such *immediate* reasoning would only be another name for what is commonly called intuition. The connexion between p and q would still be something that you could not *prove* but either saw or did not see. In arguments such as those used in mathematics the difficulty in this is veiled by the fact that everybody agrees here in what they claim to see immediately to be true, but the same unanimity does not prevail in all spheres. (In all that follows we must remember that to apprehend the logical connexion between premises and conclusion is itself to apprehend the truth of a relational proposition to the effect that the premises entail the conclusion.)

The same type of difficulty applies to inductive arguments also. It is obvious that the premisses of an inductive argument must be either given empirically or be themselves conclusions based on induction (since they will hardly be *a priori*), but this is not the point I wish to emphasize here. A more important point is that for an inductive argument to be satisfactory we must either see immediately that certain general principles, e.g. the 'uniformity of nature' or the principle of causation, are true universally, or— and this, I think, is a more plausible account—we must see that the particular kind of evidence used in a particular case makes the conclusion probable, though we may, especially if we are not versed in logic, be quite unable to explain what are the formal features of the argument which do make the conclusion probable.

It is not sufficient to say in reply that so-called inductive conclusions are simply hypotheses to be verified by experience, for induction and with it science itself are useless unless we can in advance of experience make at least reasonable judgements on the strength of induction as to what will probably happen. It will not do to wait till I have been poisoned by prussic acid before deciding that prussic acid is likely to poison me. I must have before this good grounds for believing on the strength of the unfortunate experience of others that it is likely to poison me, though this has not been verified by experience since I have never drunk the beverage in question, but I should not be justified even in making this simple inference from the experience of others without assuming something that goes beyond mere observation. Nobody has observed myself being poisoned, therefore a belief that I would under certain conditions be poisoned is not just a matter of experience but of inference. Further, most inductive conclusions at least are never verified by experience unless we make certain assumptions of a kind which themselves would have to be justified by induction. For without such assumptions my experience cannot give me any information except about my own mental state and immediate objects of experience, yet, in order to verify the conclusions, what we require is information about physical events independent of my experience.

No doubt if anybody disputes an inductive argument we can go some way to meet him by argument. We may be able to point out analogous cases where a similar conclusion to the one he disputes based on similar evidence would seem highly probable even to him, and argue that it would be inconsistent to reject the evidence in the one case and accept it in the other, but this is only appealing to the man's immediate insight into the quality of evidence proffered on another occasion. In the last resort it would seem that we must depend on the immediate insight that on given evidence the conclusion is probable, an insight which occurs in each case of a legitimate inductive argument consciously made.

The above serves drastically to limit our estimate of the power of reasoning even in theoretical matters. In practical matters immediate insight as opposed to mediate reasoning seems to have an even larger sphere, since it is required to discern and compare the values which alone give point to practical action. For, unless something is worth attaining or doing for its own sake and not only as a means to something else, there can be no point in doing anything whatever, yet all attempts by philosophers to *prove* in strict logic that certain things are good in themselves or certain actions worth doing have broken down. Further, as we shall show later, we may have an insight into individual wholes without the insight being capable of adequate explanation or adequate expression in terms of propositions about elements in the whole.

I am not claiming that all intuitions are of the same kind. The

argument shows the existence of at least four different kinds—
those presupposed in deduction, those presupposed in induction,
those presupposed in ethics, and those consisting in the apprehension of a whole as a whole,[1] but what I am concerned with here
is not to define or describe the kinds of intuition, but merely to
point out the occurrence of intuitions in the sense of cognitions
that are both non-empirical and immediate. It may indeed be
objected that the four kinds of intuition are so different as not to
deserve the same name, but at least they agree in going beyond
sense-experience or merely empirical observation and yet being
immediate, or at least only mediated in the sense of being helped,
not proved, by discursive reasoning,[2] and the same sort of difficulties arise concerning all of them. I hope to show *ambulando*
that they can be satisfactorily discussed together.

If then we mean by 'reason' mediate reasoning, the functions
we can ascribe to reason are very limited and dependent at every
stage on something else which is commonly called intuition. But,
when the most sweeping claims are made on behalf of reason, the
term is generally being used to cover something more than reasoning, though it certainly does also cover reasoning. It is used to
include besides reasoning 'intuition' or the seeing something to be
true, not because it is inferred from other propositions or established by observation, but because of its own intrinsic nature it
must be, or at least is, true. Obviously the notion is liable to gross
abuses since a person may easily persuade himself that his prejudices represent real intuitions, or allow the appeal to intuition to
take the place of a careful examination of the proposition which
he accepts and any evidence relevant to it. But the case for the
existence of intuition seems irresistible since we could not have
mediate inference without discerning the links in the chain of
inference immediately. I do not believe that intuition is limited
to a knowledge of the links between the different stages in inference, but I have emphasized the latter kind of intuition simply
because it is by considering it that we can give an actual proof that
there must be such a thing as true intuition since otherwise there is
no such thing as valid reasoning. Of the obvious objections to the
notion of intuition as yielding truth I shall speak later, but I shall

[1] 'Intuition' is also sometimes used, as in translations of Kant, to stand for a
sensory element linked up with our formal knowledge. This sense of 'intuition'
has nothing in common with the sense in which the term is being used in the
present lecture.
[2] V. below, pp. 56 ff.

B*

anticipate by saying now that I am a defender of reason in a sense which includes intuitive reason.

It is often said that what people call 'intuition' is really only 'implicit inference'. Now there is no doubt that a person may be really making an inference and yet, because the inference is made so quickly that he does not notice it or fails to analyse it, may mistakenly regard it as a case of intuition. But we cannot deal with all 'intuition' in this way. It cannot all be explained away as implicit inference, if we mean by that unconscious (unintrospected) inference or inference in which the different stages are traversed too quickly to be noticed. For, whether the inference is explicit or implicit, when we have inserted all the stages that were unnoticed psychologically but are necessary logically, each conclusion must be seen to follow from its immediate premisses for it to be a case of valid inference at all, and that it does follow from these obviously cannot be itself proved by mediate reasoning. A conclusion which is psychologically immediate may not be logically immediate, but this only puts the question further back.

At this point a new difficulty arises. If we admit intuition but claim that it is the work of reason while our opponent claims that it is the work of feeling, what is the difference between us? What are we claiming that he does not admit? If an opponent of the claims of reason just asserts that the alleged intuitions are all unfounded and that there is no justification for believing any of them the issue is plain. The advocate of reason is then simply claiming to know certain propositions to be true which his opponent thinks are not known to be true. But the opponent of reason may take a different line: he may admit all that I have said so far, but take it as showing the necessary limitation of reason itself on the ground that the use of reason always presupposes at every stage something which cannot be learnt by reason but only by feeling. In that case the issue is less clear, and it is even arguable that the two sides are asserting the same thing in different words. Both admit that the beliefs in question are not and cannot be established by mediate reasoning. Both reject any criterion for them except immediate intuition, so that in judging whether they are true or false we must simply rely on our present apprehension of propositions. If that is admitted, what is the difference between saying they are due to reason and saying they are due to feeling? Is not reason in this connexion just an emotive term which some men like to use because they like to be thought intellectual and because it gives them more satisfactory emotions if they can still speak of man in general as rational, and feeling a term which others like to use because they dislike a certain aroma of coldness suggested by the notion of somebody always acting from reason, or want to maintain that they have a good right to their opinions even though they may not be good reasoners or to defend beliefs which have nothing but their desires behind them? It must be admitted that there is a certain danger of championing reason against feeling or vice versa because we are in love with a word, but the issue between the advocates of reason and the advocates of feeling remains an important one, and there are various circumstances which make it more appropriate to describe 'intuitions' as the work of reason than as the work of feeling. For, firstly, they claim truth, and it is by definition the cognitive, and not the sensitive, side of our nature which apprehends what is true. If a person attributes them to 'feeling' there is the dangerous suggestion that these intuitive beliefs or judgements are not anything which could possibly be true, but emotions or expressions of emotions. Such a view is sometimes (I think, very wrongly) taken about ethical 'judgements', but it is clearly impossible to take this view in regard to what we have seen above must be apprehended by 'intuition', if at all, i.e. the connexion between one stage of an argument and the next. To see that p entails q is not merely to have or express an emotion, it is to know the truth at least about the relation between propositions. Some intuitively apprehended propositions at least are therefore true in the strict sense of the word. Secondly, what we apprehend is objectively valid not only for us but for everyone. If the connexion we seem to see really holds, it holds independently of our apprehension of it, and it is therefore a fact, whatever mistaken opinions other people and we ourselves at other times may have held about it and however they and we may feel about it. This objectivity and universal validity in what we intuit are suggested rather by the term *reason* than by the term *feeling*, and so the former seems to me more appropriate. Thirdly, one test of the intelligence of a person is certainly his capacity for immediate insight, and the more he has reasoned round a subject the more likely is he to have a correct immediate insight and to avoid the confusions which vitiate it. (I shall have more to say about this third point later in the lecture.) If a person recognizes clearly the points I have mentioned, and yet prefers to ascribe intuitive beliefs to 'feeling', I should not think there was any important controversy between him and me, though I should deplore the looseness of his language. What is important is the assertion that we have such knowledge or justified belief and not the assignment of it to some faculty.

It is relevant here to note that 'feel', as ordinarily used, has two quite different senses: (1) It is used in connexion with occurrences such as pains, pleasures, emotions, sensations. In this sense it would be absurd to speak of 'feeling that something is true'. (2) It is sometimes used as a synonym for 'believe'. It is most naturally used as such where the belief is strongly held and connected with a strong emotion but is incapable of logical proof, e.g. when a man says 'I feel that there is a God' or 'I feel that my wife loves me', or where it is based on a vague sense of the general situation without our being in a position to give any definite ground, e.g. 'I feel that there is something wrong with his argument'. The circumstances that I have detailed under which 'feel' is most naturally used for 'believe' explain the connexion between the two sense of 'feel', but we must remember that the two senses are very different. When we use 'feel' in the second sense we are talking about the cognitive and not about the sensitive side of our nature, not about our pleasures and pains but about our attitude to the truth or falsity of propositions, and not about our emotional reaction to them, but about our tendency to accept them as true. It seems to me that the fact that 'feel' is used in these two different senses has helped to make the anti-rationalist view seem more plausible than it really is, and we must be careful to note that, if a man ascribes an intuitive belief to 'feeling' in this second sense, he is not really contradicting the man who ascribes it to intuitive reason except in so far as the latter claims certain knowledge and not merely justified belief. The difference between certain knowledge and justified belief is no doubt an important one, but justified beliefs as well as knowledge might be based on reason, and the issue between the rationalist and the anti-rationalist is not therefore the same as that between the man who claims certainty in these matters and the man who denies certainty but admits justified belief. The person who defends intuitive reason is asserting that we can know or rightly believe some propositions which are not established by mediate inference or by observation or by any other criterion except the nature of the proposition believed in itself when we inspect it by itself. To substitute 'feel' for 'believe' is very undesirable in this as in most philosophical contexts, because of the ambiguity of 'feel' pointed out above, but, if the word is being used in the second sense pointed out, it may not amount to a genuine philosophical difference.

On the other hand we must not think of the ascription of some piece of knowledge to intuition as an explanation of it any more than it is an explanation of a man's anger to say that he has a bad temper. A faculty is not something different from its manifestations which causes the manifestations, but only a way of classifying the experiences and actions referred to it. I am not interested in the establishment of intuition as an occult faculty, but in the question whether there are actual cases of intuitive knowing. If you ask me what intuition is as a faculty apart from its manifestations I should answer: 'Nothing'; but it is very important to consider where and how far we can have cases of knowledge and justified belief based on intuition or immediate insight, as an actual act of mind, not merely a faculty. This is really a question about the justification of our ostensible knowledge and beliefs and not about a psychological capacity or disposition.

We may distinguish three main views which have been held by philosophers on this question of 'intuition'. The first is that held most explicitly perhaps by the Cartesians, but probably also by the vast majority of thinkers, at least of past generations. According to this view intuition establishes the certainty and truth of a number of separate general principles all of which are true absolutely in their own right and not because of any connexion with other propositions. These principles must just each be accepted as known without question or proof, and there is no attempt made to show that they entail each other or even to establish a systematic connexion between them. From these propositions a number of deductions are effected. In philosophy this is done with the help of a few very general and obvious empirical propositions such as: something exists, in mathematics and pure logic without any empirical or existential propositions at all. Since in the course of the deduction each stage is seen immediately, i.e. by intuition, to follow logically from the preceding one, reasoning becomes nothing but a chain of intuitions. Intuition is held to be a superior mode of knowledge to mediate deduction: God we must suppose to have intuitive knowledge, but we cannot suppose that he needs deduction in the sense of mediate inference; everything he knows must be known immediately. This view of intuition was almost universal prior to Kant, although there has always been a sus-

picious disagreement among philosophers as to what the propositions were exactly which they knew by intuition, and hardly any
philosopher has ever tried to give an exhaustive list of them.

Let us turn to a second type of view, that of extreme empiricism.
The empiricist takes it for granted that we can have knowledge
of what we immediately experience, but makes a more or less
thorough-going attempt to avoid the admission of any other kind
of knowledge as far as he possibly can. One noted, or notorious,
attempt to do this was made by John Stuart Mill. He tried to
account for alleged *a priori* propositions by maintaining that they
were really empirical generalizations, and explained their certainty
and the appearance of necessity by which they are distinguished
from admitted empirical generalizations by saying that the
instances on which they are founded are more numerous than
those which form the basis of other general propositions. As he
quite logically concluded, it follows from his view that, though in
fact 2+2 is equal to 4 in the part of the universe with which we
are well acquainted, it is quite conceivable and possible that in
the region of the fixed stars 2+2 may be sometimes equal to 5.
This view is not, I think, held by any reputable philosopher
nowadays, so I shall not trouble you by refuting it.

More important for us, because far more prevalent nowadays,
is an alternative empiricist solution of the problem of self-evident
propositions, and *a priori* propositions and arguments generally,
according to which these are viewed as derivable from the structure of language, a view from which it follows that they are totally
incapable of giving us any information about the general nature
of independent reality. I have dealt with this view elsewhere.[1] The
most fundamental objection to it is that it leads to the impossible
consequence that, since what constitutes a correct use of language
depends simply on how most people, or most educated people, use
language, it would make all *a priori* propositions and deductive
inference arbitrary, so that if a majority or if a dictator decided to
alter the laws of logic, these laws would really be different. I do
not say that the supporters of the view to which I am referring
would usually admit this, though some would, but, however its
supporters may try to escape the conclusion, I think this is the
inevitable logical consequence of their theory. It is also its *reductio
ad absurdum*.

Thirdly, another, totally different, view which seeks to dispense

[1] Aristotelian Society, *Proceedings*, New Series, vol. xl, pp. 207–44.

with immediately known propositions is the coherence theory. According to this view all true propositions form a system of such a kind that any one of them can, and can only, be justified by reference to the rest, and their ability to fit into such a system is the sole criterion of the truth of propositions. None is therefore true in its own right, but only true, in the degree in which it is true—for truth is on the coherence theory generally, though paradoxically, held to be a matter of degree—because of its place in the system. Self-evidence, therefore, becomes of psychological only and not of logical significance. A self-evident proposition is one which is so bound up with the most essential principles of our whole system of thought that we cannot really question it even if we do so verbally, and belief in it, though attainable in fact without argument, can only be *justified* by an argument which would show it to be so connected. To this view it is objected that, after all, inference presupposes certain fundamental logical principles which, just because they are presupposed in all inference, cannot themselves be established by inference and therefore must be accepted as self-evident once for all without proof if we are to have a proof of anything at all. The reply of most advocates of the coherence theory would be that these principles are proved by the very fact that they are presupposed in all thought and that there is therefore no need to accept them as self-evident without proof. For a proposition is proved if the only alternative to it is an impossible one. Now the alternative to accepting such principles as the law of contradiction is to abandon all thought or at least all thought which makes any claim to sense or truth, and this alternative is impossible. Therefore the law of contradiction and the fundamental principles of logic are after all proved, like all other provable propositions, by reference to the coherence of the system to which they belong; only, while other propositions are proved because they follow from the system, these are proved because they are the necessary conditions of there being any system. The advocate of the coherence theory would insist that it is important to realize that arguments can work backwards as well as forwards. It is a familiar fact to all that we can justify conclusions by deducing them from a principle, but it is not so readily noticed that the case for the truth of the principle itself is always in some degree strengthened, if it needs strengthening at all, by the success with which we can deduce from it conclusions both self-consistent and consistent with empirical facts. The case for the fundamental principles of logic, it may be objected, does not require any further strengthening. They are already so well known that the use of them to deduce any particular fresh conclusion does not add anything to their certainty; but an advocate of the coherence theory, if he admitted this, would hold that their certainty is just due to the fact that the whole system of our knowledge and indeed any conceivable system depends on them. Therefore they too are justified by reference to the system, only in their case one is arguing not from a part of the system to another part, but from the notion of a system to the presuppositions of any conceivable system.

It is often objected to this that we are guilty of a vicious circle if we argue both from a principle to the truth of its conclusions and from the conclusions to the truth of the principle; and since, without accepting their view as a whole, I think there is a good deal of truth in what the advocates of the coherence theory say, I shall try to answer the objection in the way which seems to me best without committing myself to saying how far the holders of the theory would accept my reply. Now in the first place it seems to me that in the case of the fundamental principles of logic there is no vicious circle because the truth of these principles, if deducible from their conclusions at all, is only so deducible because an independent premiss is introduced, namely, the premiss that there is such a thing as knowledge, or at least justified belief. (Advocates of the coherence theory, while still using the term knowledge, in many of their dicta seem to refuse to ascribe to any proposition that absolute certainty which is commonly connoted by 'knowledge'.) The argument, therefore, is not simply: The laws of logic are true, certain other propositions follow from them, therefore these propositions are true, these propositions presuppose the laws of logic, therefore the laws of logic are true because otherwise these propositions would not be true. It is: All conclusions and propositions whatever presuppose the laws of logic; if these laws, therefore, were not true there could be no knowledge or justified belief, but there is knowledge or justified belief, therefore these laws are true. There is no circle in this argument; if we accept the independent premiss that there is knowledge or justified belief we must accept the laws of logic as true, and this premiss, whether logically necessary or not, certainly seems incapable of being seriously doubted. You may be a sceptic about the existence of God, or, in your most philosophical moments, perhaps even about the existence of physical objects in any sense which implies their independence of human experience, but can you hold that every belief alike is unjustified? Can you help believing at least that you exist and in some sense have a body, that there are other human beings, that $2+2$ is equal to 4,[1] and can you help believing that you are right in believing these things? Anyone who cannot reject these beliefs must accept also what they imply, and like every other belief they must imply the laws which are pre-supposed in all thought.

At first sight the sphere of possible application of this method of argument seems very restricted. For it may be doubted whether any proposition could be said to be strictly presupposed by all others except the laws of contradiction and identity (if these are two separate laws) and perhaps the law of excluded middle. Other logical principles are presupposed, not in all propositions without exception, but in important classes of inferences. But it would be retorted that all propositions that are strictly proved are proved by showing that it would contradict the laws of thought to suppose them false, so this argument really extends to all strict proofs. Further, with many propositions which are not capable of being strictly proved, what is ultimately the same principle may be invoked where they are essentially bound up with a fundamental department of belief. For, if it is quite impossible not to believe that some beliefs are justified, it is at least unreasonable to be sceptical about the whole of an important class of inferences, e.g. scientific induction. And the same consideration may be applied to the essential presuppositions of any fundamental department of belief, e.g. belief in other minds, ethics, for many people religious belief, unless the difficulties are quite insuperable, even though no propositions falling within the department can be strictly proved. But this obviously again involves the addition of an independent premiss of a somewhat more complicated kind to the effect that the domain of beliefs in question cannot all be wrong or unjustified.

However the advocates of the coherence theory commonly regard this idea that argument works both ways as applying not only to the fundamental presuppositions of a given branch of knowledge or belief but to all argument and arguable propositions.

---

[1] I am not intending to imply that all these propositions are known intuitively. I am giving them as illustrations of knowledge or indubitable belief, not of intuition.

With any belief, as not only advocates of the coherence theory but some of its bitterest enemies, e.g. Dr Schiller, have insisted, it is the case that any deduction from it of propositions which are both mutually consistent and consistent with the rest of our knowledge and beliefs strengthens its probability in some degree, unless indeed it is absolutely certain already. This is because, if the belief were false, it would be likely, when its consequences were developed, sooner or later to disclose its falsity by leading to inconsistencies either within the set of consequences themselves or between the consequences and empirical facts, and each time we have made inferences from it without leading to such inconsistencies the less likely is it that subsequent inferences will reveal them. (The degree in which a single successful inference enhances the probability of its premiss may of course be extremely small.) The inference backwards from conclusions to premiss thus again depends on an independent premiss, i.e. the premiss that a false proposition would be more or less likely to disclose its falsity by leading to conclusions which are either mutually inconsistent or inconsistent with other well-established beliefs.

Still I cannot now accept coherence as the sole test of truth. I cannot believe that we only know that $2+2$ is equal to 4 because otherwise we could not have arithmetic or at least not a consistent arithmetic: it seems to me quite certain even apart from this further argument which might be used in its favour. We see that it follows from the nature of twoness in a more direct manner than the coherence theory suggests. It is true that we can show that the assumption that $2+2$ is equal to any number but four would lead to conclusions inconsistent with every fact of arithmetic, but this argument is superfluous since we already know it to be true that $2+2=4$ without that. And, when we make an ordinary first figure syllogistic inference, do we only know that it is valid because, if the *dictum de omni et nullo* were false, our whole thought, or much of it, would be rendered inconsistent? I doubt it. It is true that the consequences of a proposition can serve as a test of the truth of that proposition in the way indicated and that they may thus provide additional confirmation of its truth if any such confirmation is needed, but in some cases there seems to be none needed. The advocate of the coherence theory might reply that to know the truth of a self-evident proposition: S is P, is the same as to perceive the coherence between the notions of S and P and therefore comes under this criterion, but this would make the term coherence so wide as to leave it with little meaning. For to say that all *a priori* propositions conform to the coherence test in this sense would only be to say that they depend on a necessary connexion of properties, which everyone who accepted *a priori* propositions at all would admit.

But there is in any case a clear-cut proof available that even the coherence theory cannot dispense with intuition. Suppose a particular belief is accepted or a particular proposition known to be true because it coheres with the system. But how do we see that it coheres with the system? That it does so might indeed be established by a process of mediate inference, but that could only be if the various premisses used cohered with the system and the conclusion cohered with them. So we must sooner or later, and probably sooner rather than later, come to a proposition of which we can only say that we just see immediately that it coheres with other true propositions or with the system as a whole. And so we are back at immediate knowledge or intuition again. Even supposing the coherence theory has rendered it unnecessary to hold that the first principles of logic or the primary axioms of a science are just to be accepted as self-evident, we must at any rate admit that, if we are to use the coherence test at all, some propositions of the kind: p coheres with the system, or: p coheres with the system more than q, must be immediately cognized, for if we did not cognize them immediately we could not use the coherence test. I do not know whether what I have said really contradicts anything which the advocates of the theory usually wish to maintain, but it shows at any rate that they cannot get rid of intuitively cognized propositions if their theory is to work at all.

So we are driven to the conclusion that it is quite impossible to avoid the admission of an element of intuition in knowledge. Yet the position may not be quite as the members of the first school I mentioned think it to be. Let us now turn to the objections commonly brought against the notion of 'intuition'. They certainly raise difficulties which require very serious consideration. The most serious and commonly used objections are the following four: (1) Different sides in a dispute have often each sincerely claimed to know by intuition doctrines which directly or implicitly contradicted each other. (2) Some propositions, such as that every physical change has a cause, or the axioms of Euclid, which the vast majority of educated people held to be self-evident are now not generally regarded as such, and, except for the most fundamental laws of logic at any rate and a few other relatively unimportant propositions such as that everything which has shape has size and nothing can have two different colours in the same part of it at the same time, we have no agreement as to what propositions are known intuitively. (2) The criterion of intuition or self-evidence is purely subjective and psychological, and therefore cannot be adequate. (4) Intuitions are unbacked by reasons, and therefore cannot be tested.

Against the first two objections it seems to me that the advocate of intuition can only defend his position if he makes one concession. He must abandon the claim to certainty and infallibility which has been commonly advanced for intuition in the past. I do not mean that no *a priori* propositions are known immediately with certainty—I am sure we thus know the law of contradiction for example—but that we cannot claim that there is a distinctive state or act of mind, intuiting, which has the property of being always right. The term intuition is indeed commonly used in a sense in which it would be self-contradictory to speak of an 'intuition' being false or uncertain, just as it would be self-contradictory to speak of 'knowledge' being false or uncertain. That is because the term intuition, like the term knowledge, connotes not only that our attitude to a proposition is of a particular kind psychologically, it connotes also that the proposition towards which we have this attitude is true. That is commonly part of the meaning of 'I have an intuition' as it is of 'I know', but the conclusion which logically follows from this that intuitions are never false is simply a verbal one. It is on a par with: Treason never prospers, for if it prospers it is not called treason. It does not by any means imply that we cannot have the very same psychological attitude to propositions which are false, only it would not then be called 'intuition' but 'apparent intuition', just as we commonly speak of 'ostensible memory' and not of 'remembering' if a person has the psychological attitude characteristic of remembering to a false proposition. But there need, as far as I can see, be no psychological distinction between genuine and merely apparent intuitions as mental states or acts, taken in themselves, though what I shall say later on will tend to support the view that the mode of causation involved in their production is different.[1]

Further, while there may be ostensible intuitions which are

---

[1] *Vide* below, p. 39.

false, there may be others which, while falling short of absolute certainty, are adequate to provide some justification for belief. I am not indeed contending that intuition or,, for that matter, *a priori* reasoning, can be only probable in exactly the same sense as that in which the conclusions of problematic inference are only probable. In the case of problematic induction even a perfect reasoner would not be able to obtain certain conclusions if he had only our premisses, but this is not the kind of uncertainty I am suggesting here. What I am suggesting is an uncertainty due solely to the risk of our being mistaken. Our ostensible intuition (or convincing *a priori* argument) may be vitiated by a confusion of some kind, and while we can eliminate this risk in some cases, e.g. with propositions such as that: 'No S is P' entails 'No P is S', or that $2+2=4$, we cannot do it in all. In philosophy at any rate it seems almost beyond human capacity to make the fundamental notions completely clear to oneself, and so there is always the risk that an apparent intuition (or *a priori* argument) which seems to yield truth may really not do so. This does not necessarily mean that the ostensible intuition is merely worthless, it means that it involves a risk of error, to be lessened by testing and care but perhaps never completely eliminated. It may even be that the ostensible intuition actually includes error in itself, yet is far from worthless because it also contains truth. It may be, humanly speaking, impossible at the present time, or perhaps ever, completely to disentangle this truth from the error, yet the mixture of truth and error we have attained may represent a great advance towards the truth as compared with the position we should hold if we had just ignored the ostensible intuition. This is likely to be the case with most of the epoch-making philosophical and religious intuitions of great men. Not that the ordinary man, too, is without many cognitions not derivable entirely from inference or observation which, like many of those dependent on inference or observation, do not yield certainty and yet justify belief, and, while not presenting us with any completely clear definite proposition, yet enhance our knowledge and perhaps sometimes form a necessary basis of any advance in a given branch of study at all. It seems to me that such confused non-inferential cognitions form the basis, for instance, of the categories of substance and cause, not to mention the part they play in ethics or religion. Anyone who claims that the validity of the categories of cause and substance is self-evident is liable to be challenged to give a precise account of the propositions about them which he holds are immediately known, and he may then find that any tenable propositions turn out to be so complicated that it is quite unreasonable to suppose them self-evident, and will surely find that, even if he can formulate some apparently simple propositions which he thinks he knows, the question of the analysis of the concepts involved in them is very difficult and dubious. But if he admitted that our object of knowledge (or, better, 'cognition', since 'knowledge' implies certainty) is something more or less vague, not adequately stateable, at least by us at present, in a definite form of words and only capable of being understood progressively if we add to the original non-inferential cognition inference, analysis, and testing by its applications, then his position becomes much less easy to assail. To take one example, that some such non-inferential cognition forms the basis of our belief in induction must be admitted if we are to accept the results of induction as justified at all, yet logicians have certainly so far not succeeded in analysing adequately and stating definitely what is the *a priori* element in induction.

If the mode of cognition we are discussing admits of error this will explain the possibility of conflicting 'intuitions' by different persons or by the same person at different times. As for the third objection, to the effect that 'intuition' is a merely subjective criterion, we may reply that, while the state of intuiting is of course only a subjective state of somebody, so is every cognitive state, and it is clear that whatever criterion we had we could only in the last resort tell whether we were applying it by reference to our subjective state. For nobody else can do our knowing or reasoning for us, though we no doubt may, instead of knowing or reasoning, accept other people's opinions. But this does not mean that the truth of the proposition we intuit or claim to intuit is *inferred* from our subjective state. We do not argue: I feel certain of this, therefore it is true. It is not a case of inferring a necessary proposition from a contingent, empirical one about my state of mind, which would indeed be illegitimate, but of seeing a proposition to be necessary where of course the seeing is itself a subjective state of mind. From this sort of subjectivity we could only free ourselves by not using our mind. In so far as intuitions or claims to intuition are alleged to be open to the charge of subjectivity in a sense in which other forms of cognition are not, the objection resolves itself into the fourth one, i.e. that 'intuitions' are unbacked by reasons and incapable of being tested, and are therefore useless as criteria.

To this objection we shall now turn. It has been pressed most strongly in connexion with ethics, chiefly because all attempts to prove ethical conclusions from non-ethical premisses have failed. But it is very important to realize that this kind of difficulty is by no means confined to ethics, as the supporters of ethical subjec- tivism often seem almost to think. Intuition is required by all reasoning and not only by ethics. It is true that in many cases there is universal agreement as to what we see intuitively, so that the difficulty does not arise in such an acute form as it does in regard to some ethical problems, but it is certainly not true that the disagreement to which I have referred occurs only in considering questions of ethics and philosophy. There is frequent disagree- ment about matters of fact as to what has happened or will happen or concerning the causes of something, and when we have ex- hausted the arguments on a given point in these matters there still remains a difference between the ways in which these arguments are regarded by the antagonists. In any science where you cannot prove but can only make more or less probable, there will be different estimates as to the balance of probabilities. As in ethics you have to compare and weigh in the balance different values, so here you have to balance the probable arguments against each other, and in order to do that you must rely at some point or other on an estimate of their strength which cannot itself be further justified by mediate reasoning and which may still vary according to the person who makes the judgement. There are genuine differences between competent researchers as to the force of argu- ments even about matters of fact where we are estimating proba- bilities, as in historical studies. Our decision as to which of two probable arguments is the stronger may be influenced by other arguments in turn, but to be influenced by them rationally we must also estimate the weight of these other arguments, so that in the last resort it is a matter of immediate insight into their nature. Just as in a demonstrative argument you must see intui- tively how each step follows from the preceding one, so in the case of a probable argument you must rely on estimates of the degree of probability given by the argument as compared to that given by arguments on the other side, which estimates, unless the degrees of probability can be mathematically calculated, must be intuitive or be deduced from estimates which are intuitive. Again we are confronted with a situation in which we either see or do not see and cannot logically prove that what we seem to see is true.

Some people would cut the knot by just saying that the right view is the view which works, but this ignores the point that whether a view works or not is itself something which cannot be decided without reasoning and therefore, by my previous argument, without intuition. We cannot determine whether a view will or would work or even that it has worked in the past by mere observation alone. For, although we may observe the consequences of an action, we require at least some simple reasoning, e.g. an application of the method of difference, to see that what we observe is a consequence of the action and not of something else. That we require reasoning is still more obvious if what we are to decide is not whether something has worked, but whether it will or would work. So the argument I have used to show that all reasoning requires something of the nature of immediate insight or intuition can be used to show that this is the case with the reasoning by which we determine whether a belief works or would work, and we are no nearer escaping from intuition. A consideration of the likely consequences of a belief will not enable us in a dispute to decide by pure reasoning unmixed with an intuitive estimate of probabilities whether our own view or that of our opponent is true, for his estimate of the probabilities may differ from ours, and likewise his estimate of the strength of each argument that we use in favour of our estimate. We cannot go on *ad infinitum* giving further arguments about the consequences, and however many arguments we give, the difference of opinion may and often does remain. 'Working' as a criterion will not remove the difficulties mentioned even where it is applicable at all.

Now it is when two intuitive convictions, whether in the same or different people, conflict, or when we have some doubts as to whether our intuitive conviction is not confused and unreliable that tests become important, and the merit of the coherence theory in this connexion is that it has warned us against too readily assuming that our immediate intuitive convictions are certainly true, and has suggested the procedure of testing them. I think the theory is wrong in maintaining that no propositions can be known apart from the coherence test, but at least it is a valuable test. Intuitionists have often far too readily assumed that we knew with certainty where we needed an additional test, or have mistakenly ignored intuitive convictions that fall short of certainty but yet might rank as justified beliefs. Where we have an intuitive conviction of the truth of a proposition not amounting to certainty, but sufficient at least to justify our taking pains to try out what will happen if it is true, then the coherence test may prove very important. If the propositions intuitively believed, when developed, agree with our other knowledge and are capable of being made the basis of a relatively coherent system, that may perhaps be sufficient to elevate them, if not to the position of absolute certainty, at any rate to that of well-justified belief. For example, our intuitive belief in the occurrence of causation is immensely strengthened by the success of science in developing this postulate so as to make a relatively coherent system of physical events.[1] Either our intuitive conviction or the success of science might perhaps be inadequate by itself to justify the certainty we feel that causation occurs, yet together they may do so. Again, to take an ethical instance, our intuitive belief in the obligation to keep promises can be confirmed and supported by a realization both of Kant's point that the policy of making promises with the intention of breaking them cannot be consistently universalized, and, still more, by a consideration that the keeping of promises on principle and in general tends to the fulfilment of other *prima facie* duties, has good consequences, and is essential for the maintenance of the fabric of an ordered society, i.e. by the coherence of the belief with the results of the application of other ethical criteria. So we can reply to the last and most serious criticism directed against the admission of intuitions by flatly denying its truth. It is not the case, as the objector alleges, that intuitions are unbacked by reasons and therefore incapable of being tested so that there is no means of distinguishing between conflicting ones. The critic who uses this argument has confused the true proposition that intuitions are not completely established by reasoning with the false proposition that they cannot be supported by reasoning, a mistake for which however, he has the excuse that his opponents have spoken as if the intuitive mode of cognition always yielded knowledge and therefore did not require any support by reasons. As a matter of fact even when we *know* the truth of a proposition intuitively this is not incompatible with its being possible also to give reasons

---

[1] Even if recent scientific discoveries cast doubt on the *universality* of causation, they do not cast doubts on its *occurrence*, which is implied even in the admission that certain conditions render certain consequences more probable than others.

supporting it, though it does render the giving of such reasons superfluous,[1] since we know it without the reasons, and to base it on them would be to prove the more certain by the less. But the use of tests does not imply that a belief is to be based only on the tests: we have seen that all non-empirical beliefs cannot be based on inference, for even to infer we need intuitions to provide the links of the inference.

But this raises another question. As we have discovered, an important class of propositions which we must admit that we see intuitively to be true are propositions asserting the implications on which inference depends, propositions of the form: p *entails* q. How are these themselves to be tested? Are they not cases of pure untested intuition? Now in the case of the general principles of inference no test seems to be needed, since we all seem to be able to see unhesitatingly, immediately, and certainly that they are true. But if they needed testing a test would be provided by seeing that they agree with each other and that, in cases where the premisses are true and the conclusions can be otherwise confirmed, the assumption of the principles of inference leads to conclusions which are also true. As a matter of fact, we do apply a test. It is very doubtful whether we should ever have a right to accept it as *knowledge* that one proposition implied another on the ground that we saw this in one particular case unless we also saw that this implication was not peculiar to just this proposition but would also hold in other similar cases, though the two processes are not usually sharply separated except for the formal logician. This universalization is itself a test, one might call it a test by coherence with other cases of valid inference. If I felt completely certain on considering a conjunction of two propositions that they implied a third and then noticed that on considering two other propositions which were in no relevant respect different from the first two I could not see that the corresponding implication followed, my original certainty would usually disappear at once and I should suspect that I had made a mistake. Nor, on the other hand, could we attain knowledge of the general laws of inference without some reference to particular instances. For though such general laws are not mere empirical generalizations

---

[1] i.e. for establishing the truth of the proposition known. It may be very useful, even when a proposition is already known, to give a proof of it for the purpose of disclosing what is not already known, i.e. its connection with the other propositions on which the proof is based.

from particular instances, they cannot be adequately grasped till we have seen that they are capable of yielding inferences seen to be valid in particular cases.[1] So the particular instances and the general law are both required to confirm each other.

The intuitionist and coherence theories should therefore be taken as supplementary. We cannot dispense with intuition, but its results can be tested by coherence with other propositions. The intuitionist is wrong if he will not admit that his apparent intuitions may have all degrees of certainty and ignores the possibility or need of the application of further tests: the advocate of the coherence theory is wrong if he denies or ignores the need for intuition over and above any coherence test which can be applied. On the one hand some propositions may be known intuitively apart from any coherence test, though it may be doubted even with these whether they can be understood without reference to their place in the system to which they belong, and on the other hand, when some propositions are already established others may be rendered probable because they form a coherent system with them, though even here intuition is necessary to determine when coherence is achieved. The mere fact that we seem to intuit the truth of a proposition does not necessarily mean that we know it, and most cases of ostensible intuition require to be supplemented by the coherence test; but mere coherence by itself (as in a well-written novel) is no evidence of truth at all unless some of the coherent propositions are otherwise established or at least supported. They may be established or supported by experience, but where this is not the case the support may be derived from intuition and the two criteria can then supplement each other. For we must remember the logical points that, while the fact that A entails B and B entails A is itself no evidence whatever for the truth of either A or B, yet if there is already some evidence supporting A and also some independent evidence supporting B the evidence for both is rendered mush stronger by the fact that A and B entail each other, because the evidence for either of them then also supports that for the other.[2] Further, it is also rendered stronger, though in less degree, if the truth of A or B would each make the truth of the other probable, and, provided A and B

[1] W. E. Johnson in his *Logic* (pt i, ch. 8) says that they are therefore based on intuitive induction.

[2] Even the advocates of the coherence theory usually admit that it is not mere coherence which is the criterion, for human beings at least, but coherence with our experience.

might possibly have turned out incompatible, it is even rendered stronger in some degree if A and B are merely shown to be compatible with each other. In this way the coherence test may support and be supported by intuitive convictions. I have said that all reasoning presupposes intuition, and therefore it would be a vicious circle if I said that all intuited truths could be proved by reasoning and had no basis except reasoning, but it is not a vicious circle if I say that they could all be supported by reasoning. For, though the reasoning by which they are supported will in its turn presuppose, or rather be a chain of, other intuitions, two views may support each other mutually, either strengthening the evidence for the other, provided either has some independent basis itself. In this case our intuitive conviction provides the independent basis, and where this does not amount to certainty two intuitive convictions may still support each other in such a way as to justify a greater confidence in either than we should otherwise have felt.

Even where intuition is not backed by any explicit process of inference, the advocate of the coherence theory is right in refusing to regard it as a quasi-miraculous flash of insight standing by itself and not essentially connected with any thought-process at all. Intuition presupposes at least a partial analysis of the situation or a selecting of certain aspects of it, a process which presumably takes some time and may be more or less gradual, and it is certainly affected deeply by our previous experience and thought. What we see immediately may be the result of a careful survey or long experience of the whole situation or the whole system involved and yet may be incapable of deduction from definite explicit features in that situation or system.

For the advocate of the coherence theory is also right in emphasizing the dependence of our intuitions, in most cases at least, on our previous view of the system to which they refer as a whole. Only this does not eliminate the necessity for intuition, since, even if the truth of an intuition depends on the whole, we must see intuitively that its truth is entailed by the whole. Certain recent writers have identified intuition with awareness of individual, though organized, wholes,[1] and have insisted that we can have genuine knowledge of such wholes. Leaving aside the implications of this for history, aesthetics, and religion, we may note that this intuition of an organized whole or individual system

---

[1] Stocks, *Reason and Intuition*, and De Burgh, *Knowledge of the Individual*.

may figure both as a presupposition and as a culmination of reasoning. How is it that we can see, e.g. that if A is to the north of B and B to the north of C then A is to the north of C, or that a straight line in three-dimensional Euclidean space is the shortest distance between two points? Not because we see the truth of these propositions quite by themselves apart from any others, but because we see them to be involved in our general idea of space. Again, intuition may appear as a culmination which presupposes and is dependent on discursive reasoning but goes beyond anything which could, strictly speaking, be proved by this reasoning. To quote from the late Professor Stocks, '. . . intuition is needed to supplement and complete the work of reason, and it is needed because what is in question throughout is an individual response to a particular situation. But that intuition is dependent on the rational analysis, and conditioned by it: it is not a certainty, arising from mere inspection, to which reason makes and can make no contribution. On the other hand, since analysis can never exhaust the individual, no logical relation can be established between the final intuition and the arguments which preceded it. The arguments lack final cogency: they are only inclining reasons. The final intuition remains unproved and unprovable.'[1] This is most clearly so perhaps in ethics, where in cases of a real difficulty we eventually see or judge rather than prove that of the various alternative acts before us this or that one is right. We can argue in ethics and we may be influenced by arguments, but in cases where there are good arguments both for and against a particular course of action there are no rules of logic or mathematics by which we can calculate which arguments have superior weight. We ought to consider the points on each side, but we shall not usually *prove* thereby even to our own satisfaction that a particular act is right, we shall merely put ourselves into a position in which we have more chance of seeing whether it is or is not right. This applies whether we adopt a utilitarian or a deontological theory of ethics or some combination of the two, because we have to balance against each other either conflicting obligations or conflicting goods or both and there is no process of reasoning by which we can prove logically that one good is greater or one obligation more binding than another. We are dependent on a view of the situation and of the consequences of the act *as a whole*: in order to form that view, we need to attend to arguments which direct our atten-

[1] *Philosophy*, vol. xi, no. 43, p. 298, or *Reason and Intuition*, p. 15.

tion to particular aspects of the situation or of the consequences, but, while it is true that in order to form an idea of the ethical significance of a whole we have to take account of all those parts which possess value or disvalue, we cannot deduce its value from them. Arguments which do give a knock-down proof in ethics always take for granted certain ethical assumptions which are not provable, however legitimate and true.

The coherence test is specially valuable as confirming philosophical intuitions because of the uncertainty to which the latter are liable. I have often thought that a philosopher who is expounding a system ought always to separate quite definitely the propositions which he holds to be intuitively seen to be true from those which he holds to be inferred, and have felt vexed with philosophers for not doing this, but while I still think that a great deal more ought to be done in this direction than is done by many most eminent philosophers, I can see now that the dichotomy is not an absolute one. A philosophical theory may be and commonly is accepted by its author both as the development of his intuitive convictions and on account of grounds, and success in working out the intuitive convictions coherently is in itself a ground for the view. To take one controversy as an example, many philosophers, called 'idealists', would claim an intuitive insight that matter implies mind or experience; but they would rarely rest this view on the intuition alone but on their ability to work out from the intuition a coherent system of philosophy which will be compatible with the facts and explain them better (make more of a coherent system of them) than the views of their rivals, while most 'realists' would regard our instinctive common-sense belief in the independent existence of matter as at least some prima facie evidence for their view and also combine with this a justification of 'realism' by showing that the hypothesis of independent physical objects gives a good causal explanation of experience, i.e. makes a coherent system of our experience. And also a philosophy may, like Spinoza's, find its culminating point in an intuition which goes beyond the reasoning that has preceded it, though it might never have been possible but for that reasoning.

So inference and intuition are linked together. Inference always presupposes intuition to provide the links in the inference, but on the other hand inference is needed to support, prepare for, and develop intuition. This is so in four ways:

1. As we have noted already, what we think we see immediately

without proof can also be tested mediately by its coherence with other acceptable beliefs and perhaps also by other arguments which are most appropriately put under some other heading than 'coherence'. These tests may give positive support to the intuitive conviction and may often be necessary to raise it to the level of a well-justified belief. Intuition of a truth together with arguments for it may be sufficient to justify its acceptance where neither would have been sufficient alone.

2. Further, a process of reasoning often is necessary to make clear to ourselves what it is that we really see intuitively. Our apparent intuitions about probability, cause, substance, goodness, God, need to be analysed and separated from what is irrelevant, and this process cannot be carried out without reasoning.

3. Even where an intuition is not directly supported by other arguments, it must be remembered that the more we have studied a subject and thought rationally about it, using our powers of inference, the more likely we are to be in a state of mind in which we shall intuit rightly. A person is not likely to have new, clear, true, and fruitful intuitions in regard to a subject if he has made no study of that subject.

4. False intuitive beliefs commonly arise either out of some intellectual confusion or out of some prejudice due to the influence of emotion or desire, e.g. wishful thinking, and a process of negative testing of alleged intuitions is badly needed to remove these irrelevant causes of belief. It may even be doubted whether there ever is a case of an irreducible conflict between ostensible intuitions which could not ultimately be traced to either of these causes.[1] It is quite certain that we can often change a person's view as to what he sees intuitively by removing these irrelevant causes, the intellectual confusion through a process of reasoning, the emotional influences through psychological treatment, personal influence, or preaching. It no doubt is beyond any human power to apply these remedies successfully in all instances, but this is a purely empirical limitation and a matter of degree. There is no reason to conclude that on principle they are ever inapplicable.

It is possible to deal on these lines with the acute practical dilemma which arises when two people claim to have ethical

---

[1] I am not here thinking of cases where a person merely fails to intuit the truth of something which another intuits. These may be merely cases of lack of experience or of ability in the direction required and may not need any such positive explanation as I have suggested for cases where different people claim to have contradictory intuitions.

intuitions that are incompatible with each other. It is one of the
chief causes of scepticism and subjectivism in ethics that in such
cases there seems to be a complete deadlock, neither side being
able to prove the other wrong or do anything to bridge the gulf
between them. But, although in a particular case the deadlock
may well be in practice irremovable, it can be accounted for in all
sorts of ways and there are many things which can be said, provided the other side will listen to them. The dispute may arise
because one side is lacking in the experience required to make a
judgement, for to estimate the intrinsic value of an experience you
must have some knowledge of what that experience is like. In such
a case the remedy is to supply the man with the experience in
question or, failing this, to describe it, if possible, in a way which
will make him realize its valuableness, a task which is, however,
usually more likely to be fulfilled by a great writer than by a
philosopher. Or the judgement that something is good or evil
may have been due to a concentration on one side of it while
ignoring others, e.g. there is no doubt that war does lead a number
of persons to perform actions of higher ethical value than any that
these persons would have been likely to perform in peace time,
and those who mistakenly regard war as good rather than evil (if
there are still people who sincerely take this view) do so because
they have concentrated their attention on the fact which I have
just mentioned and not attended enough to the evils involved in
war. The remedy in each case is to call attention in an emphatic
way to the ignored good or evil, a task that may again often be
achieved better by a poet or a novelist than by a philosopher.
Thirdly, the difference may be due to genuine intellectual confusions such as the philosopher could remove. In such cases the
person intuits something true, but confuses it with something else
which is not true, or thinks he intuits something when he is really
inferring it mistakenly. Examples are the confusions which have
led to hedonism, and the belief that one knows certain ethical
laws to be universally and absolutely binding when what
one has really seen is only that their breach is intrinsically evil or
prima facie wrong. Fourthly, there may be verbal misunderstandings, i.e. cases where the disputants are not really contradicting each other but only using words in a different way, e.g.
'virtue' may be 'intrinsically good' in one sense of 'virtue' or one
sense of 'good' and not perhaps in another. Here again the
philosopher may help. Fifthly, a mistaken intuition may be due to

psychological causes not obvious to the person who has it, such as
habit or a 'repressed desire', or to causes which the person is
conscious of but does not regard as having influenced his beliefs,
e.g. liking for some other person, conscious desire. The discovery of these is rather the task of a personal friend or a psychologist than of a philosopher, but it must be remembered that
the mere fact that some possible psychological cause of error is
present does not necessarily prove the belief to be wrong. There
are always psychological factors present which might conceivably
have led to error, but we cannot say, e.g. that all pleasant beliefs
are unjustified because with a pleasant belief it is always conceivable that the person who holds it might have been prejudiced by
desire. Finally, disagreement may be and very commonly is due
to the fact that one (or both) of the parties to the dispute does not
really wish to know the truth and would much rather risk being
in error than risk surrendering a comfortable or congenial belief.
Such disputes clearly throw no discredit on the competency of
reason as such, only on the rationality of particular men, and
require a preacher or moral educator to settle them, not a theoretical moralist or philosopher.

To the negative test of trying to discover and remove causes
which may have given rise to error can be added positive arguments of many sorts. For it is certainly not true that we cannot
argue in ethics. Ethical arguments consist to a large extent in
predicting consequences, and this is a matter for causal reasoning
ultimately based on empirical generalization; but the work of
reasoning in ethics does not stop there, for it is not the mere fact
that certain consequences are likely to follow which is relevant
to the rightness or wrongness of an action, but the goodness or
badness of the consequences. Whether the utilitarian view that
the only ultimate ground of rightness is to be found in consequences be true or not, the philosopher or ethical reasoner can
help otherwise than by mere prediction of consequences. He can
list the values affected in order to call attention to some that are
very apt to be overlooked, and classify them in order to give some
clue as to their relative importance. He can apply the coherence
test to the rival contentions and see how far either of them is
capable of taking its place in a coherent system of ethics. He can
argue from the analogy of other cases where one side had admitted
or might be expected to admit a contrary view to that now put
forward by it. He can help by distinguishing degrees of binding-

C

ness in different obligations,[1] by pointing out what would happen
if everybody acted in the way proposed, by framing an ideal and
then viewing the proposed action in the light of the ideal, by sorting
out relevant and irrelevant facts, perhaps most of all by asking the
right questions. Even if owing to the many difficulties in the path
agreement is not always obtained in practice by these methods,
that may be because it is very rare to find a person who both can
and will make the best use of the methods, or be as receptive to
them as reason requires, when they lead to results conflicting
with his desires or prejudices. The remedy for our ills in ethics
and in politics—which is only a department of ethics—is not less
reason but more, a reason which is neither so sceptical that it
requires everything to be empirically given or formally proved,
nor so credulous that it is a mere slave to the suggestive power of
some superficially impressive personality or to the reasoner's
own desires, a reason which includes both critical reasoning and
wise intuition. For though good will is the prime necessity and
reason without will is paralyzed, will without reason is blind.

[1] We use a good many criteria besides the mere appeal to consequences for
deciding, e.g., which of two conflicting promises is more binding.

III

KNOWLEDGE OF PHYSICAL OBJECTS

From the time of Descartes onwards it has been one of the chief puzzles of philosophers to see how we could justify the claim we ordinarily make to knowledge of the physical world, and it has since then generally been held, even by 'realists', that there is some degree of uncertainty attaching to all physical object propositions, however slight it may be. But a modern school of philosophers have proposed at one fell swoop to eliminate all doubts on the subject, not indeed as merely ungrounded, but as meaningless, by laying down the principle that all meaningful statements must be capable of verification or falsification by sense-experience and concluding that, since philosophers have no dispute as to the facts of sense-experience, their disputes are either verbal or meaningless. That the school in question, in so far as it carries out its programme consistently, also throws out a great many babies with the bath-water seems clear to me; but I do not wish to discuss these now, and if the verificationists to whom I am referring have really succeeded in showing that any general doubt as to the existence of physical objects is unmeaning, they will have earned the utmost gratitude from philosophers for removing one of the chief difficulties that for many generations has beset them. What a large proportion of philosophical labour has been expended either in justifying the belief that we have knowledge of 'independent' physical objects or in showing that it cannot be justified! And now we are saved all this labour by the single verification formula, which enables us to say that there is none but a verbal difference between the contending schools, that to assert the existence of physical objects in any sense in which their existence cannot be verified is to talk nonsense, and that to say that we can doubt the existence of physical objects is also meaningless. True, we shall have to content ourselves with a view which does not admit anything in the notion of a physical object beyond a class of propositions about human observations, actual or possible; but since to assert anything else would be meaningless, why worry? Since any alternative suggestion has either no meaning at all or the same meaning as the verificationist suggestion, there is literally nothing about which to worry. However, there is a fatal snag in such a comforting view: the verificationist principle on which it is based cannot be proved and would in fact contradict itself if it were true, for it could not be verified itself and so would on its own showing be meaningless, and a statement cannot be both meaningless and true.

As a matter of fact the full-blooded verificationism of which I have just been speaking, and which I criticized in an earlier article in this periodical,[1] has now commonly been abandoned in favour of what might be called methodological verificationism, a way of approach which is not committed to the truth of the verification principle but treats the latter rather as a slogan suggesting the desirability of asking about all assertions—if true, how could they be verified, than as an established proposition. Such a method of procedure may be useful for some purposes; but it must be remembered that, unless we hold the verification principle to be not a methodological fiction but a *true* proposition, we are not justified in accepting the truth of any proposition because it has been deduced by an argument in which the verification principle was a premiss. That it can be deduced from a premiss which is not true is no justification of any proposition. We cannot rule out the possibility of doubts about physical objects by a straightforward deduction from the verification principle unless we are justified in thinking the latter itself is true and not merely methodologically useful. But it may still well be the case that the conclusion that any general doubt about physical objects is meaningless is true, though the verification principle from which it has sometimes been deduced is false. This view indeed attracts me much more than most other points in the verificationist philosophy. Only, if it is true, we shall have to find other arguments for it than any that could be based on the assertion that all meaningful statements must be verifiable by sense-experience. Having considered such an argument I shall turn to another type of view which involves the same conviction in the certainty of physical object propositions without, however, asserting that denial or doubt is *meaningless*.

People sometimes assume that the doubt can be dismissed just because it 'makes no practical difference'; but it may be retorted that, if a person is really interested only in questions which do

---

[1] V.46. Above pp. 15–33.

make a practical difference in the ordinary, narrow sense of 'practical', he is not the sort of person who should study philosophy at all, because it cannot possibly interest him. I should have thought it had been believed for centuries that philosophy could not help one to predict particular physical events or psychological experiences; but I cannot see any ground for concluding from this belief (which I share) that 'philosophical assertions' are either merely verbal or meaningless, unless we assume the verification principle to be true, an assumption which I have rejected. That philosophical study may have an indirect practical effect of a different sort surely cannot be denied, for obviously it can affect one's general attitude to life and therefore one's emotional reactions and practical decisions: many of the most important events in history on most recognized criteria of importance have been partly determined by general ideas about religion, ethics, or politics which, though not mainly the fruit of philosophical reflection, were influenced, at least indirectly, by the latter (though usually not nearly so much as in my opinion would have been desirable). It may be retorted that theories about the grounds for holding that physical objects exist are not, like ideas about God, going to cause any revolutionary changes in human life and society; but, since all parts of philosophy are liable to reveal unexpected interconnections, we can never be sure that philosophical considerations which originated in some sphere of thought as far removed from the ordinary thoughts of practical life as are the questions which I am discussing in this article may not indirectly affect men's views on subjects of practical importance by suggesting and supporting a particular mode of thought which may be applied in other fields. Just as it has been commonly said that the scientific discoveries which have been of most enormous practical importance have usually originated from lines of research which seemed to the researcher incapable of yielding any practical effects at all, so in philosophy we have no right to assume that ideas of practical importance may not emerge from or be affected by studies in fields that appear to have no practical bearing whatever. Most of the great philosophers of the past have thought it worth their while to devote very careful attention indeed to the theory of physical objects and the theory of knowledge; and since they would at least claim that their philosophy is a systematically inter-connected whole, it follows that considerations arising from these fields are likely to have influenced other parts of their philosophical teaching more practical in their relevance. To look too closely for practical results in one's philosophy and aim too directly at them is not the best way of obtaining them. Philosophy cannot indeed be practical in the sense in which the art of making shoes or the science of physiology is practical; but if 'practical' means 'relevant to human happiness and misery' there is hardly anything more practically important than have been certain philosophical or quasi-philosophical ideas.

The verificationist, whether dogmatic or methodological, has at least shown one thing, namely, that the general doubt about the existence of physical objects is a different kind of doubt from the doubt about the existence of particular objects when there are particular reasons for doubting it. The philosophical doubt about physical objects differs from such doubts, which occur at the level of common sense, in four respects. (1) It is not an emotional but only a theoretical doubt: the philosopher *feels* quite certain about what he says he doubts, at least when considering it outside his study in the hurly-burly of practical life and probably even in most philosophical discussions themselves. (2) It has no *direct* practical effect, i.e. philosophers who profess the doubt are just as keen to avoid moving motorcars and bombs and to eat food as are philosophers who do not profess it or ordinary practical men. (3) It is not based on the same kind of grounds as ordinary mundane doubts, e.g. doubts as to whether the lake a man seems to see in a desert is not really only a mirage. (4) It is characterized by extreme generality—if it affects any, it affects all physical object propositions. But to say that it is a different kind of doubt is not to say that it is no doubt at all. Or, even if we say that human beings are psychologically incapable of doubting all physical object propositions, it may still be true that they are really doubtful and that we can see that they are so, though we cannot hold this proposition in mind for long, apply it in practice or feel as if it were true. Still less does the psychological difficulty of entertaining a doubt make the doubt meaningless.

Now I should myself like to be able to accept the suggestion that the doubt in question is meaningless, for then I should have a clear justification for holding as indubitable many things which almost all philosophers would like to hold indubitable but cannot prove, for if the doubt as to physical objects may be dismissed as meaningless we should be justified in treating in the same way any professed doubt as to the existence of other minds than the speaker's own or any suggestion that memory is always untrustworthy. We should then discover a justification for Dr Moore's view that we know (in the strict sense of 'know') many common-sense propositions about these matters, a view which he holds without having been able to give any argument to justify it except a reference to other common-sense propositions about which the question could equally well have been asked how we know them, as when he proves that external objects exist by merely pointing out that his hands exist.[1] But I cannot get away from the fact that I see quite clearly that the statements that memory is always untrustworthy or that the existence of any physical object is doubtful, whether true or false, have at least a good plain meaning, however hard it may be to furnish a quite adequate philosophical 'analysis' of their meaning. I must therefore reject the proffered consolation and face my doubts hoping that they may after all turn out, not indeed meaningless, but unjustified.

However, there is one argument used in favour of the view that such doubts are meaningless which I must first discuss. It is urged that doubt is only significant when there is some particular reason for doubting and some conceivable criteria which could be relevant to that doubt. And even people who do not hold the verificationist principle in general may contend that in the case of physical things at any rate we are justified in saying that the reason for the doubt and the criteria for settling it must be empirical because, whether there are questions which can be settled by other than empirical criteria or not, at any rate empirical criteria are the only criteria which can settle questions about the existence or properties of physical things. Everybody admits that it is not senseless to doubt whether the man in the distance is Smith on the ground that I am looking through a dense mist which distorts what I see, that a person I see in the distance even under normal conditions sometimes turns out on closer inspection not to be the person I first took him to be, and that I have heard from a fairly reliable source that Smith sailed for Australia yesterday. But it is contended that it is senseless to raise the doubt whether anything I see ever is as I see it on the ground that there can be no conceivable empirical criteria which would be relevant to that doubt. There are no possible experiences, it is said, which could cast doubt on all physical object propositions, only on some.

[1] *Philosophical Papers*, p. 146.

You cast doubt on some only by reference to other physical object propositions and therefore you cannot cast doubt on them all.

In reply I should flatly deny that empirical circumstances cannot be relevant to the general doubt. In fact the philosophers who have cast doubt on our certainty as to physical objects have usually done so on the ground of particular empirical circumstances, e.g. dreams or the occurrence of what subsequent experience shows to be 'illusions'. Now it may be held that the empirical evidence given does not justify their conclusion that all physical object propositions are doubtful. I shall have something to say about that later. But this can at any rate only be settled by an investigation of the particular grounds given and not by a general argument against the possibility of doubt. Further, it is quite conceivable that illusions and dreams might have been much more frequent and much more difficult to distinguish from what we regard as veridical perception than is actually the case. Suppose when we looked at what we took to be the same place we very rarely had an experience in the least similar twice running, suppose it were completely impossible to arrive at any sort of agreement between different men as to the physical things around us, suppose what I took to be the same physical object behaved like water one moment and like steel the next without there being any discernible regularity whatever in these changes, suppose I seemed sometimes to have the body of a toad and sometimes of an elephant and sometimes no body at all. Under these circumstances it is surely plain that a doubt as to the reliability of any apparent perceptions of physical objects would be justified, whether it is or is not justified today. Now the occurrence of such circumstances is perfectly possible logically. It may be doubted whether life could have established and maintained itself under such conditions and so as to whether we should have been there to doubt the existence of physical objects; but I am not sure whether any argument against the supposition to that effect does not vitiate itself by already presupposing the existence of a physical world, and in any case it is *logically* possible that life might have existed under such circumstances for anything we can see. And we can surely imagine a state of affairs in which, though things did not go to the extreme which I have suggested, the reports of different people on things they observed were more difficult to reconcile than they actually are, a state in which illusions were more frequent and more puzzling, a state in which everybody was apt to have hallucinations and dreams without warning in the middle of their waking experience. Consequently, even if we now think that the argument of the sceptic fails so completely as to leave us still in possession of absolutely certain knowledge of physical objects, we can easily imagine circumstances in which the element in our experience that we call 'illusion' was so much more prominent and baffling than it is that we should have to admit that the existence of physical objects was more or less doubtful and that no physical object judgements were absolutely certain. Contrariwise, if we are already of the opinion that no physical object propositions can be known with absolute certainty, we can imagine a state of affairs in which illusions, dreams and discrepancies between different observers were much less prominent than they are, and we should then have to admit that under such conditions physical object propositions, if not absolutely certain, would be at least nearer certainty than they are in fact for us. This is sufficient to show that empirical circumstances are relevant to the doubt in question, and so the doubt cannot be dismissed on the ground that they are not. The argument which I have quoted in favour of this dismissal could at the best only apply against a person who said that, even if there never were any dreams or perceptions which our subsequent experience inclined us to describe as illusory, physical object propositions would still all be doubtful, and who raised doubts without giving any empirical evidence in their favour; and I do not think that it would even apply against him, because the apparent inadequacy of any conceivable empirical criteria to establish physical object propositions with certainty is of itself a strong argument against the certainty of the latter apart from any evidence based on illusions, etc.

Could my point be met by admitting that empirical criteria are relevant to the doubt but still denying that it is a meaningful doubt on the ground that empirical criteria, though relevant as increasing or decreasing probability, cannot settle the question asked by the doubter completely and prove with certainty either that physical objects do or that they do not exist? No, clearly not, for if the doubt is meaningless no empirical criteria can possibly even be relevant to the degree of doubtfulness to be attached to the propositions doubted, since it is then senseless to say that they are doubtful at all. Further, the whole argument rested on the supposition that physical object propositions are propositions

c*

of such a kind that their truth could be determined by empirical criteria and no others. Therefore, if it is true that the use of empirical criteria could not under any conceivable circumstances remove the doubt, once it was raised, it follows that physical object propositions are all really uncertain; and on the other hand, if there are conceivable empirical criteria which could remove them, the statement that they are all uncertain may be false but could not be meaningless.

As a matter of fact, as we have seen, the doubt is itself based mainly on empirical circumstances in the sense that they provide premisses from which we may plausibly deduce that the propositions are doubtful. It remains true that our decision should not and could not depend wholly on the empirical evidence taken as brute fact, but on an estimate of the bearing of the latter. Philosophers do agree as to the empirical evidence but differ as to the conclusions they draw from it. This in itself is not peculiar to philosophers; it is often the case also with, e.g. historians, who estimate differently the bearing of acknowledged facts in making their rival theories probable or the reverse. However, it would be unreasonable to deny that there is some difference, hard perhaps to define, between the relation which empirical evidence can bear to philosophical conclusions and the relation which it bears to doubtful historical or other factual conclusions deduced from it. But I do not mean to say that philosophical doubt about physical objects is the same kind of doubt as ordinary doubt about the nature or existence of some particular objects; all I mean to point out is that, if the doubt is dismissed as senseless or not worth considering philosophically on the ground that it would be a doubt to which empirical evidence was irrelevant, the premiss is just not true, so that we need not accept the conclusion even if we granted, which I should not grant, that the truth of the premiss would entail it.

It may be objected that we can only doubt physical object propositions on the strength of other propositions about physical objects, and that therefore it cannot be legitimate to doubt all physical object propositions but only some of them. 'How can we know that the flat sense-datum is not part of the surface of the cricket ball, unless we know that there really is a cricket ball and that it really does have a surface which is spherical? Or how do we know that the reflection of the glove is dislocated as to position and reversed as to right and left, unless we know where the glove itself is and how its parts are arranged?'[1] I should, however, agree with the author from whom I have just quoted in dismissing this objection, though perhaps with somewhat less respect than he shows for it. In the first place, the fact that I *seem* to see the same object on different occasions as possessing qualities which are not compatible with each other might be held sufficient of itself to justify doubt.[2] Assumptions about physical objects play a large part in the argument from illusion as commonly stated; but the argument is not wholly destroyed when these assumptions are taken away. Indeed it may be held that the mere fact that we cannot *prove* the existence of physical objects, if this is a fact, is in view of the impossibility of holding it to be certain that all cases of ostensible perception are cases of direct knowledge sufficient to cast some doubt on all physical object propositions. I am not arguing that the sceptic's argument is successful; that we have to consider later. But at least it is meaningful, and is not in all its forms based on the assumption of the truth of any physical object propositions. But, secondly, I do not think that the fact that physical object propositions formed part of a sceptic's premises would necessarily vitiate or render uncertain his conclusion in so far as drawn from these premises. If it can be shown from what he says that a witness contradicts himself this is a good argument for attaching doubt to everything the witness says unless confirmed from other sources, and the sceptic is trying to show that perception is an unreliable witness by showing that some physical object propositions based on perception are incompatible with some of our perceptions. A *reductio ad absurdum* is always recognized as a legitimate form of argument, and a *reductio ad absurdum* consists in showing a view to be false by assuming it to be true and then deducing from this assumption consequences which are absurd or incompatible with the assumption itself or with well-established facts. This is not exactly the argument in question about physical objects, for it is not intended by such arguments to show that the belief in physical objects is logically absurd or even false, but that it is not certain; but the principle is similar. The argument is: even granting the truth of the ordinary belief in the physical world, it follows that

---

[1] H. H. Price, *Perception*, p. 34.

[2] No doubt it would be logically possible to reply that the object had changed, but this would not remove the doubt raised, for nobody could hold that it was *certain* that the object had changed in this way.

the belief still cannot be certain. (And if it is not true, there can be no question of its being certain.) The sceptical arguments to which I have referred may not be right, but at least they escape the charge of depending for their validity on the truth of the view which they are intended to assail, except when gratuitously mis-stated by the persons who use them.

Let us now turn to another kind of view which dismisses philosophical doubt in these matters as illegitimate, namely, the view put forward by Dr G. E. Moore. Without claiming that doubt is meaningless, he does insist that we have certain know-ledge of many physical object propositions. In order to maintain this position it is essential, as he recognizes, to distinguish between the proposition that I see it to be logically impossible that *p* could be false and the proposition that I certainly know *p* to be true. But in holding that we can know with certainty what it is logically possible might not be true he is in agreement with most philoso-phers, for most philosophers have maintained that we can know with certainty many propositions about my present state of mind and immediate objects of sense and yet they have not held that these propositions are logically necessary, still less that we could see them to be so. I know now that I am feeling cold, but it is perfectly possible logically, for anything I can see, that I might instead be feeling very hot. Not only does Dr Moore hold that we can know with certainty what it is logically possible might not be true, but also that we can know with certainty what it is *logically* possible we might be wrong in thinking we knew. (For these two statements are not indistinguishable. It is logically possible that I might not be in existence, but it is not logically possible that I could think I existed and yet not exist.) But again this is quite in accord with the views of most philosophers. Most philosophers, I think, have held that we could by memory know with absolute certainty some propositions about the past (even if other memory-propositions were only believed), although they could not show any logical impossibility to be involved either in the non-happen-ing of the event a man was convinced he remembered or in his thinking he knew it had happened though it had not really done so. As a matter of fact, since, e.g. feeling cold is different from judging that I feel cold, I should hold that there would be no self-con-tradiction even in the supposition that a man was mistaken in his judgement as to his immediate sense-experience, so that we have even here a case of *knowing* where it is *logically* possible we might be mistaken; but I am not sure whether most philosophers would agree with my view. However, the majority of philosophers have not when discussing philosophy claimed strict knowledge of propositions about physical objects, as does Dr Moore.

If we cannot see the denial of a physical object proposition to be self-contradictory, how can we know the proposition to be true? In *Contemporary British Philosophy*[1] Dr Moore says that we know such propositions without knowing how we know them. In *Proof of an External World*[2] he claims to be able to prove with complete adequacy and certainty that there are external objects by just pointing to some particular physical objects which we can see, but admittedly leaves unanswered the question how we know that these particular objects which provide the premiss of the proof exist and seems to suggest that this question neither admits of nor needs an answer.[3] This position seems to me not satisfactory unless our knowledge here is direct, and so many difficulties have been raised in the course of philosophical controversy against the latter supposition that even in that case a defence against these objections is urgently needed. If we do not know physical object propositions directly—and some of the propositions which Dr Moore cites as known in *Contemporary British Philosophy* he admits we do not know directly[4]—it is surely incumbent on the philosopher to explain the logical nature of the arguments by which they can be established and show how it is that such arguments yield not probability but complete certainty.

It seems often to be assumed that, if we adopt a phenomenalist view of physical objects and analyse them in terms of the sense-data of human beings, all difficulty in supposing propositions about them to be directly known disappears. But this is by no means the case. For, even if we analyse such propositions in terms of human experience or sense-data, they still go beyond my own sense-data, so that I cannot claim that the content of even the simplest of them is entirely given in my present experience. Even such a statement as 'There is a table' includes on the phenomenalist view propositions about the experience or sense-data of other human beings besides myself and about hypothetical observations of my own, i.e. it asserts not only that I have table-like sense-data now, but also at least that other human

[1] Ed. J. H. Muirhead, *2nd Series*, p. 206.
[2] In Philosophical Papers, pp. 146 ff.   [3] id. p. 149.   [4] P. 206.

beings would have similar sense-data if they looked under certain conditions and that if I varied the conditions I should have certain other sense-data which I am not having now, for instance, tactual sense-data or visual sense-data obtained from a different point of view. If physical object propositions were merely statements about one's present experience and immediate objects of sense, there would be no distinction between propositions about physical objects and propositions about dreams. Therefore, if we claim to know physical object propositions, we are claiming to know something that is not logically necessary and is not given in our present experience, whether we adopt a realist or a phenomenalist view of physical objects. But this claim is not necessarily to be rejected offhand.

In an unpublished paper[1] read at Cambridge several years ago to the Moral Science Club, to which Dr Moore has kindly given me leave to refer, he defends his position against some stock objections by the sceptic. I have not the paper in front of me but am dependent on a restatement of the argument which I made in a course of lectures that I delivered, so it is very possible that it may not be in all respects a completely accurate account of what Dr Moore said, e.g. I seem to remember that he was concerned more with memory than with physical object propositions in his paper while I have only developed these arguments in regard to physical objects. But I think that it represents adequately arguments that he used, and even irrespective of the question whether he used them the arguments are certainly important and deserve discussion and, if possible, a reply, which in the absence of publication they are hardly likely to obtain from anybody else. Dr Moore first considers the argument from dreams as used by, e.g. Descartes. It he thinks can be stated in some way like this.

A person who seems to himself to be perceiving a chair may not actually be perceiving one, for he may seem to perceive a chair in what is only a dream.

I am a person who seems to be perceiving a chair now.

Therefore, I may not now be perceiving a chair.

Now, Dr Moore contends, the first premiss may mean one of two things. It may mean 'Some people who seem to themselves to be perceiving a chair are not actually perceiving a chair'.

---

[1] A paper by him containing similar points has since been published in his *Philosophical Papers* under the heading *Four Forms of Scepticism*.

But in that case the argument breaks down because 'may' cannot possibly bear that sense in the conclusion. I cannot say, 'Some of me is perceiving a chair'. Even if that objection did not hold, he might have added, the argument would in that case commit the fallacy of undistributed middle, being of the form *MoP SaM SoP*. He compares the argument to: A human being may be female, I am a human being, therefore I may be female.

Secondly, he says, the major premiss may mean merely that it is logically possible that a person who seems to himself to be perceiving a chair is really not perceiving a chair. Then there is no flaw in the argument, but the conclusion is not incompatible with Dr Moore's view, for he does not hold that it is logically impossible that we could be deceived as regards these physical object propositions but only that we know in some cases that we are not so deceived. As we have seen, he is contending that we can *know* even where it is logically possible that we might be wrong.

I cannot, however, help viewing this reply with considerable suspicion. The difficulty is not merely that some experiences which seem to be instances of perceiving, e.g. chairs are not really so. It is, I think, that there is no internal difference which we can detect between dreams and waking experiences, illusions and veridical perceptions, that enables us to distinguish them. The argument: Parents may have a female child, A and B are parents, therefore A and B may have a female child—is valid enough. 'May' is to be understood relatively to the evidence available, and I think that the argument leading to the conclusion that I may be female sounds absurd only because I already know that I am not female. If what is stated in the second premiss, namely, that I am a human being were really all that was known of me, it would be perfectly legitimate to conclude that I 'may be female'. And what is meant by 'may be' here is not, I think, either that it is logically possible, or that some people are female, but that relative to the evidence it is not certain that the person concerned is other than female. Interpreted in this way the major premiss of the sceptic's argument about physical objects becomes: From the fact that a man seems to himself to perceive a physical object it never follows with certainty that he is really perceiving that object, and the conclusion becomes—it is not certain that I am perceiving a chair. Dr Moore would no doubt say that this begs the question; but there is a reason given for the major premiss, namely, that we also seem to perceive physical object in dreams, when we are not really perceiving them. Why does this seem to provide a ground for the sceptic? Not merely because some members of the class, ostensible perceptions, are not real perceptions of physical objects. If there were a clear criterion internal to the experience by which we could distinguish those members of the class which are not real perceptions of physical objects from those which are, the argument would lose at least a good deal of its point, but the trouble is that no such criterion is available. The argument may therefore be restated as follows:

There is no empirically observable difference in the experience itself between perceiving a physical thing in waking life and seeming to perceive a thing of that sort in dreams.

'There is a physical object of a certain kind' is empirical knowledge if it is knowledge at all, therefore there must be an empirically observable difference between an experience in which I know this and an experience in which I do not.

Therefore I cannot say that I now know that there is a physical chair here, when I cannot, faced with just the same experience, know it in dreams.

This argument seems to me formidable. No doubt empirical tests that fall outside my present experience could be applied in order to confirm that there was a chair here; but Dr Moore's claim is that I can sometimes know the existence of chairs by just seeing them without applying further tests, and also I might have a dream in which I seemed to be applying these further tests as much as ever I do in waking life. It may, however, be objected that it is not certain that we ever do have dreams in which there occur experiences exactly the same as any we have in our waking life. It may be for anything we can show to the contrary that there is always a difference of some sort in the way a dream feels as compared to the way in which a waking experience of similar content feels. As far as they can remember this is undoubtedly the case with some people; but there are others, vivid dreamers, who could not be sure of this but would rather be inclined to deny it, saying that some dreams seemed just as real as waking life. However, no one can be confident enough in his memory of dreams and his ability to notice his feelings while dreaming for him to be entitled to say with any assurance whether the experience of seeming to see, e.g. a chair in a dream is or is not the same in quality as is the experience of seeing it in waking life. It is therefore by no means sure that the first premiss of the argument is true, and so the conclusion is not proved. But at any rate the premiss *may* well be true, and if it is true it seems to me that the conclusion follows. No doubt it might be the case that some experiences of perception in waking life exactly resembled experiences in dreams but that the members of the former class which did so were not cases of knowledge. It would generally be admitted that there are cases of perception, e.g. at a distance or in a mist, where we are not entitled to be sure that the kind of object we think we see is physically there at all, and it might be that the only experiences of perception in waking life which resembled experiences in dreams were of that kind. In that case I do not think that Dr Moore's position would be threatened, since he does not claim that all cases of ostensible perception are cases of knowledge. But if there are cases of apparent perception in dreams which exactly resemble internally the kind of experience I now have when I seem to perceive the chair, it is very difficult to see how I can possibly know in the strictest sense of 'know' that I am perceiving a physical chair. It is agreed that the knowledge of physical objects is based on our experience in perceiving; but if so how could the same experience be a case of absolutely certain knowing on one occasion and a source of error on another? It might well still lead to true judgements on some occasions and to false on others; but since the same empirical criteria do not in that case always go with true physical object judgements, we could not say that we were entitled to be absolutely certain that our experience justified the judgements about physical objects. We are therefore confronted with an argument which, if its premisses are true, leads to the conclusion that we do not know any physical object propositions with absolute certainty. The second premiss is clearly true; but it is uncertain whether the first is or is not true. If it is true it follows that we do not know physical object propositions with absolute certainty; and since it is doubtful whether it is or is not true, it seems that we must conclude at least that we do not know that we know them with absolute certainty. Most people undoubtedly have dream experiences which bear a considerable resemblance to those of waking life, and the suggestion that dream experiences still really *always* feel somewhat different is not supported by experience but is a mere supposition. I should therefore conclude from the argument that it is at least very uncertain whether we ever know physical object propositions in the sense of 'know' which connotes absolute and complete objective certainty. (That we are often subjectively certain is not disputed by anybody.) Some philosophers say that this is the only proper sense of 'know'; and if so we shall then have to conclude that it is very uncertain whether we know any physical object propositions to be true at all.

The second argument of the sceptic which Dr Moore considers is the argument, also suggested by Descartes, that we cannot have certain knowledge of physical objects because it is always possible that there may be a demon at work who is deceiving us. He replies that the statement that there may be a demon who is deceiving us in our perceptions may mean two things. It may mean, firstly, that this supposition is logically possible; but that is not the point at issue. Dr Moore admits that it is logically possible that there might not be a chair there when he seems to perceive one; but he holds that this is compatible with his knowing in the strictest sense that there really is a chair. Secondly, it may mean that the supposition is not formally incompatible with anything he knows; but this, he says, begs the question. For, if he does know that there is a chair, he does know something formally incompatible with the supposition that a demon is deceiving him in the matter.

In considering this reply the doubt that strikes me is as to how I could know in any sense which connotes absolute certainty that there is a chair here without *first* knowing that a demon is not deceiving me. If I know directly that there is a chair here this, I think, would be quite possible, and I then do not see any objection to Dr Moore's reply; but, if the proposition that there is a chair here can only be justified by some process of induction, as Dr Moore seems to think most likely from his treatment of the next sceptical objection, I do not see how such a conclusion could be established inductively with certainty without first eliminating the rival hypothesis that a demon is deceiving me. And there are unsolved difficulties in holding that I can know physical object propositions directly.

The third sceptical argument is to the effect that physical object propositions are all uncertain because they can only be justified by some sort of inductive argument and induction can never yield certainty. Dr Moore replies that this argument involves four assumptions: (1) that I do not know the propositions in question directly; (2) that they are not logically entailed by anything which I know directly; (3) that if (1) and (2) are both true, physical object propositions can only be established inductively; (4) that inductive arguments can never give certainty. Dr Moore asks whether it is as certain that all these four assumptions are true as it is that he knows there is a chair before him. He is convinced that it is not, and if so the argument must be rejected as sacrificing the more certain to the less certain. Of the four assumptions in question, which he admits are severally all very plausible, he is least disinclined to doubt the fourth; but he thinks any one of them much less certain than is the proposition that he knows that there is a chair.

Now Dr Moore's whole argument here is founded on the conviction that we know physical object propositions in the *ordinary* sense of 'know', not in any special philosophical sense of 'know'. Therefore, if the ordinary sense of 'know' does not involve the complete and absolute certainty claimed, the basis of the argument goes. It is this proposition that I shall maintain. I shall not contend that I do not know that I am sitting in a chair; but I shall claim that 'know' as commonly used is to be analysed in a way which is compatible with admitting the force of the arguments that Dr Moore has rejected. But the going is very treacherous here, and it is necessary to make very careful distinctions if we are not to fall into a trap. For that a person 'knows' is a surprisingly complex proposition. I had better therefore rather risk going too slowly than going too quickly, and in order to make my position quite clear I had better start by raising certain points that are too elementary to be in themselves very interesting to the reader.

There is no doubt that the expression 'A knows that S is P' cannot be correctly used unless two conditions are fulfilled. (1) A proposition about A's state of mind which can be expressed by saying 'A is subjectively certain' must be true. (2) It must also be true that S really is P. If I am A and 'know' is in the present tense, it is not indeed possible for me to separate (1) and (2). For to be subjectively certain that S is P involves affirming at least to myself that S is P, so that I cannot affirm (1) without also affirming (2). This, I think, is the explanation why the two propositions are both expressed by the same sentence 'I know'. But I might distinguish the two at some later time and say 'I was certain that S is P but S really is not P'. In that case I should certainly not say that I ever knew that S is P but only that I thought I knew. Similarly, I can make the distinction in regard to other people and say that they are certain of something which I do not think true, but I shall not then (unless I am speaking ironically) say they know, but only that they think they know. I shall later make a distinction between a more popular and a stricter sense of 'know', but what I have said so far applies to both senses. In both senses it is the case that 'A knows that S is P' entails 'S is P' whereas 'A believes that S is P' or 'A is certain that S is P' does not entail 'S is P'.

The entailment in question is explained by philosophers in two ways. Firstly, it may be held that the proposition 'A cannot know that S is P unless S is P' is only an analytic, verbal one following from the fact that 'S is P' is part of the meaning of 'A knows that S is P'. On this view knowledge is always true for the same reason as that for which treason never prospers, i.e. only because we do not call it knowledge if we do not think it true. But, secondly, some philosophers, e.g. Cook Wilson, have held that there is a certain state of mind, knowing, such that it is absolutely impossible for a person who is in this state of mind to be mistaken as to the truth of the proposition towards which his act of knowing is directed. In that case the entailment would presumably be synthetic *a priori*, i.e. a certain fact about one's mental state in regard to the proposition that S was P would entail that S was P. I do not wish to discuss here the issue between the two rival views, but I am inclined to prefer the former. If it is adopted, 'A knows that S is P' will be a highly complex proposition including both a proposition about A's state of mind and the proposition that S is P itself besides other constituents which I shall next mention. Such different propositions came to be conjoined and expressed by the same form of words, I think, because when the first person singular of the present tense is involved they cannot, as we have seen, be separated.

But I have not yet mentioned all the conditions which must be fulfilled if we are to say correctly 'A knows that S is P'. Suppose S was P and A was certain that S was P but he was certain of it because of a fallacious argument. He could not then be correctly said to know that S is P. I should not 'know' that the square of 11 was 121, however certain I might be about it, if I only thought it to be true because I believed that the square of 11 was greater by two than the square of 9 and that the square of 9 was 119. Or, again, suppose S was P and A was certain that S was P but had no *reason* at all (as opposed to a psychological 'cause') for his certainty. In that case he would still be said to *know*, if 'S is P' were held to be a self-evident proposition or a proposition which could be established by his immediate perception, as could, e.g. the proposition that he is or is not feeling cold, but not if it were held to be a proposition of a kind which could not be legitimately asserted except on the strength of reasons. Again, he would not be said to know if he was certain of it for reasons which really only made it probable. We may express all these conditions by saying that we can only speak of 'knowing' that *S* is *P* where '*S* is *P*' is *objectively*, as well as subjectively, certain. I do not put forward this account as a *definition* of 'know' but as a rough explanation sufficient to make clear the use of the term. There are grave technical difficulties about giving a definition of 'know'.

Now philosophers have usually insisted that we must have absolute and complete certainty if we are to speak of 'knowing' at all; but this is not in accord with the most common usage of 'know'. It would certainly be according to any standard an incorrect use of language to employ the term 'know' even of another person where the proposition said to be known is not thought by the person who uses the term to be true, or where though it is probably true its probability falls *much* short of certainty; but we do often speak of 'knowing' where it would be admitted that certainty was not absolute. Thus we should use the term 'scientific knowledge' without hesitation, although all or almost all the propositions of natural science covered by this term are not known with certainty but are very probable hypotheses or empirical generalizations. Again, suppose I hear on the wireless an official statement that some person of importance in Britain has died and am asked later whether I know that he has died. Almost everybody would say they did 'know' under these circumstances, yet it clearly cannot be absolutely and completely certain that a single official statement might not be mistaken. We have thus a distinction between a stricter sense of 'know' which philosophers have usually employed and a looser sense in which the word is actually used in everyday speech. If 'know' is commonly actually used in the second way, I do not see how philosophers can have any right to say that theirs is the only proper sense of 'know'. This is a question of language, and in language the standard of propriety is the general usage of the educated. We may distinguish the two senses by saying that in the stricter sense of 'know' the term is admissible only if we have complete subjective and objective certainty, while to use the term in the looser sense it is sufficient that there should be 'practical' objective certainty and absence of real doubt. We commonly say we 'know' that S is P where we are practically certain, even if there is a theoretical possibility of error, provided it is very slight. If later on it does turn out to be the case that S is not P, or even if I discover reasons which leave room for a substantial risk that S is not P, I shall then deny that I ever knew that S was P; but as long as such evidence against it is not forthcoming, and what evidence there is makes it practically certain, we are content to speak of 'knowing'. No doubt whenever we do this we run a slight risk that our statement will not be true, for if it turns out that S is not P after all we shall, even according to the less strict sense of 'know', have to deny that we knew; but then we do commonly make statements in regard to which there is a *slight* risk that they will not turn out true, and this does not mean that the statement 'I know' will be false because there is a slight risk that I am wrong. If the risk materializes it will be false, but the odds are *ex hypothesi* very much against that happening, and if it does not materialize and S is P the statement will be true. If we were using 'know' in the strict sense there would be not merely a risk but a certainty of error every time we used it in the absence of the completest certainty, objective and subjective, that S is P.

It is a very common circumstance for a person, when he says he knows something, to be only vaguely and not explicitly aware of the reasons for accepting its truth. Most of the people who said they 'knew' that so-and-so had died because this had been announced on the wireless would not be distinctly aware, at the time at least, of the reasons which justified a more confident acceptance of this information than of a statement on the wireless by some politician that, e.g., imperial preference is a good thing. And certainly most people when they claim knowledge of particular physical propositions are not distinctly aware of the circumstances which justify them in passing beyond their own sense-data. Yet if 'know' is to be used in the stricter sense, I think it can hardly be applied with consistency to anybody who is not quite clearly aware of the reasons which justify him in asserting the truth of the proposition of which he claims knowledge. In view of this and of the philosophical difficulties raised it seems to me very difficult to maintain that in the stricter sense of 'know' we know any physical object propositions at all. It also seems ridiculous to me, as it does to Dr Moore, to say that I do not know whether this is a table or whether I am standing or sitting; but this, I think, is because we are here using 'know' in a second and less exigent sense, which is also the sense in which most people in everyday life use the term. There are still philosophical difficulties which I have not been able completely to solve about holding that we know any physical object propositions even in the looser sense of 'know', but despite the difficulties I cannot help being convinced that I do know them. Any argument to the contrary, however plausible, is at the worst less certain than that I thus know them. I wish at any rate to make it clear that any dispute between Dr Moore and me is not as to whether we know physical object propositions but as to the analysis of the term 'know'. Similarly, I should say that it would convey quite a wrong impression to say that all physical object propositions are only 'probable'. We commonly use the term, 'probable', not for what falls very slightly short of certainty but for what falls a great deal short, and therefore for me to say that it is only probable that there is a table before me would be to express a much lower degree of certainty than I feel. For the same reason it would be wrong of me to say in ordinary conversation even that it was not certain; it is practically certain. But, if I am talking philosophy, this is not wrong, for it falls short of absolute hundred per cent certainty. Dr Moore's whole argument depends on the assumptions that we know physical object propositions and that 'knowing' connotes absolute certainty; the former assumption I accept but the latter I reject, and if this course is adopted it becomes unnecessary to find arguments to justify their absolute certainty against the sceptic.

Philosophers who take the synthetic *a priori* view of the connection between the mental state of knowing and the truth of the proposition known are very inclined to say that there is only one correct sense of 'knowing' and that the usage I have suggested is just wrong, but if it is an ordinary usage it is difficult to see on what grounds it could be condemned as wrong. But no doubt it would follow from their view that in cases where we 'know' only in the looser sense our state of mind, and not only the objective relation of the proposition claimed to be known to the evidence, is different from what it is in the cases where we 'know' in the stronger sense. For if it were the same in the first case as it is in the second, we should have objective certainty. But this should be, even for them, no reason for rejecting the looser sense: obviously our mental state of practical certainty, if not identical with, at any rate bears some considerable resemblance to the mental state of actual certainty, otherwise the two would not be, as they are, liable to be confused with each other, and this would explain why the term 'know' was used in both senses.

It may even be contended that the notion of absolute certainty has no meaning as applied to physical object propositions, provided it is thought that these can only be established by induction and are not directly known. For it seems to be involved in the meaning of induction in the sense in which the word is used here that it cannot give complete certainty, since further tests which would increase the degree of certainty are always possible. If not analytically included in the meaning of 'induction' it is a synthetic *a priori* proposition involved in its meaning in the sense of following necessarily from it. It may therefore be said that it was not appropriate to express what I had to say by saying that physical object propositions are not absolutely certain, since many of them are certain in the only sense in which certainty can be applied to what is established by induction, so that to deny certainty of them is like denying goodness of food because food cannot be good in the sense in which a moral man is good. This criticism would clearly be justified if I were using 'absolute certainty' in the sense in which this is applicable to *a priori* propositions; but that is not the only sense of absolute certainty. 'Absolute certainty', in a somewhat different sense, also applies to directly cognised empirical propositions about one's present mental state and immediate objects of sense; and since it is logically possible that physical object propositions could be known directly, the question whether they are absolutely certain in this sense is a quite legitimate one. In fact the question whether physical object propositions were ever absolutely certain would resolve itself for me into the question whether they could be directly known in the strict sense of 'know'. My answer, which I have not time to discuss here, would be that they are directly cognised but not in such a way as to give absolutely certain knowledge.

This answer is given from a realist point of view; but I think it very important to realize that the acceptance of a phenomenalist analysis of physical object propositions would not make it any easier to hold that they were ever know directly but would rather have the reverse effect. If physical object propositions are analysed phenomenalistically they are analysed in terms not only of my present experience or sense-data but in terms of the sense-data of other persons and of my future possible sense-data. Now, while it may be claimed without absurdity, though perhaps wrongly, that I am directly aware of an independent physical object when I see the table, it can hardly be claimed that when I see it I am immediately aware of the sense-data of the other people in the room, still less (when I am alone) of the hypothetical non-existent sense-data of the 'normal observers' who would see it under certain conditions or of the sense-data that I shall or should have under hypothetical conditions not yet realized. This, though not logically self-contradictory, is quite obviously false. The point I have just raised seems to me very important because the chief motive for adopting the phenomenalist analysis of propositions about physical objects seems to have been that it would enable one to claim knowledge of physical objects. But in fact, if 'knowledge' is used in the strict sense, it is even more difficult to claim this than it is on the realist view, for while, if you are a realist, it is just possible, though difficult, to claim that we can have direct knowledge of physical objects it is quite impossible on the phenomenalist view.

If we take the view that all physical object propositions are based on induction, it follows logically, I think, that they can never be absolutely certain in the sense in which directly known propositions about one's present state can be, though it remains true that there is a sense of 'certain' in which they can very well be certain, i.e. the sense which I have expressed by the phrase, 'practically certain'. It may therefore be argued that it is meaningless to deny that they are absolutely certain, since absolute certainty is just a predicate that has no sense in this connection at all. But this does not follow. For:

1. The denial of a logically self-contradictory proposition is not meaningless. If it would be meaningless, which I do not admit, to say that some physical object propositions were absolutely certain in the sense in which propositions about my present state can be, the statement that they cannot be absolutely certain in this sense would become the statement that it was meaningless to say they were, and a statement that something else is meaningless is not without meaning itself. It has a meaning even to say that 'abracadabra' means nothing, and since it has been at any rate supposed that the notion of absolute certainty could be

applied to physical object propositions, while as far as I know it has never been supposed even by philosophers that 'abracadabra' meant anything, a proposition denying meaning to the one would have a utility which the denial of meaning to the other would not have.

2. The proposition denied is not logically self-contradictory, since it is logically possible that physical object propositions might be directly cognized with certainty.

3. There is in any case a perfectly good meaning in saying that all physical object propositions are uncertain, whether there would be a meaning in saying that some are absolutely certain or not. For it is clear that, if physical object propositions can only be justified inductively, however many tests we apply, their degree of certainty may always be increased still further by applying others, and this entails a standard of certainty which is never completely reached. It may be held either that this standard is derived from other branches of knowledge, or that it is an unrealized idea formed as a result of the observation that one physical object proposition is more certain than another, as the idea of perfect goodness may be formed even in the absence of any experience of its realization by noting that one man is better than another and that, however good any man we encounter is, there is always a better possible. The same consideration prevents us saying that some physical object propositions are at least as certain as they could conceivably be, it being assumed that they could not conceivably be certain in any sense of 'certain' other than that in which inductively established propositions can be certain, i.e. practically certain. For this practical certainty is not a fixed quantity which cannot be exceeded but a matter of degree. However certain the proposition that there is a table in front of me is in view of the evidence at my disposal, its certainty could be increased by additional tests. This sounds very odd, but I think only for the same sort of reason as it sounds odd to talk about the heat of something which is very little above absolute zero. Just outside the study of physical science we are not practically interested in very small degrees of heat, and describe things which possess very little heat as not hot at all, so outside philosophy when the uncertainty falls below a certain limit we take no notice of it and describe the proposition as certain. But that the certainty cannot be complete I think follows from the nature of induction, if the physical object propositions are based on this. We can in

that case see that the premisses just do not entail the absolute certainty of the conclusion.

Therefore, if we have absolutely certain knowledge of physical objects, it must be direct. That we should have such knowledge is logically possible, but does it in fact occur? The view that we have such knowledge is defended by Professor Aaron in a recent number of this periodical.[1] If it is claimed that the knowledge is direct the last two of the objections to its absolute certainty which Dr Moore and I have discussed disappear, i.e. the objection from the possibility of a deceitful demon and the objection from the nature of induction. There remains the objection from dreams, which seems to me strong, and that from illusions, which makes it exceedingly difficult to say what it is we know with absolute certainty. I know that there is a table before me. But the colour of the table is generally held to be a subjective appearance and would probably appear quite different if I looked through a microscope, its shape and size vary with my position, its texture would again appear quite different if I could see the ultimate particles. What is there left that is absolutely certain? The occurrence of illusion is not incompatible with the view that we have a direct cognition of physical objects which gives us an element of truth mixed with the illusion, but is it compatible with the occurrence of a direct knowledge that is absolutely certain? In the absence of correction by experience and instruction we are just as convinced of the physical existence of qualities like the colour of the sky or of mirror-images to which we later do not assign physical existence as of the qualities which we say really belong to the physical object. I am only justified in being even practically certain that there is a table here because such experiences have not deceived me in the past but have been confirmed by coherence with others.

[1] Vol. LI, No. 204, pp. 311 ff.

IV

MENTAL ACTS[1]

Philonous. Surely there are such things as philosophers have called mental acts. Surely we know, infer, believe, doubt, will, decide, etc.? The *cogito, ergo sum* of Descartes already proves the existence of at least some of these acts, and we are aware by introspection of the others. For instance I decided to write this article while listening to a discussion on Mental Acts at the joint session of the Aristotelian Society and Mind Association of 1947. I knew perfectly well at the time that I made the decision then, yet at the time I took no external action—that only began some time later—I knew it by introspection. And I certainly know whether I am believing or doubting a proposition that is proposed to me, and I know it before I have taken any action on the belief, so that we cannot reduce believing to a kind of overt action. Introspection, so far from being uncertain, is the most certain of all avenues of knowledge. It is in fact infallible, and we discover the existence of mental acts by introspection.

Empiricus. But what are these mental acts? Can you give any description of what it is like to know, decide, etc.? You can mention the occasions and effects of your knowledge and decisions, you may (unless you are a behaviourist) perhaps tell me of the images which accompany them, you can at any rate repeat the subvocal language used by yourself in connexion with them, but you cannot tell me what they are like in themselves. You may say they are indefinable, but does not your inability to describe any one of them raise suspicions? We are justified in assuming indefinable entities only if we have a clear experience of what they are like, since otherwise the words just have no meaning, and have you this experience? You may claim to know them by introspection, but many people who are quite as good at introspection as you—in fact many expert psychologists, not to say philosophers—have denied this introspective knowledge of them.

---

[1] This article was written before the publication of Ryle's *Concept of Mind*, but it seems to me highly relevant to Ryle's account. For a more specific attack on Ryle's book v. my article in *Clarity is Not Enough* (ed. H. D. Lewis, 311 ff).

When I look for them and try to examine them, they seem to vanish into a diaphanous nothing. Introspection is up to a point clear and certain. I can know that I have a pain, I can know that I have certain sensations (or at least sense-data), but when I look for an act of knowing I cannot find it. Now you may say I am mistaken, you may protest that they are there although I cannot find them, but should not the mere fact that many people cannot find them when they introspect cast doubt on their existence? If there are such things they must be extremely common, one for every time we know, etc., and, if so, surely everybody would, at least sometimes, be able to detect them? There is no doubt that pains occur; if acts of knowing were possible objects of introspection like pains, there should be no doubt that they also occur. Such common and fundamental elements of mental life as these are alleged to be surely could not be missed? Further, an examination of language reveals that psychological terms such as 'knowing' or 'believing' or 'desiring' do not stand for single acts or events of any sort but for dispositional states. We can say truly that somebody knows, believes or desires something even if the person happens to be in a state of dreamless sleep when we use the words. Therefore, though these words no doubt stand for something, they do not stand for mental acts, and the fact that we can sometimes know that we know something does not prove that there are knowing acts.

This dialogue expresses one of the fundamental differences of modern philosophy. The conflict has, I think, no single source, but is bound up with a whole mass of complications and misunderstandings, no doubt too intricate to be ferreted out adequately in a single article. Yet without solving it we can have no tolerable theory of mind. It is therefore very disappointing that relatively so little has been done by philosophers to come to terms on the subject. The wide divergencies between philosophers and the incredible assertions that were made on one (the anti-act) side in the discussion to which I have referred while the other remained largely unexpressed, though no doubt accepted by very many, have prompted me to make an effort to come to the rescue.

Now, I think, Philonous had better admit that our psychological terms are not, as they stand, usually just names for mental acts. To say that I know or believe or desire something is not just to say that I perform an act of knowing, etc. It is rather to say that I have a certain disposition. The same applies to words for emotions—being angry is not a single mental act—only here what the words referred to would be called not a 'disposition' but a 'state of mind'. This is because to say that a man is angry usually implies that there are actual qualities of angry feeling, or at least irritability, in his experience throughout the time when he is described as being angry—we cannot be angry in a dreamless sleep—while to say that a man knows, believes or desires something does not imply that he is conscious of it in any way all the time during which he can correctly be described as knowing, believing, or desiring it. There are, however, some psychological terms which do seem to stand, at least sometimes, for mental acts. Thus the word 'see' in the non-physical sense of 'see' stands for a definite experience which would seem to be detectable introspectively when we say after a period of puzzlement: 'Ah, this is clear to me now'. Whether this experience is best described as an act is another question, but there does seem to be a definite experience which we can get hold of here. This suggests that Philonous might equate the mental act primarily concerned in knowledge not with what is meant by 'knowing' but with what is meant by 'coming to know'. To 'see' in the sense in which I have just used it is to come to know the relation of something, e.g. the relation between a premiss and a conclusion. And he might contend that also words like *decide, choose, will*, stand for mental acts and not dispositions. Other words for which he might plausibly advance this claim are *perceive, recollect*, and *entertain* (in the rather technical sense of entertaining propositions). *Remember* and *infer* seem to be used in both ways. But even if there were no single words which stood for mental acts, it would not oblige us to deny mental acts or dismiss the term as meaningless. It may well be the case that a word implies or presupposes something for which it does not itself stand. An example is provided by the use of colour words. There is no case of a single word standing for a single determinate shade of colour, yet the use of our ordinary colour words such as red, yellow, etc., presupposes such shades. The terms have meaning only as covering a range of such shades. If nothing had a determinate shade of yellow at any moment, nothing would ever be yellow at all. Similarly, Philonous might say, 'know' does not stand for any single mental act, but if there were no mental acts of a certain kind we could never 'know'. And logically, it would seem, the use of a dispositional word must presuppose awareness of certain occurrents or events. For a 'disposition' seems to signify simply the tendency for certain events to occur: it is nothing actual.

But Empiricus may advance a different interpretation of the disposition words. He may say they stand not for a disposition to perform certain mental acts but for a disposition to overt action. Thus 'believing' has been regarded as a disposition to act as if what we are said to believe were true. And those like him have used as an argument for their view the fact that, if a person says that he believes *A* but acts as if he did not, we should be inclined to say that he did not believe *A*. It might be retorted, however, that this is only because we regard his act as external evidence for his beliefs and so infer the latter from the former. With this reply I should be inclined to agree. The inference we can indeed easily see to be a somewhat precarious one in view of human inconsistency and the fact that we are liable to be swayed by various desires to do what we believe to be imprudent, thus acting as if *A* were not true while believing *A*. But if action as though what we are said to believe were true were what is *meant* by 'believing', there would be nothing precarious about the inference in question. Empiricus might try to meet this objection by introducing the word 'tendency' and defining belief in terms of a tendency to act in a certain way. But suppose I act as if *A* were not true, although I believe *A* to be true. Suppose, for instance, on the authority of a doctor I believe that drink is very bad for my health and yet go on drinking. In that case it might well still be admitted that I have a tendency to abstain from drink, since if I were not otherwise attracted by it I certainly should abstain in order to save my health. I therefore have a tendency to act as if *A* (the proposition that drink is bad for my health) were true. But I have also in the supposed case a tendency to act as if it were false, for I go on drinking. Therefore I by definition both believe and disbelieve that drink is bad for my health, and since I act on the whole as if it were not, the disbelief may be said to be more marked than the belief. Yet there is surely no contradiction in saying that somebody believed all the time that drink was bad for him and never disbelieved it at all, yet went on drinking. Another difficulty is that it is hard to see what can be meant by acting as if *A* were *B* except *acting as if I believed A to be B*, in which case the definition becomes circular. The fact that *A* is *B* will not affect the actions in question unless I believe *A* to be *B*, though it may affect their results. The fact that a certain medicine will cure a certain disease will not affect my actions when I get the disease unless I first believe that it will or at least may cure it, though it will, of course, affect my success in attaining my object if I do take the medicine in question. Again, I often believe propositions on which I never have occasion to act, e.g. most of the information I obtain by reading newspapers and history books. In order to meet this objection belief is defined in terms of hypothetical action. But here Philonous has a strong point—Surely I can know directly (sometimes at least) that I believe something, yet I never know directly (though I may infer) that I should, if something happened which has not happened, do some particular thing. Hypothetical propositions about contingent future facts (at least apart from the sphere of 'psychical research') are never known in this direct way. Empiricus may possibly then reply that at least I act on the belief in one way, namely, I formulate it in words at least to myself when I believe it; but this account seems to involve him in a vicious circle, for merely saying something is compatible with not believing it and we have to add 'saying it in the belief that it is true'.

Similarly, he will commit a vicious circle if he includes under the actions which constitute belief drawing inferences from the proposition believed, for to infer is not merely to pronounce them, but to pronounce them believing or knowing them to be true. The same criticisms may of course be brought against the parallel account of knowing: in fact, philosophers have usually not spoken of 'acts of belief' but of 'acts of knowing'. I do not myself, however, think that there is any psychological difference between subjectively certain belief without a shadow of doubt and knowledge. The difference is that the terms *knowledge* and *know* have both a psychological and a logical meaning at once. They connote not only that we are subjectively certain but that the certainty is justified, and it is the presence of this second, non-psychological element which constitutes the difference between them and *subjectively certain belief*. But, if there are cognitive acts which yield certain truths, there are surely also cognitive acts which involve the possibility and even the actuality of error. So I shall continue to discuss the matter in terms of believing, though philosophers have not usually spoken of acts of belief. They have spoken of 'acts of judgement', which covers not only knowledge but also uncertainty and error, and they might just as well have said 'acts of believing'. Both with believing and knowing, we must clearly reject any account of them purely in terms of action or hypothetical action.

It is more plausible to say that *part* of what we mean by 'believing' is acting as if p were true. Indeed, in some cases it seems to be the major part. Thus I can say without hesitation that you believe that the floor will not suddenly explode beneath you, though you have probably never contemplated this eventuality at all, and therefore cannot in any case have performed a mental act of believing that it will not happen. Since there is consequently no mental act or psychological event of any sort directly involved, it would indeed seem plausible in such cases to say that all that was meant was that you acted as if the floor would explode, e.g. remained sitting unconcernedly and did not rush out of the house. I think, however, something more is involved in the statement than this. Part of the meaning, I think, is here to be found in hypothetical *mental* processes. In saying you believe this I mean to say not only that you act externally as if you believed it, but also that you (*a*) would have an actual conscious mental belief in its truth if the question were proposed to you, (*b*) would be surprised if something happened incompatible with what I have said you believed. We fortunately have the capacity of acting as if we possessed a number of beliefs which we do not consciously possess, and with most of such beliefs we should, if questioned, have a conscious belief in their truth. In the relatively rare cases where a question was met by a denial of the belief, it would generally be said that the person who uttered the denial did not hold the belief or had ceased to hold it; but there might be people who (without accusing him of lying) still said that he believed the proposition in question if he went on acting as if he did. But they would in that case probably preface the word believe by 'really', thus implying that they are using 'believe' in not quite the ordinary sense. Take another case: F. C. Schiller told a story of an orthodox Christian who was asked what he thought would happen to him when he died and answered, 'I suppose I shall enter into a state of eternal bliss, but I wish you would not talk of such depressing topics'. Did he or did he not believe that he would enter into a state of eternal bliss? Most people (provided they trusted his veracity) would say he 'believed it in a way' but did not 'really believe it'. But there are two ways of interpreting this. It may be said that the notion of believing includes acting and feeling in a way

D

which would be rational if the belief were well-founded, or it may be said that it does not include this but that such behaviour and feelings are evidence for the belief being present, though not part of what is meant by 'belief'. In the latter case we may say that, though the belief must be present in some degree for the man introspectively to discover it, it is evidently not present in full degree if his actions or feelings are flagrantly inconsistent with it so that we are justified in that case in saying he does not *really* believe it. Obviously we must not in either case press this too far; men are very liable to be irrational, and it would be quite ridiculous to say a person did not believe *p* because he did not draw and apply in his actions all the inferences which a perfectly rational being would draw from *p*. It is, however, only a verbal dispute in which of these two ways 'believe' is to be used; the important point is that 'belief', even if it does include in its meaning a reference to outward behaviour, includes something else besides. That seems quite obvious, and it is at least as obvious with 'knowing', yet if this is admitted it does not necessarily follow that this something is a mental act or acts.

But let our friend Empiricus speak for himself. If he is sensible, he will admit the presence of something that can be introspectively discovered, but he will deny that it is a mental act. Believing itself, he will continue to insist, is a dispositional term, and similarly knowing, and on this linguistic point he is certainly right; but he may admit that events sometimes occur in connexion with believing and knowing which cannot be observed by the ordinary physical senses, and can normally only be observed by the person who is said to believe or know and not by anybody else. (I say 'normally' only to avoid implying a denial of the occurrence of telepathy.) Yes, he will say, when I have a belief I sometimes do not observe anything at all, but sometimes at the time when I acquire the belief I observe the occurrence of verbal or other imagery. But what of this? Images are admittedly no more like mental acts than are sense-data. But surely, Philonous asks, the belief requires not merely imagery but assent to what is conveyed by the imagery? And he can support his argument by pointing out that I may, confronted with the same verbal imagery, either believe, disbelieve, or merely entertain the proposition in question. Empiricus may then go a step further: he may admit the occurrence of belief-feelings. It would be in the highest degree paradoxical and un-empirical even for an 'empiricist' to deny that we

do have such feelings, however they may be analysed; and why
should he? In regard to the same imagery, he can say, I may have
a feeling of conviction or its opposite or a feeling of doubt or no
feeling at all. In the first case I can be said to believe, in the second
case to disbelieve, in the third to doubt, and in the fourth merely
to entertain the proposition. If you care to call this feeling a
mental act you are at liberty to do so, but there is no more point
in doing this than in applying the term to any other feeling. A
throb of pain would not be called a mental act by anyone, nor
would a throb of emotion. And feelings of conviction or doubt
are only emotions, a point which is usually overlooked because
they are in most (though not in all) cases such very mild emotions.
This is in fact too simple an account, but the complexities which
come now do not necessarily weaken the case of Empiricus. It
may be pointed out that there is not always a distinctive feeling
in cases of belief or disbelief; but where the feeling is not present,
he may reply that 'belief' or 'disbelief' is being used in a hypothetical sense as meaning that the person will, if certain circumstances arise, act in a certain way or have a feeling of a certain
kind or both, the feeling being 'conviction' if the belief is challenged and 'surprise' if it prove false. I do not ordinarily have an
introspectively discernible belief-feeling when I am told some
particular unimportant fact by a friend or do a simple sum in
arithmetic, but in both cases there would be more or less surprise
if the belief proved false, and other circumstances might produce
a feeling of conviction, if e.g. the belief was unreasonably challenged by someone. If both criteria, the criterion of action and
the criterion of ability to evoke surprise or conviction, are sub-
sequently satisfied, we shall assert without hesitation that belief
is present; if only one is, some people will prefer to make this
assertion, others not, and some will hesitate, but the difference
between these parties will merely be the verbal one as to how
much they include under the term 'belief'. But when we have
granted imagery and feeling, what else is there to introspect?
Is there anything at all? There are cases of belief, all must admit,
where we cannot detect a distinct belief feeling, and that is a
reason against just identifying belief with the feeling; but even if
we admitted mental acts, since belief is a dispositional term, we
could not just identify it with the mental acts. We should in any
case have to define it in terms of *hypothetical* mental acts. And,
where we cannot detect a belief-feeling, can we detect a mental

act either? Can we in these cases detect anything at all in our mental process but imagery? Further, even if we suppose that there is a mental act present in all cases, is that anything but supposing that there is always present some peculiar kind of feeling like the feeling of which we are aware in some cases of belief, only in a less noticeable form? What could mental acts be but some kind of feeling?

To this it may be replied that, even if called feelings, cognitive acts are such peculiar kinds of feelings that at any rate they deserve to be put in a separate class distinct from all other feelings and that the difference is indeed so great that it is misleading to suggest they are as like headaches and emotions of anger as is suggested by calling them by the same name, feelings. For they are concerned with truth and falsity in a way in which no other feelings are, and their essential nature lies not in what they feel like, but in a unique kind of relation to a proposition. Headaches and emotions of anger do not apprehend truth, assent to propositions, or commit errors. There is an empirically given difference in nature of a kind which justifies the traditional division of mental process into the three sides, cognitive, conative and affective, and makes it most inappropriate to lump them all together as feelings. Further, though a feeling of conviction may accompany believing or knowing, can it be identified with the cognitive act of knowing or coming to believe? The feeling may be so weak as to be almost or quite indiscernible in many cases where knowledge is regarded as absolutely certain, and it seems that it may be present very intensely (as in cases of nitrous oxide intoxication) where nothing is believed. And we are aware that we know or believe something in a great many cases where we do not detect anything at all in the way of a belief feeling or emotion of conviction. As I have said, I certainly am not aware of such a feeling each time I am told an unimportant fact by someone, yet in the absence of any special reason for doing otherwise I believe what I am told about matters of fact and know directly at the time that I believe it. In doing sums in arithmetic which give not merely belief but knowledge I do not usually have any detectable feeling of conviction at all, yet I am aware at the time that I know. This awareness cannot be reduced merely to the presence of imagery, for two reasons at least: (1) the same imagery may be accompanied by knowledge, belief, disbelief, doubt, and suspension of judgement; therefore imagery cannot

explain the distinction between these mental states; (2) in order
to judge, believe, or know we require not only images but an
awareness of what the images mean. This awareness of meaning
may be interpreted to a certain extent in terms of other images,
but we cannot go on with this to the end, and there are very
many cases where we have none but verbal images and could
not have any others that would serve our purpose at all. Nor
can meaning be interpreted in terms of imagery together with
action, at least unless we mean by 'action' the mental action
of thinking in certain ways, which itself would involve mental
cognitive 'acts'. We cannot reduce this thinking to merely talking
to ourselves, whether physically or mentally, for the same difficulty
will then again arise of explaining in such terms what is meant
by saying that the words we use in this speech have a meaning.
If we open a book on philosophy at almost any place, we shall
find a sentence which is such that its meaning cannot be expressed
in any imagery that does not consist of words or other symbols
unlike in character to what they represent (since it concerns what
cannot be pictured in terms of the senses), and which is also such
that belief in its truth could not be connected directly with any
resultant physical action except the action of repeating the words
to a questioner. If it is then said that the meaning can be translated
in terms of action by bringing under the latter head the making
of the inferences we should make if we believed it true, this
presupposes a mental process of thinking not reducible to either
outward physical action or hypothetical action or imagery. For
if we say that the making of the inferences just consists in the
using of words, we have provided no means of distinguishing
between nonsense-syllables and words which have a meaning not
expressible in terms of imagery. There are philosophers who
would welcome the conclusion that all metaphysics is nonsense,
but their own philosophical books or discourses would likewise
have to be regarded as nonsense, and about this their enthusiasm
would not be so great. Their philosophical sentences are no more
capable than the sentences of metaphysicians of being interpreted
solely in terms of images or outward actions or both. Nor are the
sentences which cannot be expressed by non-symbolic images
confined to philosophy—they are ubiquitous in mathematics
except where we are dealing with groups small enough for us to
have in our mind all at once, they are almost ubiquitous in
economics and politics, and very abundant in physical science and

history. Many attempts have been made to analyse meaning in the way indicated, but the examples given almost always concern sensible objects, and the extraordinarily difficult task of dealing in this way with the other kind of propositions in detail has hardly been attempted, as far as I know. (I think myself indeed that the attempt breaks down even as regards sensible objects, because all propositions about such objects involve the use of general terms and I do not see how the meaning of general terms can be adequately handled in that fashion.) So we have to admit besides images an awareness of their meaning which cannot itself be analysed in terms of images. If we care to call this awareness of meaning a feeling we can do so, but it is an odd kind of feeling!

At this point we had perhaps better consider an attack made on mental acts from another quarter, namely by certain 'idealists'. They do not try to explain away mental acts in terms of imagery and physical behaviour, but they do try to explain them away in terms of 'ideas'. But it seems to me that an idea as distinct from an image—and they do make that distinction—is not an existent entity discoverable in introspection. Images I know and experiences of thinking I know, but not any third kind of entity, ideas distinct from either of these. Suppose I think of something that cannot be adequately imaged. Firstly, I have the thinking as a mental process; and secondly, I have the image of certain words or whatever other image it is that I use for the purpose; but I cannot discover any other entity by introspection. We may speak of the idea as 'the image together with its meaning' or 'the image used to mean something', but this does not introduce a fresh entity but merely consists in viewing the image in a certain relation. An allied tendency with certain idealists like Bosanquet is to include in the self the objects of its knowledge and indeed everything in which it is interested, so that the self has no fixed boundaries and no specific subject-matter that could not also belong to the not-self on another occasion when the self happened not to be interested in it. For mental acts and processes they then substitute the 'ideal self-development' of these objects. This seems to me to be talking in metaphors: there are cases where the welfare of another person may become as important to a man as if that person were an essential part of himself, but that does not make the person actually a part of himself; and the object does not alter and develop through my coming to know it better (except as regards the relational characteristic of being better known by me). My feelings, thoughts, etc., are not their objects, and do not include their objects. It seems to me that idealism carried to the point of refusing to recognize the distinction between the mental attitudes towards *A* and *A* itself can only make nonsense of any account we give of the world of experience.

To return to the main line of argument, we may sum up the trend of this article so far in dialogue form.

Empiricus. Knowing, believing, etc., do not stand for mental acts because the words may be correctly used of persons who are at the time admittedly not even conscious of what they are said to know or believe.

Philonous. This is only because they, like many other psychological terms, refer to dispositions, but there could not be the disposition if there were not sometimes acts. A mental disposition just means that the person to whom it is ascribed, though he may not be mentally active in the way referred to at the moment, will under certain conditions be mentally active in this way. As a matter of fact there are psychological terms such as 'see' in the non-physical sense of 'see' which refer directly not to mental dispositions but to mental acts.

Emp. I admit that dispositional terms such as belief involve a reference to action, but the action to which they refer is the physical action a man will undertake if he holds a certain belief.

Phil. This is a vicious circle: the action is only undertaken because the man holds the belief in question and therefore presupposes a belief distinct from itself to account for its occurrence.

Emp. Would you really admit that a person held a belief if it were the case that he would under no circumstances act as if he held the belief? And do you not on the other hand constantly ascribe beliefs to people on the strength of their outward actions even if it is highly doubtful whether they have ever formulated to themselves and given assent to the beliefs in question? If so, does it not follow that the chief part of what is meant by ascribing a belief to somebody is that he behaves in a certain manner?

Phil. I admit that, if a person does not act in accord with a belief, I may have doubts as to whether he holds the belief, but this is only because a man's actions are indirect evidence for his beliefs; and this evidence must not be pressed too far, since we are all liable to inconsistency. And, in the cases where I ascribe a belief to somebody without committing myself to the view that he has ever consciously accepted the belief, what I mean may be explained not in terms of hypothetical outward behaviour but in terms of hypothetical mental acts of judgement.

Emp. But I am not committed to analysing belief wholly in terms of outward action. I am quite prepared to admit imagery and, where a person consciously believes something, he no doubt has certain images, at least of a verbal kind.

Phil. The belief cannot possibly be identified with the images. For with the very same images I can either believe, disbelieve, doubt, or suspend judgement. Further, the images can only function in my thought if I am aware of what they mean, and we cannot reduce this awareness of meaning to other images.

Emp. On second thoughts I find there is something else which I can sometimes detect introspectively besides these images. I can also detect a feeling of conviction, a kind of (usually mild) emotion, in some cases of belief, But this is certainly not detectable in all cases of belief, and it is certainly not appropriately called a mental act any more than are other emotions.

Phil. No doubt these feelings of conviction sometimes accompany belief, but besides these there is an 'act of judgement' (for some obscure reason philosophers do not speak of 'acts of belief'). 'Belief' stands normally and primarily for a disposition to perform these mental acts. That it does not stand for the feeling of conviction is shown by the fact that in cases where we believe something with the greatest certainty the feeling of conviction may be extremely weak as a feeling or non-existent.

Emp. I do not claim to analyse 'belief' merely in terms of feelings of conviction but in terms of these plus outward action plus imagery. If we take only one of these of course the account given is deficient, but the three supplement each other's deficiencies.

Phil. They cannot help each other out in this way. For (1) outward action is insufficient because we often do not act on a belief. Therefore the belief will on the behaviourist view have to be defined in terms of hypothetical action. But I can know directly whether I believe something and cannot know directly my hypothetical future actions. Now imagery will not help here because the same imagery may accompany both belief and doubt, therefore I still could not know directly whether I believed. Nor can feelings of conviction, since I can know directly that I believe something in many cases where I am not aware of any feeling of conviction whatever. Even if it is possible that the feelings are really there and have been overlooked by us, their presence will not explain our knowledge that we believe, since we at any rate do not know them to be there. (2) To say that believing *p* means acting as if *p* were true is to commit a vicious circle, for to act as if *p* were true can only mean acting as if we believed that *p* were true. It cannot mean acting as if we had images of *p*, which is quite compatible with our disbelief in *p*, and feelings of conviction will not help, since we have seen that we may believe without these feelings being there, or at least that we can know we believe without knowing the feelings to be there.

Emp. In cases of belief where there is no feeling of conviction, I do not think myself that I can detect anything relevant at all except imagery. But have it your own way. Suppose there is something else which you please to call a mental act. Would it not be just another feeling? If so, is anything gained by positing it, and if it does occur does it conflict with my account on principle? Would it not merely show at the most that I had given an inadequate analysis of the feelings empirically present, as might a man who, e.g., ignored the 'goosefleshy' sensation in giving an analysis of fear? What would it be like to discover a mental act that was not a feeling at all?

Phil. If an act of judging or knowing is a feeling, it is a highly peculiar kind of feeling. For, look, it apprehends truth and includes awareness not merely of images but of what the images mean. An act of judging is thus a great deal more than a mere 'feeling', if the term 'feeling' is to have any definite meaning at all. It is most misleading to use the word feeling of the acts since that suggests they are something like a headache or an emotion of anger, while they are generically different from any such things. Of course you can, if you like, lump together all mental occurrences under the heading feeling, but you will not gain anything by doing this, and will only waste a valuable word which might be used to express distinctions within experience.

Emp. But at any rate it seems to me that the occurrence of these events so different from ordinary feelings is not in any way verifiable. When I try to detect them introspectively I cannot do so, and I do not see by what process we can *infer* a quite new kind of thing, as they would be, not analysable in terms of anything we immediately experience. And I do not see in the least why they should be called 'acts', even supposing they occur.

Let us now consider the last remark of Empiricus, which

D*

brings us back to the most fundamental issue. We must admit in the first place that there is at any rate a certain inappropriateness about calling these phenomena 'acts.' I do not know how the term first came to be used for them, and I for my part wish it had not been chosen. It is unsuitable in two respects. Firstly, it suggests instantaneity, where what we should rather have in mind is a *process* of thought. Secondly, 'active' suggests volition, and I think had better be reserved for cases where volition is involved. No doubt the experience of knowing or believing is commonly closely connected with volitions which play an essential part in bringing it about. In order to acquire knowledge or belief we have to direct our attention to something, and this direction of attention (usually, though not always) at some stage involves volition. But the actual knowing or believing is itself not willing. I can will to direct my attention in a certain way. I might even will to ignore certain inconvenient arguments, i.e. refuse to attend to them. But I cannot, strictly speaking, will to believe. Whatever the nature and place of free will in ethical action, free will does not come in here. And, even if I could will to believe or know, the believing or knowing itself would not be an act of will. It is therefore better to speak of cognitive states or processes than of cognitive acts.

Now that we can introspect cognitive processes, processes of thinking about something, surely cannot be disputed. An attempt is made to reduce these to imagery, including words, but surely the imagery does not merely occur? Surely we do something with it when we think, and the doing this is the mental process. The mere fact that imagery can only be used as meaning something, and that this something in very many cases cannot itself be translated in terms of imagery should be sufficient to show that we must admit over and above the images mental states and processes involving the apprehension of what is itself not an image but the meaning of an image. But it is a different thing to say we have a definite single mental act or state which occurs in all cases of knowing and could itself be called knowing, and similarly with believing. The answer to this question is, I think, that in some cases we have it and in others not. I sometimes have a definite experience at a given time of recognizing the truth of something or seeing something to be true. That might be called a mental act (if we ignore the suggestion of 'activity'), as opposed to an ordinary mental process, for though not strictly instantaneous or timeless and therefore still a process, it sometimes seems to be completed in one specious present and is at any rate very much shorter than most mental processes of which we speak. But we need not suppose that such 'mental acts' occur in all cases of knowledge or belief. Sometimes we just take something which we are said to know or believe for granted in our thoughts without ever (as far as we introspectively notice) expressly seeing it to be true. The critic of mental acts is right in holding that the terms 'know' and 'believe' are to be dispositionally interpreted, but I insist that they should be interpreted not, primarily at least, as dispositions to physical behaviour, but as dispositions to think. And, if we take the word 'see' (in the sense in which we see the answer to a problem), this does not usually stand for a disposition, but rather for something such as those had in mind who asserted mental acts. I do not understand how anybody can deny our ability in some cases to discover introspectively that such events occur. And for reasons which I have given, I do not see how they can possibly be reduced to behaviour-tendencies or to imagery or both. Imagery is not enough; I must understand the imagery and see that it applies to something.

How is it, then, that there has been all this difficulty about 'mental acts'? Is not the very fact that there has been such disagreement about them and that many experts have not (or think they have not) detected them introspectively an argument against them on the ground that, if they were there, they would have been noticed by everybody, as I made Empiricus urge in the second paragraph of this article? If we experience cognitive acts, why should we have doubts about their existence, when nobody doubts the existence of pains? Now it may, of course, just be an ultimate fact that the sort of phenomena of which we are talking are difficult to observe while other phenomena are not. If this is an inexplicable fact, it is only in the same position as any ultimate causal law, according to the empiricist at least, and therefore the empiricist in particular has no right to make it an objection against his opponent. Why should it not be an ultimate causal property of mental acts that they are harder to observe than, e.g., pains or visual sense-data, as it is an ultimate property of certain wave-lengths that they produce the sensation of yellow? The fact that others have failed to find them suggests that we should exercise extra care in making sure that we really have detected them, but if we are sure either that we have done this or that they are necessary to explain our experience we need not be too upset by the fact that not everybody has succeeded in discovering them. The given argument against mental acts is therefore far from conclusive, but it should at any rate warn us to be cautious.

It is not, however, necessary to treat it merely as an ultimate inexplicable fact that some people find great difficulty in introspecting these mental events. The position is eased when we note the following points:

(1) There can be no doubt that everybody (except real behaviourists!) can introspect cognitions and beliefs as well as he can introspect pains, in the sense that he can become aware otherwise than by inference or the outer senses that he knows or believes something. The doubts regard the *analysis* of this fact of knowing or believing.

(2) Cognitive acts are too linked up with their objects for us to be aware of the acts by themselves, but we can be aware of them in conjunction with their objects. I cannot know what knowing or judging is like *per se*, because it does not exist *per se*, but I know what it is like to judge something or know something to be true. There would be similar difficulties about determining what the mental state of feeling pain is apart from the felt pain. It is not the former but the latter as a sensory datum, or rather the two in conjunction that we are thinking of when we speak of physical pain, while in the case of pain in the wider sense of 'unpleasure' we are saying that our whole experience has the characteristic of painfulness. Nobody would think of looking for pain *in vacuo* apart from some experience which has other characteristics besides being merely painful, for pain in either sense is patently only a universal characteristic, therefore we are not tempted here to make the mistake which we make about acts of cognition when we look for them as if they were something separate and not merely distinguishable from the object cognized.

(3) No doubt, as has often been pointed out, the subjective side of cognition is apprehensible in a different way from either the imagery or the objective side. People who have denied the subjective side may have been looking for the wrong thing in the wrong way, expecting, like Hume, to find some sort of image or combination of images.

(4) Once we have taken the imagery away, we are left with something unanalysable that cannot be further described. But

some concepts must be unanalysable, otherwise you have a vicious infinite regress, therefore we need not be put off by this.

(5) As we have seen, language raises many complications that obscure the issue. We must admit that the opponent of mental acts is partly right in that the term 'act' is not appropriate as applied to cognitions, and that the words used of them are mostly dispositional, and are to some extent (though, I think, much less so than is very commonly supposed) liable to include in their meaning not merely a reference to the mental events themselves but to behaviour. In many cases of 'knowing' and 'believing' there is, I admit, probably no conscious act to be observed, only an unconscious taking for granted in our thought. These complications do not arise with 'pain', which is not a dispositional term.

I have been discussing 'cognitive acts', but it seems to me even more unreasonable to make the corresponding denial in the case of conations. I do not, however, say that an introspectible act of volition accompanies every overt action or every direction of mental attention, any more than an 'act of cognition' is present whenever we come to 'know' or 'believe' something. With actions where no real alternative presents itself volitions perhaps do not occur as distinguishable psychological phenomena. But where there are alternatives before our mind we can assuredly introspect choices either at the time of action (volitions), or prior to action, no immediate action on them being considered possible or desirable at the time (decisions). These can be suitably termed 'acts' in a sense in which cognitions cannot, because they are directly brought into being in order to produce effects. But we should make a distinction between specific acts of choice and a continuous purposive process. The latter should not be reduced to a mere series of the former.

With cognition similarly we should distinguish a continuous process of thinking from particular 'cognitive acts'. The former should, I think be regarded as basic rather than the latter, and the process of thinking out a problem should not be reduced to a mere series of such acts. The latter play rather the part of beacons and turning-points in the process than that of being the sole material which constitutes it. It is only at comparatively exceptional moments, as when we 'see a new point', that we are aware of such an act, and we need not suppose that they are always occurring though we are not aware of them. In a sense

I am indeed continuously aware that I am writing an article on mental acts and that I am in my study, but I need not therefore suppose that I am all the time performing an unintrospected act of awareness of my surroundings and my purpose like those 'acts' which I detect introspectively when I ask myself a definite question about them. To say that I am aware throughout of my environment and purpose (in the 'background' of consciousness) is rather to talk about a relation which the process of thought continually bears than about a series of mental acts superadded to it.

But, after all, if we do discover 'mental acts' by introspection, what is that but discovering some kind of feeling? What would it be like to be aware of a mental act that was not a feeling? Is not to know that I know or will just to know what it feels like to know or will? In a sense the people who take this line are right. To know what an experience is, is to know what the experience feels like, and it could not be knowing anything else in so far as it is a knowing of the experience itself and not merely of its objects, unless we include under 'knowing what an experience is' knowing its causal properties. We are not, as might be held in the case of physical objects, knowing any property which could exist unfelt, for feeling is the determinable of which all particular experiences are determinate values. But we have not said very much when we have said this. It does not add much to the notion of an 'experience' to say that it is a feeling in a sense of 'feeling' so wide that it seems plausible to say that all experiences are just made up of feelings. It would indeed be saying a good deal if we could reduce all experiences to sensations of a recognizable kind which could be correlated with some definite sense-organs, but this cannot be done. Even if 'feeling' does carry with it a vague reference to the body and even if we suppose that every event in our mental life may be correlated with some event in the brain, the correlation is at any rate not obvious to inspection as it is in the case of the pain caused by burning a finger or with sights and sounds. And if we say that everything in experience is a feeling or feelings, we must not confuse this wide sense of 'feeling' with the more specific sense of 'feeling' in which emotions and pains are feelings but judgements and volitions are not. Feeling in the former sense is synonymous with experience in general, in the latter sense it stands for very specific kinds of or phases in experience.

As a matter of fact, each of the three traditional basic terms of psychology has a wider and a narrower usage. If it can be contended that all conscious mental states are varieties of feeling, it can be likewise contended that they are varieties of cognition, as was done by Descartes. Any state of consciousness may from one point of view be regarded as a cognition, an awareness of something. Thought may obviously be brought under the cognitive side, sensations have been commonly classed by psychologists as cognitions (of sense-data), pleasure and unpleasure can be regarded as qualities of the cognitive states, and emotions towards an object as more complexly qualified awareness of that object or ways of thinking about that object. Of course, if we bring in their external manifestations, emotions are much more; but it might be contended that this is all they are on the inward side. Conation (desire and choice) presents most difficulty to such an account, but choices and decisions might be regarded as changes in our way of thinking of certain possible acts, and desires as tendencies to think in a certain emotionally toned way about certain objects. They also lead to action, but it is because we think first in a certain way that we act (except in cases of 'automatic action', which is not in the full sense action). I do not say that this is the most natural, illuminating and satisfactory account of mental processes; but it is, I think, a possible one, and it brings out certain points of value.

Thirdly, we may make not feeling or cognition but conation fundamental in our account of mental life. We can indeed hardly make cognition and sensation just varieties of conation, but we may argue that conation is the fundamental aspect of the self on the ground that cognition is a function of attention and that pleasure and pain can themselves be analysed in terms of the conative attitudes of liking and aversion. To find an experience pleasant, it might be said, is to have a positive conative attitude to its quality as experience at the time it occurs, to find it unpleasant a negative. (Of course we might have a negative conative attitude towards the pleasant experience on other grounds, e.g. that we thought it would have bad effects or was based on something of which we morally disapproved.)

The truth seems to be that we may use each of these three terms, conation, cognition, and feeling, either in a wider or in a narrower sense. If we use it in the wider sense, each stands for an aspect of all events in our mind and not for a species of mental events to which some belong and not others. Thus we might think of feeling as constituting the stuff which makes up all our mental life. We might perhaps think of cognition as constituting a certain relation of our experience to the real (including sense-data, which we must remember are not *parts* of mind, and in the case of introspection an aspect of the mind itself other than the aspect we are describing as a cognition of it). And we might think of contation as constituting the connecting-link which organizes all our experience (*cf.* Leibniz). Attention is guided by purpose, and attention organizes our mental content and decides what we shall cognize; our temporary and our permanent dispositional purposes determine what we shall think and feel.

But the narrower sense is at least equally legitimate. If pains, emotions, and the seeing of answers to problems are all felt and so in a sense feelings, the third is so different from the other two classes that it deserves a different name. To call it a feeling may indeed have disastrous philosophical results, as it did with Hume, for whom it connoted that all beliefs, being mere sensations or feelings, were strictly speaking irrational (though scientific beliefs were still more rational in some relative sense than superstitions). Even if the three aspects be present in all human experiences, at any rate one is liable to be more prominent than the other two. If we experience a twinge of toothache we know that we have it, but that aspect is subordinate to the feeling. When we discover a particular emotionally indifferent fact we feel something, but feeling is subordinate to the knowing, and when we attend in order to find out the truth about something conation is present, but it is a mere subordinate means of cognition. When we choose or desire something we are aware of what we choose or desire, but the fundamental, the interesting fact is our conative attitude towards the object, not the mere fact that we are aware of it and think of it. So cognitions, conations and feelings may be also used as class terms for species of mental events as well as for different aspects present in all mental events. And the term used in the narrower sense of a mental event will be selected according to which of the three aspects predominates in that event. Its use will not deny the presence of the other two aspects in the event, but it will imply that in this event they are unimportant or at least subordinate.

Cognitive processes are thus felt experiences, but they deserve treatment as a special class among felt experiences. If you call them feelings, you have to admit that they have the property of yielding truth and falsehood in a unique way which is not common to all experiences. And, if you admit this, it does not perhaps matter very much whether you do or do not call them feelings, provided you are careful to explain how different they are from other 'feelings'. A 'cognitive act' we may then regard not indeed as something which exists *per se* in its own right but as a real element abstracted from a cognitive process, and perhaps the same applies to conative acts *mutatis mutandis*.

V

A NEW FORMULA FOR THE SYLLOGISM
IN TERMS OF THE ORDINARY SENSE
OF 'IMPLICATION'[1]

Recent advances in symbolic logic have been effected largely by
men who believed that the best way of treating arguments was
extensional rather than intensional, but I am not convinced that
this is more than a historical accident and that an at least equally
satisfactory logic might not be built up on an intensional basis.[2]
Extension after all seems posterior to and dependent on intension
rather than vice versa. Membership of a class depends on qualities
and relational properties, and universal propositions on connections of properties. So I shall try to give an intensional account of
the syllogism which will strictly prove the validity of all the
recognized figures, leaving it to someone who is more expert than
I am in other branches of logic to apply similar principles there
if he should deem it worth while. I shall not make use of 'implication' in the Russell sense, which is essentially an extensional
conception; but shall return to what is still the normal meaning
of the term outside formal logic, and treat this as my fundamental
concept. In this sense of 'imply' P implies Q when and only
when there is a special relation between P and Q such as would
entitle us to infer Q from P in the event of P being true. This
relation I shall signify by an arrow pointing in the direction of
the proposition which is implied. I might have called it the
relation of 'entailing', but although this would be again in accord-

---

[1] *Analysis*, vol. 12 no. 1, p. 9 ff. (1951). This article is revised, chiefly though
not wholly because W. Kneale suggested a better mode of symbolism.

[2] [I note that in an article published in *Mind*, vol. 76 no. 303, p. 346 ff. Storrs
McCall proposes a treatment of syllogisms in some respects very similar to mine.
The time factor puts out of the question any influence of his on my original
article, nor was my revision of it thus influenced. I did not notice his article till
I was on the point of sending my final version in, and I did not consider it
desirable to go into the technical question as to which of us had produced the
more satisfactory formulation.

Going further back W. Kneale pointed out to me that Leibniz also had the
idea of producing a logic which treated the syllogism as a matter of intensional
connection (v. Kneale, *Development of Logic*, p. 339).]

ance with ordinary usage, it might confuse those who limit 'entailment' to cases of formal and logically necessary implication. I mean to cover not only those but all cases where we deem ourselves entitled to infer one proposition from another, whether because of formal logic, because of a supposed causal or other not formally necessary connection, or because of some authority which we accept. It is a pity that the word 'implication', which was and still is so generally used to express just this, has been by its diversion to another sense spoilt for formal logic. For a general term to express any relation justifying inference is needed by the logician.

Most modern logicians have treated universal propositions as not having existential import, but they have adopted a different line as regards particular propositions. I propose to give a non-existential interpretation of the latter also. It will not of course express their full meaning, but neither does a non-existential interpretation of universal propositions, and I think both express an important part of the meaning, though no complete logic should fail also to include the existential interpretations and point out the logical consequences which result when propositions are interpreted in the latter way. Now the non-existential element in the universal proposition all s is p seems to me to be adequately conveyed by the hypothetical: if x is s, then it is p. This is not equivalent to: $(x$ is $s)$ implies $(x$ is $p)$, in the Russell sense, because we certainly do not regard as true all hypothetical propositions in which the antecedent does not stand for a fact. Such a proposition may be true, but only if there is a special relation between antecedent and consequent such that, if the antecedent had been a true proposition, we should have been entitled to infer the consequent as true also.[1] This relation I have decided to express by an arrow, so 'All s is p' becomes: '(x) $(Sx \rightarrow Px)$', using Sx to stand for 'x is s' and Px for 'x is p'. But it will be more convenient if I am allowed to abbreviate still further and just substitute S for the function 'x is s' etc. By '$S \rightarrow P$' I shall mean that any true proposition formed from the function 'x is s' by making a substitution would be so related to the corresponding proposition formed from the function 'x is p' that the latter could be inferred from the former. It will be an advantage in clarity of exposition to retain the letters S P M so familiar to students of the syllogism. I shall use a bar above a term to mean 'not'.

[1] I am not intending this as a *definition* of a hypothetical. If so, it would be circular.

But how are particular propositions to be interpreted non-existentially? We are told that the particular is the contradictory of the universal. Well, what is the contradictory of $S \rightarrow P$? Surely: P does not follow from S, or: S is compatible with $\overline{P}$. So we have corresponding to the four traditional kinds of categorical propositions (a) $S \rightarrow P$, (e) $S \rightarrow \overline{P}$, (i) $S \Rightarrow \overline{P}$, (o) $S \Rightarrow P$. It may be objected that I have eviscerated particular propositions to such a point as to deprive them of all value, but it is very often of some considerable use to know that two things are compatible. A patient may very much want to know whether pursuing his ordinary occupations is compatible with his return to health or a jury whether the evidence is compatible with the prisoner's innocence. In science it is often a most important step to show that two things were compatible which had been supposed incompatible, and many men have been very worried indeed as to whether freedom is compatible with causality or the goodness of God with evil. A discovery of consistency is indeed usually valued not for its own sake but rather as a preliminary to establishing further truths, but that this is the case with particular propositions has long been a commonplace in logic.

Now it is not possible in the space to demonstrate by my method or any other all recognized valid syllogistic moods, but this would also be unnecessary. They fall into three distinct groups, and if I demonstrate one or two of each of the three, it will be quite clear how the others also could be demonstrated by applying the same method. The first group is the one in which both premisses and conclusion are universal. The Barbara mood becomes: $M \rightarrow P$, $S \rightarrow M$, therefore $S \rightarrow P$. This may be proved as follows: Suppose S true for any particular value of x, e.g. Socrates. Then M is true also for that value, since $S \rightarrow M$ and if M is true so is P. Therefore $S \rightarrow P$. Obviously there would be no difference of principle if for P we substituted $\overline{P}$, but the argument would break down altogether if for $S \rightarrow M$ we substituted $S \rightarrow \overline{M}$ (c.f. rule that minor premise of first figure must be affirmative), unless we substituted $\overline{M}$ for M also in $M \rightarrow P$, in which case $\overline{M}$ would be the middle term and the minor would under the old formulation be treated as affirmative. Second figure syllogisms with a universal conclusion can be demonstrated equally easily but not quite in the same way. Here $S \rightarrow M$ and $P \rightarrow \overline{M}$ or vice versa. Therefore if both S and P were true for the same value of x, there would be a contradiction $(M \overline{M})$. Therefore $S \rightarrow \overline{P}$ (sEp).

The second group consists of syllogisms in which one premiss is particular. Let us take the third figure syllogism: some m is not p, all m is s, some s is not p $(= M \overrightarrow{\rightarrow} P, M \rightarrow S, S \overrightarrow{\rightarrow} P)$. This may be proved as follows: Suppose $S \rightarrow P$. Then since $M \rightarrow S$, $M \rightarrow P$, which contradicts the major. If we took, e.g., the mood AII in the first figure, the proof would be somewhat different in character. The mood runs: $M \rightarrow P$, $S \overrightarrow{\rightarrow} \overline{M}$, therefore $S \overrightarrow{\rightarrow} \overline{P}$ Proof: Suppose $S \rightarrow \overline{P}$. Now $M \rightarrow P$, therefore $\overline{P} \rightarrow \overline{M}$, therefore S implies $\overline{M}$, which contradicts the minor premiss.

The third group consists of syllogisms in which there are two universal premisses and a particular conclusion, e.g.: $M \rightarrow P$, $M \rightarrow S$, therefore $S \overrightarrow{\rightarrow} \overline{P}$. This class of syllogism have been pronounced invalid by modern logicians because they interpreted universal propositions non-existentially and particular existentially, thus rendering an existential conclusion impossible. Since I am interpreting both premisses and conclusion non-existentially, this does not apply to my account, and I can prove these also, but to do so I shall have to make one additional assumption which will appear directly. For the mood AAI in the third figure the proof is as follows. The mood runs: $M \rightarrow P$, $M \rightarrow S$, $S \overrightarrow{\rightarrow} \overline{P}$. Now suppose S did imply $\overline{P}$. Then since $M \rightarrow S$, $M \rightarrow \overline{P}$. But one premiss was $M \rightarrow P$. Therefore M implies both P and $\overline{P}$. The conclusion that S cannot imply P is thus proved by a *reductio ad absurdum* if we grant that M is not a self-contradictory concept; similarly with AAI in the fourth figure. Here $P \rightarrow M$, $M \rightarrow S$, $S \overrightarrow{\rightarrow} \overline{P}$. To prove the conclusion suppose $S \rightarrow \overline{P}$. Then, since $P \rightarrow M$ and $M \rightarrow S$, we have $P \rightarrow \overline{P}$. As I have said however I have to make an assumption with this group which I did not have to make with the two other groups, namely that m or, in the case of the fourth figure mood AAI, p is not a self-contradictory concept. If the assumption is not made somebody may well use the premisses, e.g. $M \rightarrow P$ and $M \rightarrow S$ to show not that S and P are compatible but that there can be no cases of M. For the validity of my proofs depends on the assumption that M cannot imply both X and not $-X$, or P imply non-P, assumptions which hold only if these propositions are not self-contradictory.[1] The

---

[1] I am indebted to Prof. W. Kneale for a comment on this point.

proofs of syllogisms in the first two groups do not require this assumption, but use logical principles which would be valid even if one or more of the premisses of a syllogism were self-contradictory. For a self-contradictory proposition can still imply something, and the relation of implication is still transitive. Also we can still argue from $A \rightarrow B$ to $\overline{B} \rightarrow \overline{A}$ even where A is self-contradictory, otherwise we could not use a *reductio ad absurdum* argument. I did indeed assume that two contradictory propositions could not both be true, but I did not assume in the proofs of the other groups of syllogism that the premisses of the syllogisms were not self-contradictory. All squares are circles, all triangles are squares, therefore all triangles are circles, is a perfectly valid syllogism in the sense that the conclusion would necessarily be true if the premisses were. The additional assumption I made with the third group may seem avoidable if we adopt the method of proof corresponding to the traditional one of reduction to the first figure. The use of this method depends with the moods of which I am thinking on our ability to convert. Now to convert a universal negative is to say that because $S \rightarrow \overline{P}$, $P \rightarrow \overline{S}$, an obviously valid inference, while to convert a universal affirmative is to say that because $S \rightarrow P$, P is compatible with S, which again seems obvious, since to assert compatibility is to make a weaker statement than to assert entailment. But it is really obvious only if we grant that S is not self-contradictory, because if it were S might imply both P and not-P. So we cannot escape making the assumption in this way. Subject to the assumption however the ordinary rules about conversion and the traditional square of inference can be seen to be justified in my account. We can indeed see more clearly than on an ordinary formulation some points, e.g. that an O proposition cannot be converted, for $sOp = S \overset{\longrightarrow}{} P$ and $pOs = P \overset{\longrightarrow}{} S$, and it is obviously the case that all implications are not necessarily reciprocal.

I do not think that in these demonstrations I have assumed any logical axioms except the three traditional laws of thought (or two if the law of identity is dismissed as saying nothing). But it is interesting to note that the proofs of all three classes of syllogisms presuppose the validity of the traditional first figure (with universal premisses and conclusion) in the form—if $S \rightarrow M$ and $M \rightarrow P$, then $S \rightarrow P$, thus justifying the old view of the priority of the first figure, for the principle of transitivity is necessary for all syllogistic inference. I have given what I took as a proof of this transitivity by saying that if S is true of any x and S implies M it follows (from the meaning of implication) that M is true of it and then repeating the process with M and P. This argument does not seem to me at any point to presuppose a prior assumption of transitivity, i.e. it does not itself need to assume already the principle that if $S \rightarrow M$ and $M \rightarrow P$, $S \rightarrow P$ in order to justify itself, but somebody may contend that what I have done is rather to point out that the transitivity principle is self-evident than to prove it. In that case we should have to regard the moods Barbara and Celarent as not demonstrated themselves but as just the affirmative and negative forms of a self-evident principle on which all syllogistic inference depends. Some of the proofs also make use of the principle that if one proposition implies another the falsity of the second implies the falsity of the first. This principle need not be taken as just self-evident but can be demonstrated as follows. Suppose a proposition X implied another proposition Y and suppose Y to be false, then if X were true Y being implied by X would also be true and so the same proposition would be both true and false. The principle is thus demonstrable by reference to the law of contradiction. So none but the most fundamental laws of thought are presupposed in my demonstrations. I do not think that even the commutative laws arc, only the traditional two or three 'laws of thought'. The principle that, if P implies Q and P is true Q is true, has sometimes been put forward as a separate independent axiom or postulate, but I do not see that it need be, for it is surely included in the meaning of 'imply' (both in the Russellian and in my sense of 'imply'), so that it cannot be denied without self-contradiction. I should therefore claim that my method can give what, as far as I know, the old syllogistic logic never provided, namely a strict demonstration that the valid moods do prove their conclusions and not merely a demonstration that some moods are invalid. No doubt logic as developed today on the orthodox lines can also provide such a demonstration, but for reasons which I gave at the beginning I should regard my account as more fundamental.

If the propositions in question are interpreted existentially, it is easy to make the requisite additions. With the universal propositions we simply add to the original non-existential interpretation the proposition: S is true for some values of x. A particular proposition interpreted existentially becomes 'S and P not only can be but are true in at least one case for the same value of x.'

If these interpretations are adopted, syllogisms can be treated in the classical way. In the Barbara mood all *s* is *m*, if there are cases of *s*, becomes '*S* is true of some cases of *x* and *S* implies *M*;' from this and '*M* implies *P*' it follows that *S* implies *P* and that *P* will therefore be true of some actual cases, i.e. at least those cases of which *S* is true. We may note that it is here only necessary to assume that there are some cases of *S* being true, the rest following. In the third figure it is however necessary if we are to have a valid existential conclusion that cases of *m* should be primarily given as existing also. This then will imply the existence of cases of *s* which will also be cases of *p*.

VI

CAUSALITY AND INDUCTION

In this article I am venturing on a field which has been very well trodden in recent years by people who are far more expert than I am myself in the detailed work required. My justification is that I do think these people have in common certain general philosophical assumptions that unduly circumscribe the possibilities to which they have to adapt the more specialized doctrine of logic and scientific method. They rule out dogmatically certain ways of solving their problems and I shall suggest these ways for their consideration. They assume in particular that the problem of induction is not to be solved by positing a necessary connection between cause and effect, they assume that there can be no such necessary connection. For most modern logicians the supposition that there is a synthetic *a priori* proposition to the effect even, e.g., that the same thing cannot be both red and blue is suspect, but the supposition that there can be a necessary and *a priori* connection between different things or different events is just meaningless and absurd. Such a suggestion must then be ruled out even if it should help to solve the problem of induction; they seem to know it *a priori* to be impossible. But it must be admitted that these logicians have not solved their problem, and most of them are conscious of this, though they often try to meet the situation by the time-honoured expedient of crying 'Sour grapes'. It is admitted by them that induction cannot be justified by any process of argument evident to reason and they can only escape the dilemma by persuading themselves that it does not need to be so justified. In other words they have to rest content with arguing in a way which on their own showing is not rationally justified and say that this is a logically impeccable procedure. I am not content with such arguments, and when I say this I am not being irrational or indulging in any extraordinary paradox.

Now those who maintain that induction is not justifiable in the sense of logically justifiable are not thereby exonerated from explaining in what sense it is justifiable. They cannot say that it is never justifiable at all. For, in the first place, they cannot possibly really believe this. They cannot believe that there is no justification for supposing that, if they jump from the top of a skyscraper, they are more likely to hurt themselves than if they remain seated at home. And, secondly, if they take this line, they will be unable to make a distinction which they certainly do make, the distinction between forecasts based on induction which are scientifically acceptable and forecasts which are 'superstitions' or simply silly. If inductive inferences are never justifiable, science and superstition are in the same boat; to distinguish them scientific inferences of the kind competent people consider rational must be justifiable in some sense in which the silly ones are not. Now it is usually the main object of the type of philosopher whose views I am discussing to provide a philosophy of science. It is therefore urgently incumbent on him to explain as far as possible what the sense is in which good inductions can justify their conclusions and bad inductions cannot. Unfortunately far too little work has been done on that topic.

One alternative is to say that 'justifiable' just means 'practically useful'. But this does not seem to me any help. For it is not enough that the conclusion established by induction should have been practically useful in the past. It is no practical use knowing that something has been useful in the past if this is no guide to future utility. But to argue from practical success in the past to practical success in the future is already to use an inductive argument in a sense not itself definable in terms of practical utility. To say that it has been useful in the past to refrain from drinking prussic acid is not to say that it will be useful in the future. On the contrary the latter is an inference, and not an analytic inference, from the former. And if we admit inferences from what has been practically useful in the past to what will be practically useful in the future we are already admitting induction with all its problems. It is no easier to see how we can infer inductively that, because something has been useful in the past, it will be useful in the future, than to see in general how we can infer that, because something has been true of events of a certain kind in the past, it is likely to be true of similar events in the future. The problem is the same in both cases. This is, if possible, even more obvious when 'practically useful' is defined as 'enabling one to make true predictions'. But in any case, as Lord Russell says,[1] 'it is nonsense to pretend that science can be valid practically

---

[1] *Human Knowledge—Its Scope and Limits*, p. 524.

but not theoretically, for it is only valid practically if what it predicts happens, and if our canons (or some substitute) are not valid, there is no reason to believe in scientific predictions.' Further, if 'inductively justified' be defined as 'practically useful', we are confronted with a vicious circle. For 'practically useful' cannot mean here 'just what will in fact be practically useful'. Obviously a belief or class of beliefs which it was unjustifiable to hold on the evidence might by good luck turn out practically useful. We must then mean 'what we are inductively justified in believing will be practically useful' (or on some variations of the theory 'what belongs to a class of propositions of which this is true').

But suppose we mean by 'practically useful' just 'practically useful in the past.' This brings us to another type of theory according to which to say on inductive grounds that something is probable is simply to sum up the evidence 'on which' we say 'the conclusion is based.' Such a view is really implied in, e.g., the solution advanced by C. Lewy in *Analysis*,[1] where he says that there is a contradiction in saying

(1) Whenever I have heard barking in the past there was always a dog somewhere near;
(2) I am hearing barking now;
(3) I have not good reason to believe that there is a dog somewhere near now.

The contradiction is, it appears from the context, meant to be a verbal one. One of the things that there is a good reason . . . *means* is that (1) and (2) are true, and the other things it means are similar propositions about past events. Obviously (1) is inadequate as it stands, but even if it were expanded to cover all possible propositions which could serve as inductive evidence for the conclusion it would still be merely a compound proposition about observed events and not about the as yet unobserved event which we infer as probable. If this were so, to say that there is a good (inductive) reason for beliving in the occurrence of some future (or unobserved) event would simply be to say that observed events of a certain kind had occurred; to say that I will die would be simply to say that other men had done so; to say that there was a

[1] Vol. VI, 87ff. I doubt whether he would now accept this solution, but some people would.

danger of war simply to say something of past wars. That is surely incredible. When a man makes predictions about the likely length of his life or about the issue of war and peace, his interest does not lie in what happened in the past but in its bearing on the future. He is not asking for its own sake whether people died from his illness in the past or under what conditions wars broke out before 1951—such questions would not give him the anxiety and emotional excitement which he feels—he is asking about a future event. And I do not see how a statement about a future event can verbally contradict a statement about the past.

A further difficulty arises. According to this view to say that an event is probable is to say that certain observed phenomena (which we call the evidence) are of a certain kind? But of what kind? We cannot answer: 'such as to justify us in inferring that the event called probable will occur', if this view is to be advanced as itself a solution of the problem of the justification of inductive arguments. And it is difficult to see what other characteristic they have in common in respect of which we could lump them all together or call them evidence. The general course adopted by holders of such a view seems to be to abandon the search for a common element and say that there could only be an *extensive* definition of 'evidence' and 'probable', i.e., a definition by giving a list of the sort of data which would commonly be described as constituting evidence in support of something or as making something probable. In that case the only link which put them all in the class of 'evidence' would be a verbal one, that they were all called 'evidence'. For if the definition is purely extensional, not intensional, there is no common characteristic or relation asserted when we describe different data as evidence for something except the characteristic of having the same word applied to them. But in that case are we to say that what most people call good evidence or what most people call probable must necessarily really be so? That would be attributing scientific infallibility to the majority. Or are we to say that what competent scientists call rationally justifiable is necessarily really so? That would be a vicious circle, for the ultimate criterion for calling anybody a competent scientist is that he is rational in his inductive reasoning. And it is surely obvious that we are not talking primarily about human language when we estimate the probability of future occurrences. Whether there is likely to be another war is not a question of linguistic correctness.

Some would still perhaps give a definition of inductive probability in terms of the feeling of confidence that we have when we make judgements which we regard as probably true. But this clearly will not do. The fact that a gambler has feelings of confidence when he makes forecasts about the success of a horse does not make his belief inductively grounded or the horse's success really probable. The correctness of our calculations about probabilities is by no means always in proportion to our feelings of expectation. If, on the other hand, we substitute 'rational confidence' for 'confidence', we are admitting inductive inference to the unobserved with all its problems. A rational confidence would be a confidence which such inference justified.

In the absence of a definition of what is meant by 'inductively justified' those who insist that induction cannot be logically justified will be driven back to saying that inductive conclusions are justifiable in their own way, but that we cannot explain further what that way is. This is to have recourse to the indefinable and to say that inductive justification is an ultimate unanalysable concept, as a different school has said about 'good'. Further, it would presumably have to be not only indefinable but *non-natural*, since it has never been identified with any *simple* feeling or sense-quality, and it cannot, if it is indefinable, be identified with any *complex* empirical concept. Some of the logicians who have said that induction does not need logical justification might not mind this conclusion, but most assuredly would. They are very averse to non-natural indefinables and the thought that they had added to the number of these would bring them bitter remorse. I am less hostile to such entities, but still I do not relish increasing their number unnecessarily. And I am clear that we must not accept one unless we are satisfied that we have direct awareness of the characteristic or relation in question in some sort of experience. (I do not mean 'sense-experience'. After all to see that one proposition logically entails another is an experience, though I should not call it a sense experience. To *see* that something is intrinsically good is even on a non-naturalistic view an experience, though 'intrinsic goodness' itself does not on such a view stand for an experience.) Unless we have such an awareness of something, it is no use saying it is indefinable because we shall then not in the least know what it is we are talking about, and since it is plain that we do know what 'inductively justifiable' means we must suppose either that we have this awareness here or that it is definable in some fashion or other. Now I am not myself satisfied that we have such an awareness in the case of the attribute 'inductively justifiable', and therefore I am not prepared to accept it as indefinable. I know what is meant by saying that a conclusion is 'deductively justifiable', i.e., that it is entailed by its premises, but I am not aware also of another kind of justifiability, that of induction, in which the premises do not entail the conclusion. I frankly do not understand what this means. Consequently I am as regards this indefinable in a similar position to that in which naturalists say they are as regards the indefinable or indefinables of ethics, except that I am not influenced by any general presupposition to the effect that non-naturalist concepts must on no account be admitted.

But what many people who deny the need of justifying induction mean is perhaps simply that we just see in particular cases that the evidence justifies the regarding as probable a particular conclusion, that there is no need or possibility of justifying it by general principles and no more to be said about it except to ward off philosophical errors. There is an important element of truth in such a contention. The actual inductive predictions we make are not the result of inferences from an axiom such as the uniformity of nature applied to experiences. Their relation to such an axiom is certainly not like that which the inference: 5 were in the room an hour ago, 7 more have gone in and none have come out, so there are 12 in there now, bears to the principle of pure arithmetic that $5 + 7 = 12$. In order to make the inference we do not need to envisage any general axiom as a premise. Rather do we see directly that the particular data are such as to make a certain conclusion probable. I do not mean that it is a case of mere self-evidence unaffected by prior experience. On the contrary, previous experience in the main determines what data we take as adequate, but the process must have started somewhere, and whether an appeal to self-evidence is an adequate answer here for the philosopher or not, it is clear that to the ordinary man it seems evident that particular evidence justifies a particular conclusion long before he has thought of the general axioms on which this depends (if he ever does so). Any such axioms we must regard rather as generalizations from what we see in particular cases, than as premises from which ordinary inductive conclusions are deduced (except at a very sophisticated level). I do not mean by this indeed that they are empirical generalizations; in that case I should be open to the objection that I am establishing by induction the principles on which induction itself depends. Either we must regard them as inductions only in a quite different sense, what Johnson calls 'intuitive inductions', i.e., universal propositions which we first see to be true in particular instances and then realize are of such a nature that they are valid universally and not only in these particular instances. (I think, however, that 'induction' is a misleading term here, and it is certainly most important not to confuse it as thus used with the more usual sense of 'induction'.) Or, if we do not think we have this intuitive insight, we must regard them as postulates, i.e. propositions which we can in no way see to be true but which are presupposed in a good many beliefs that we cannot help holding. Or, thirdly, and this is the view I favour, we may claim to have a confused intuitive awareness of something here, we do not quite know what, which the philosophers have not yet succeeded in analysing adequately, though we have a vague general idea of its nature. But, however that may be, it must be remembered that even great scientists rely rather on a trained insight, the fruit no doubt partly of experience, as to the bearing of certain evidence than on a logical deduction from the uniformity of nature and the principle of limited variety, etc. But the logician or philosopher cannot stop here. He cannot just say that we see in each particular case what follows inductively as a probable consequence and leave it at that. Clearly the different examples of inductive arguments have something in common, and he will try to find out what it is. Further, it is surely plain in induction as in deduction that the real logical basis of an argument is what it has in common with other arguments of the same form. It is on this and not on its particular content that the validity of an inductive inference depends. It is not because of the particular nature of burning, but because it has been conjoined with fire in the past, that we conclude that, if we put our hand in the fire tomorrow, we shall be burnt, and there are countless cases of induction in which what is logically precisely the same argument may be used. It is true in deduction also that insight into a particular argument is psychologically prior. Uneducated people can argue correctly in syllogisms though they do not know logic. For a long time the distinction between the premises and the principle of an argument has been recognized. But the fact that we can use a particular argument without recognizing its principle does not prevent the principle, the form which that argument has in common with others, being *logically* prior. Thus the reason why the argument in the traditional example about mortality is valid is not because it is concerned with Socrates, men and mortality in particular, but because it exemplifies the *dictum de omni et nullo* or whatever improved formulation logicians prefer to give of the principle in question. Similarly: There seems to have been no relevant change in the situation except that I put my hand in the fire, my hand did not hurt before but now does hurt, therefore fire applied to a hand probably causes pain, is valid because it is an instance of the Method of Difference, though it is a method of argument much more difficult to apply in many cases because of the doubt as to what is relevant. I suppose if we had not relied on other people's authority and had been strictly logical as to inferences from our own experience, we should have to put our hand in the fire several times before we were adequately satisfied as to this causal property in fire. Further, it seems plain that the form of argument called the Method of Difference is not valid in its own right but depends on some more general principle which it has in common with other inductive methods. The great difference between induction and syllogisms here is that in the case of the latter the principles were already clearly seen by Aristotle more than 2,000 years ago and logicians are agreed as to what they substantially are (though not as to their best formulation), while no such agreement prevails as regards induction. It is an interesting and important subject of research to determine the logical principles governing induction, and it may even affect scientific practice beneficially; but good reasoning is quite possible without any explicit idea of general principles, at least in cases which are not very complex.

Further, it must be realized that those who say that inductive inference is justified in its own way but that this is *toto genere* different from that of deductive, are making a rather strange claim. They are claiming that we are entitled to infer B from A without there being any logical relation between A and B. We certainly make inductive inferences in the sense that we believe B because of A and at the same time hold that it is the relation to A which justifies the belief. Nor can anyone really believe that the inferences are never justifiable. But if we hold that we are sometimes entitled to believe B because of A, this seems to involve already the admission that A entails the probability (though not the certainty) of *B*. A valid inference the premises of which did not entail even the probability of the conclusion would be a funny inference indeed. Its validity would certainly call for explanation.

A different view, more like the older theory, is suggested by Lord Keynes,[1] Lord Russell,[2] and Mr Kneale.[3] It is that there are some axioms on which induction depends which are neither evident *a priori* nor capable of establishment by empirical observations but known in some other way, not further explained, and from these axioms the validity of inductive arguments could be deduced. Certainly it would be quite impossible to claim that Keynes's Principle of Limited Independent Variety, i.e., the principle that the universe is simple enough for our inductions, could be seen to be self-evident; and though it would not be so absurd to make this claim in regard to the propositions of Russell and Kneale, it would be very daring. If they are seen to be true at all, it does not seem to be a case of seeing their logical necessity. One cannot be happy about falling back on a mysterious third kind of cognition different from both the well-authenticated kinds, *a priori* and empirical, but if the logical difficulties raised about induction prove insoluble we may have to fall back on this view.

Another suggestion, also made by Mr. Kneale,[4] is that the principles of induction might be justified, not because they are seen to be objectively true, but because the policy of assuming their truth and acting accordingly is the only policy by means of which we can hope to discover laws of nature, if there are any laws. Now this no doubt gives the reason why the scientist should adopt his hypotheses in the first place. They should be possible theories which he holds in mind in the first instance, not because they have been proved to be probable, but because we need to have some hypothesis in mind to be tested if we are to have any good chance of eventually finding the right one by observation. I, too, think that there is a preliminary stage in induction in which the premises from which we draw conclusions are not validated; but the whole point of this procedure lies in our hope that what we first adopt without validification will later be rendered probable by the fulfilment of the predictions based on it or refuted by their non-fulfilment, and this assumes that verification of predictions

[1] *A Treatise on Probability.*   [2] *Human Knowledge—Its Scope and Limits.*
[3] *Probability and Induction.*   [4] *Probability and Induction*, pt IV.

E

can enhance the probability of an hypothesis. But how this can be is just the problem or the major part of the problem of induction. We must remember that in the absence of some special assumption the fact that a hypothesis has applied in the past is no argument whatever even for the probability of its applying in the future. At any rate Mr Kneale's suggestion is at the best *a pis aller*, and falls very much below what we cannot help believing in ordinary life. We cannot help believing that fire will really burn and do not merely act on the policy of assuming that it does so. It will not be necessary to have recourse to his explanation as the final account if my positive argument to justify induction, which will follow, is accepted. But let us first examine further the concept of causation.

The attitude of most[1] modern logicians to induction has as its background a theory of causation approximating to the regularity view, but it is worth noting that the motives which inspired the great scientific advance of modern times were not exactly those which a regularity theory of causation would encourage or countenance. The main original motive in looking for causes (insofar as it was not merely practical utility), was to find *reasons* to explain events, but according to modern theories causation has nothing to do with 'explaining' or 'reasons for' anything. Yet it was largely because it was thought to give the reasons for phenomena that science was deemed an inspiring pursuit and one the advantages of which were far from being exhausted by its practical value. When, e.g., eclipses were ascribed to a shadow cast by the moon or earth, it was thought that scientists were giving the reason for what happened. This is mistaken according to the usual modern view. They have merely arranged the facts in a practically convenient way. I feel a certain scepticism as to whether this is what scientists really believe when they are working out their science, but at any rate it is what most of them (under philosophical influence) say when they give a general account of the epistemology of science, and it is the view of any philosophers who can claim at all to be in the fashion. But it must be made clear that it is far from being the universal view, the common-sense view, the only conceivable view, or indeed a view held at all by any appreciable number of people before Hume. This is not to say that the view is false, but I have, I think, more substantial grounds for

---

[1] Kneale is an honourable exception.

rejecting it, and one of the chief of these is that its rejection will relieve the problem of induction.

The first point I wish to make here is that, without necessarily going so far as to say that a cause is only a species of logical ground, we must at least admit there to be a marked analogy between them. The most important feature about causation, both in theory and practice, is that it enables us to infer one proposition from others. In deductive reasoning also we do this, and so causation must be regarded as in the most important aspect at least analogous to the relation between premises and conclusion in deductive reasoning. I may have gone too far when I committed myself to saying elsewhere that causation involved a relation of logical entailment, but at least one can hardly deny that the two relations bear a very strong analogy to each other. They are both relations on the strength of which we can validly make inferences (at least unless we are going to be sceptical about the whole of science). Whether we say that the cause entails the effect and *vice versa* or not is largely a question of language or at least of emphasis. If we say that it does, we must admit that this differs in important respects from other kinds of entailment; and if we say it does not, we must admit that there is present at least a relation *like* entailment, but it can hardly be a difference of principle which we say but rather a difference of expression and emphasis.

Secondly I wish to defend the attempt to justify induction by an argument from inverse probability. Many regularities are, in fact, given in our experiences. There are many cases where a B in all or almost all observed instances follows an A. For instance, every time I put my hand near the fire it feels warmer than before. Now suppose we only took account of two alternatives—feeling warmer and feeling colder. This is certainly inadequate, there is also the alternative of feeling no change in temperature, to say nothing of all the other changes which might conceivably take place in my hand in respects other than temperature. But at any rate, to take those into account would only strengthen my argument. At least we know that the antecedent probability of its feeling warmer on a particular occasion cannot in the absence of any relevant causal law be greater than one in two. Therefore the antecedent probability of its feeling warmer in the absence of a causal law on all of twenty occasions when I put it near the fire is already less than $1/2^{20}$ or less than 1/a million. But the experiment has been tried by people not twenty but millions of times. If the constancy of the result were not explained by some causal connection, it would be an incredible coincidence even more improbable than having all the trumps in one hand at bridge several times in succession. So in such cases the probability of there being some relevant causal law seems to follow clearly. And once we have thus justified the acceptance of some causal laws we can discover more by using these to help us in making inferences which verify further hypotheses. Thus in view of causal laws already established we may be able to infer that a hypothesis has certain consequences, i.e., if it were true, such and such verifiable effects would follow. We may then find by observation that these occur to such an extent as to justify us in asserting the probability of the hypothesis. Thus if we grant some laws on the strength of the first argument, we are able to infer a good many more. So, if I am right, we have a justification of induction which does not assume anything except the principles of probability on which the inverse probability argument is based, principles which unlike special inductive presuppositions such as the uniformity of nature or the principle of limited independent variety seem quite clearly evident in the strictest logical sense. It is quite evident that in the absence of any reason favouring one alternative the odds against one of several possible alternatives repeating itself even twenty times in succession are more than a million to one. The argument, if valid, shows not indeed that every event has a cause—it has no tendency to do this—but that it is extremely probable that there are some causal laws, at least of a statistical kind. (Whether such a statistical law could be ultimate may, however, be doubted.)

This argument is of course not original.[1] It is far too obvious to be that. But it needs renewed discussion because it has been commonly rejected by recent philosophers on various grounds which seem to me fallacious.

(1) It has been objected that the notion of probability or improbability already presupposes causation, so that the argument becomes a vicious circle. But this is refuted by the fact that the notions can be applied in mathematics where causation is not in question. It is more improbable that any given number above 14 will turn out to be a prime than not and increasingly so as the number increases; in the absence of any special knowledge the probability of the result of a calculation that yields a whole number being even is 50 per cent; the repeated exemplification

---

[1] V. W. P. Montague, *The Ways of Things*, pp. 182ff.

of a mathematical law in the absence of any direct proof or disproof increases the probability that that law is true. And I ask you to consider the argument on its own merits. Is it not very improbable that by sheer chance every time or almost every time a person put his hand on a red hot coal he should happen to have felt pain at the same time if there were no causal connection? And if this is so fantastically improbable, is it not an argument for causation? (2) It is objected that we cannot conclude that, because arguments of this type may be legitimately used, as they commonly are, to establish a particular scientific hypothesis, they can therefore be used as a valid ground for the acceptance of the notion of causal law in general. It does not necessarily follow that, because a certain type of argument is valid within the inductive system, therefore it could be used as a justification for the system as a whole. This, of course, is true as far as it goes. But it does not entitle one to conclude that the argument thus used is invalid without a consideration of the logic of the special case. A type of argument that is valid in one context might well not be valid in another, but we cannot possibly say that, just because the context is different, it must be invalid. The difference in the context may or may not be relevant to its validity. That it destroys its validity can only be shown by calling attention to the *special points* in respect of which it affects detrimentally the logic of the argument, and I cannot see that there are any such. Whether we are dealing with a particular causal law or considering the general argument to establish that there are some causal laws, it remains true that it is immensely improbable that the same kind of event would repeat itself many times on a certain kind of occasion unless there were a causal connexion involved. But I have conceded too much. In fact, so far from the context being quite different in the two cases, it seems to me that the context is the same (except insofar as other arguments are introduced based on previous inductions), and only the purpose different. The argument for any particular causal law must from the nature of the case be at the same time an argument that there are causal laws. The argument for the causal law that fire burns flesh based on a number of occurrences of burning too great to be dismissed as a coincidence is at the same time an argument for the more general proposition that there are some causal laws. The argument for the one conclusion cannot be valid without the argument for the other being so too. There are more subtle ways of establishing causal laws, but if

some could not first be established by the method of which I have
spoken, I doubt whether these more subtle ways could be of any
avail.

(3) It is objected that an argument such as I have used is valid
only if we presuppose that any law in question has a finite probability prior to the argument. This view is taken by Lord Keynes,
and most subsequent writers on inductive logic have agreed
with him on the point, which seems to be implied by the fact that
the mathematical formula used to compute the probability
resulting from an argument makes it a function not only of the
evidence which forms the basis of the particular argument but
equally of the probability which the hypothesis had prior to the
argument. This seems plain enough where the argument is concerned with something of which we had previous knowledge.
Thus in considering whether a man has committed a theft it is
obviously right to consider not only the fact that, say, he is one
of the only two persons who were in a position to steal the money,
but also our previous knowledge of his character which might
make the probability of his having done such a thing immensely
lower than 50 per cent. We should rightly require stronger
evidence to establish the existence in the American countryside
of a lion than of a stray dog because the antecedent probability
of the former is much less than that of the latter. But this reference
to antecedent probability only takes us a step further back: it
amounts, in fact, to an appeal to previous inductive arguments to
supplement the one before us and the probability the previous
arguments give would in its turn seem to depend on a probability
established by still earlier arguments. But obviously this process
cannot go on for ever. Sooner or later we must come to a point
where there is no further argument available to give the hypothesis which we want to establish any antecedent probability.
And this would apparently be the position as regards the first
causal law which we tried to establish by the argument from
inverse probability given above. And, since any multiple of zero
is still zero, we are apparently not in a position to give the hypothesis any probability at all even at the conclusion of an argument,
unless at the beginning we knew it at least not to be impossible.
And how could we do this without any previous argument, which
would again depend partly on the antecedent probability of its
conclusions? Further, even if we assume it not to be impossible,
it is still, in the absence of further evidence, only one of an

infinite number of alternatives, so that its antecedent probability would still seem to be not indeed o but $1/\infty$, a fraction which still could not be multiplied so as to produce an appreciable result, however favourable the subsequent evidence. The effect of this line of criticism would be to render all inductive arguments invalid unless we make some assumption about Nature such as Keynes' principle of limited independent variety. For we cannot supply, as has been suggested, the required antecedent probability by argument from analogy, since arguments from analogy too depend for their validity partly on the antecedent probability of the conclusion.[1] And in any case it is difficult to see how we could find any analogies to support the first causal law we established. What we want is to be able to fix the absolute probability of a hypothesis prior to any argument for it or at least to know that this is a finite quantity.

It might perhaps be said in reply that our strong instinctive belief in causation gave us not indeed certainty, but at any rate the finite probability required (which need only be very small, since the denominator of any fraction on the other side would from the nature of the evidence be rapidly multiplied thousands of times over); but apart from any such contention it seems to me that the argument is vitiated by a serious confusion about the nature of probability. I say this with hesitation in view of the very formidable authorities on the other side, but I cannot see any valid reply to the counter-objection I am going to make. In the first place, I would point out that the argument is one of a very curious kind. It amounts to saying that, because there was no evidence in favour of a proposition before we argued about it, there can never be any for it or at least never any of appreciable strength, and this surely cannot possibly follow from such a premise. But, it will be said, we have mathematics or formal logic here against us, the conclusion about the weakness of inductive arguments has been strictly proved. To this we may provisionally reply that an argument which establishes such a conclusion could not be either mathematical or merely analytic. If we are to get such a result at all, there must be some non-mathematical synthetic assumptions lurking undetected in the alleged proof, such as an axiom about probability. Now that the weakness of an argument cannot be established by the mere fact that *prior* to the argument there was no evidence for the conclusion (as opposed to positive

---

[1] Keynes, *Treatise on Probability*, p. 258.

evidence against it), is surely as evident as any axioms on which the
quasi-mathematical proof is supposed to be founded could be.
Surely it is obvious that the mere fact that there was no evidence
for something before there was any argument for it (a tautology
if ever there was one), could not constitute a positive objection
against accepting any subsequent arguments for it (unless indeed
there is reason to think that, if it had been true, we should have
previously discovered evidence for it, a point which does not arise
in the present case). This is emphatically not the sort of thing
that could be established by logic. I know that modern logicians
are very suspicious of appeals to self-evidence, but at least they
often find a *non sequitur* evident, and this one surely is so. A
logician may hesitate to say that it is self-evident that q follows
from p, but he does not hesitate to regard it as self-evident in
innumerable cases that a certain proposition q does *not* follow
from another p, and here it is evident indeed that our q does not
follow from our p.

But I shall not stop with an appeal to self-evidence, but shall
attack what seems to me to be a positive fallacy in the argument.
It is plain, as no one else has more clearly pointed out than Lord
Keynes himself, that probability is always relative to some data,
normally of course, the data accessible to the speaker at the time
he makes a probability judgment. What is deemed probable is in
itself neither probable nor improbable but just a fact or not a
fact, but there may be data which 'probabilify' it or the reverse.
This explains how, e.g., the defeat of Germany might have been
improbable in 1940, probable in 1944, and just a fact in 1945.
Something can be probable relatively to one set of data and improbable relatively to another, as New York can be north relatively
to Washington and south relatively to Montreal. But if probability
is a relational property, how can there be any meaning in the
notion of a probability antecedent to any data supporting or
making against it? Such a probability would be like the notion
of a place which was north without being north of anywhere else.
It would be like asking about the degree of superiority of something to which nothing was inferior. And how can the fact that we
cannot answer a meaningless or self-contradictory question,
namely the question what the degree of this probability is, be
regarded as a difficulty for any argument whatever? It seems rather,
to any logical conscience which is not quite unduly sophisticated
that, while the antecedent probability of a hypothesis should be

considered in the sense that we must not be concerned only with whatever argument is before us at the time but also take into account any previous arguments affecting its probability, we ought not to regard the latter as either favourably or unfavourably affected by the mere fact that there is no other evidence on the matter, unless owing to the particular circumstances of the case there is reason to think that, if the conclusion were true, we should have been likely to discover the positive evidence for it. We must not allow ourselves to be misled by the argument that for anything we can tell the truth of the hypothesis might be impossible and in that case it could not be probable. At any rate, we do not *know* it to be impossible, and therefore its probability is relatively to our available data not zero. The chance that it might be impossible for all we know is only a ground for saying it is not certain.

It may be retorted that I have only jumped out of the frying pan into the fire. The difficulty was that the probability of the conclusion of any inductive argument had to be measured by a fraction which was a function of a probability that might be zero or $1/\infty$. I have met this by saying that to talk of the probability in question was self-contradictory or meaningless. But is it not the case that we still cannot logically regard inductive arguments as giving any substantial probability to their conclusions any more than if the original objection about *a priori* probability had been accepted? According to this objection we could never assert that the probability given was of any finite degree, but according to my criticism are we not still debarred from asserting it? For, while the original objection makes this probability the result of a multiplication sum in which one factor might be zero or infinitesimal, I have made this factor the result of a meaningless question or a self-contradictory operation. The only difference, it might be urged, is indeed to the disadvantage of my view as compared to the other, for while Lord Keynes's objection led only to the conclusion that inductive arguments *may* fail to give their conclusions any finite probability, my view leads to the conclusion that they *must* fail to do so. For to succeed they would have to answer a question which cannot from the nature of the case be answered. But all that follows, I retort, is not that inductive arguments give no substantial degree of probability, but that the common method of measuring this mathematically has broken down because it is seen to depend on there being an answer to a self-contradictory question. But there is no reason why there should not be argu-

E*

ments giving inductive probability which cannot be put in mathematical form or why the argument from inverse probability should not belong to these. It is certainly not the case that all types of inductive argument have been successfully formulated mathematically, e.g., this has not been done with analogy. It may seem as if the upshot were the same whether the probability of something be held to be a multiple of zero or of $1/\infty$ or whether it be held to be a multiple of some quantity which could only be ascertained by asking a meaningless or self-contradictory question, but this is not the case.[1] If the first proposition is true, it follows that the probability given at the conclusion of the argument is zero or at any rate so small as to be negligible; if the second is true, it only follows that the probability cannot be ascertained mathematically at all. We may still be able to see by a non-mathematical inference that it is far above zero, and if there is a regularity repeatedly exemplifying the law this is surely so.

But how then explain that mathematics works at all in this connexion? Surely the actual mathematics by which the conclusion was reached cannot be impugned. I do not wish to impugn it. What I suggest is that mathematics cannot be used to fix the degree of probability of the hypothesis or law, but only the degree to which the verification of predictions made from a hypothesis or the occurrence of a regularity apparently exemplifying a law increases the probability already given by any previous evidence to the hypothesis or the law. If there is no previous evidence, the calculation cannot be made; but it does not follow that the new evidence does not make its conclusion probable, only that we cannot calculate the relation of this probability to the old evidence for the same reason that we cannot answer the question whether a bachelor loves his wife. It is not that the question is too difficult to answer, but that it simply does not arise. We should not be too disappointed at the lack of mathematical precision, since we might well know that a probability was overwhelmingly strong without being able to calculate precisely its degree. Indeed, even where there is previous evidence, we could in any case hardly hope to be able to calculate the antecedent probability of the

---

[1] It is not maintained by, e.g. Lord Keynes that in fact it is zero or infinitesimal but only that it may be so: but if he is right, his argument does show that the inverse probability argument has failed to establish an appreciable probability for its conclusion. My reply is that it merely shows that this probability cannot be exactly formulated or proved mathematically.

hypothesis with mathematical exactitude, so that we could really do the sum included in logical disquisitions on the subject.

We may therefore agree with Lord Keynes, etc., if they merely mean that the inverse probability argument cannot be adequately formulated mathematically, but not if they mean that we have no good evidence for saying it can be seen to make its conclusion very probable indeed. The mathematical formula may be retained (or at least judged on its own merits), as giving the relation between the probability of a hypothesis relative to other arguments in case such are available and its probability relative also to a set of instances 'corroborating' it in the way this is done by inverse probability arguments, i.e., the extent to which the former is increased by the addition of the instances. But in cases where there is no other argument available, one term of the relation is just missing, and therefore the mathematics does not prove that the probability is zero, but is just inapplicable. The formula determines the relation of Y to X; and if there is no X, it has nothing to determine.

We need not be surprised that the logic of the inductive jump from the experienced to the unexperienced is not itself capable of exact mathematical formulation. But, mathematics or no mathematics, it surely remains true that it would be an extraordinarily unlikely coincidence for A to be followed by B 1,000 times in succession if there were no causal law connecting the two. Though we cannot give an exact numerical estimate of this probability, we can even impart a legitimate mathematical flavour by comparing it to probabilities which can be estimated mathematically. Thus, since in the absence of a necessary law there are far more than six possible ways in which a stone might act and one has been observed to behave in accordance with the law of gravitation in far more than a hundred instances, we can say that the probability of its having behaved like this if there were no such law is far less than the probability of a dice player throwing a six a hundred times in succession, unless there be strong positive objections to the law.

So I am inclined to accept the inverse probability argument as providing a justification of induction. But what is established by it? If the regularity theory of causation were true, the argument would be quite absurd. For it would amount to this: Other things being equal, it is extremely unlikely that B should have followed A in our experience 100 times and never failed to follow. Therefore we must suppose that B follows A not only 100 times but always (or almost always), which should be more unlikely still. For that the event which we call the effect always or almost always in fact follows what we call the cause is on the regularity view all that a causal law could mean. The unlikelihood of B regularly following A can be removed by the postulation of a causal law on one condition and one condition alone, namely, if the causal law be regarded as explaining the regularity, and I do not see how it can do this unless we suppose a connection between cause and effect such that the latter springs from the nature of the former. (Of course there are regularities which are not themselves causal, but these too require causation to explain them, only for this purpose we must go further back. The regular sequence of B on A may be explained by A causing B, but it may also be explained by, e.g., A and B both being caused by C, or again A might be caused by C and B by D and C might cause D.) Thus it seems to me that the argument from inverse probability can only be legitimately used to establish causal laws if we assume a view of causation according to which it is at least closely analogous to logical entailment, and that it does establish them in this sense (at least unless we adopt Berkeley's view that the events are *directly* produced by God, in which case we might suppose the latter to produce them in a regular sequence for some purpose of his own without there being a necessary connection between cause and effect.)

Further, the same view that the causal relation is at least closely analogous to that of logical entailment seems for another reason also, already mentioned, to be a necessary presupposition of induction. For, if induction is valid, we can argue from the cause to the effect (and vice versa), but if I can legitimately argue from A to B the relation between A and B must at least be closely analogous to that of logical entailment. This may be made clearer still by considering the difficulties of the regularity theory. It is essential to induction to suppose that what happened under certain conditions in the past is likely to happen under similar conditions in the future, but on such a theory how could we possibly be justified in believing this? We cannot establish it empirically, for it is needed to enable us to infer what has not been experienced from what has; and how can we argue from the conditions to their consequences if we do not suppose a necessary connection between conditions and consequences? Yet, if we are entitled to suppose a necessary connexion, the problem presents no difficulty. Where there is a necessary connexion between A and B, B will follow on A. My contention is that our judgment that there are such necessary connexions in nature, which is at least part of what we ordinarily mean by causation, is justified by the occurrence of repeated regularities which would be incredibly unlikely co-incidences unless capable of explanation, and that this provides an adequate justification for induction. If B necessarily follows from A, there is every reason why it should occur if A occurs; if we think it probable that it necessarily follows from A, we are entitled to think it probable that it will occur if A occurs, or even only if we think it follows from A and C, provided we have good grounds for believing that C occurs too in most cases of A. But in the absence of any assumption of necessary connexion the mere fact that B has always followed A could give no ground for expecting that it will do so on future occasions.

Three obvious and common objections to my view remain to be tackled. The first is that it cannot be any help to induction to postulate necessity, since we must admit that we cannot see the necessary connexion behind particular laws, at least with physical causation. I reply that my view is suggested not as an amendment to the ordinary methods of induction but as a postulate without which none of them would be justified. The detailed methods of science will not in any way be affected as long as we are incapable of seeing *a priori* the necessary conditions which we postulate, for in the absence of this insight we can only establish them indirectly by observing regularities and by using 'Mill's methods' or any improved version of these which modern logicians are able to suggest. But if we did not implicitly assume that there were some necessary laws for these methods to discover, we could not be justified in supposing that the fact that something has happened under certain conditions in the past is evidence which gives even any probability to the supposition that it will happen under similar conditions again. As regards causal laws we are now in a similar position to that of the ancient Egyptians and Babylonians about geometry. They did not know how to prove the geometrical propositions which were later proved *a priori*, but they did estab-lish some of them, as empirical generalizations, and as regards the causal laws of the physical world that is the best we can yet do. But we can never, I contend, be justified in passing from the observed to the unobserved, unless we are entitled to postulate, though we do not see it, a relation like that of logical entailment between what we regard as the cause and what we regard as the effect. The reason for that is simple: we claim to be entitled to infer the effect from the cause and the cause from the effect, but no inference can be valid unless there is a relation like that of logical entailment between its premises and its conclusion. I have already given an independent argument from inverse probability for the view that there are necessary connexions in the physical world, but even apart from this the fact that such a view is necessarily presupposed if induction is to be justified seems to me an important argument for its truth. For, that no induction is justified is something which no human being can really believe.

This brings me to the second objection, which is that my theory would conflict with the merely probable character of induction. For, it is said, alleged *a priori* arguments and propositions are either certain or just fallacious, there is no intermediate term. But a person who uses this argument must be overlooking the point I have just made, namely, that my view would make no difference to the ordinary methods of induction, since we cannot see the necessity involved even if it is there and consequently in discovering it have to rely on the same indirect methods which have always been used. For reasons that can easily be seen and are the same on my view as those given in any ordinary logical textbook, these methods cannot establish the existence of a causal law with certainty but only with probability. From my theory it would follow that the law could be seen to be certainly true only if we ourselves had *a priori* insight into its necessity, but I have admitted we have not. If we cannot see whether there is a necessary connection between A and B and cannot hope to prove it *a priori*, all we can do is to find out whether A and B empirically go together in a sufficient number and relevant kind of instances, and in doing so we can never be completely certain that we have not overlooked some other factor.

The third objection is one not against my theory of causation, but against any attempt to justify induction logically by an argument from the theory of probability. It is to the effect that any justification of induction would make it a mere species of deduction. To this I might reply—Why should it not be? The old logical division between induction and deduction as two co-ordinate species of inference may not do justice to the facts, and it has never proved easy for logicians to maintain. And even if induction be regarded as ultimately a species of deduction, there are important differences which provide a justification for its separate treatment and distinguish it sharply from all other kinds of deduction. For, unlike all other kinds, it depends on the assumption of a necessity which we do not see, and this makes its conclusions always less certain than its premises, whereas in ordinary deduction (except for the risk of having made a mistake), they are equally certain. However it seems to me that it would only be if we committed the fallacy of turning the principle of an argument into its premise that induction would become deduction. For I am not suggesting that arguments from the general to the particular should replace the arguments from the particular to the general in ordinary use. I am only saying that the use of these latter arguments is to be ultimately justified only by a deductive argument from the theory of probability.

Even if there is a logical necessity in the physical world behind causation, it is not at all surprising that we should not be able to discover it. For

(1) It is generally held that we cannot know anything of the internal nature of physical things, and if so, we cannot possibly expect to see what this can or cannot entail.[1]

(2) We are never in a position to state *the whole* cause of an event, but if causation involves entailment, it will clearly always be not part of its cause but its whole cause which will entail an event.

NOTE ON THIS ARTICLE (1968)

There are few philosophical issues that are more important than the one about causality raised here: if I was right we ought to go back to the old view according to which the world, permeated as it is by causation, is, at least to a very large extent, a rationally connected system, a view totally different from any which most of the present generation find convincing. This is also the part of my philosophical views which has encountered most opposition; but I am still convinced at least that the arguments I have given do show the presence of necessity of some kind in causation. Whether it is quite the same kind of necessity as that of logical entailment is more questionable. It is urged that, even if there is

---

[1] I claim that we have some limited insight into psychological causation, the only kind where we can be aware of the inner nature of the cause (v. my *Idealism*, pp. 176–81).

a necessary sequence, it need not be necessary in the sense that the effect follows *a priori* from the cause. My reply to this is that I do not understand in the least what sort of necessity this non-logical kind could be. The only element which can to my mind be intelligibly understood as making something necessary seems to have been removed. It must be admitted, however, that causal entailment, if it occurs, differs from all other cases of logical entailment in that here what is entailed is not simultaneous with but succeeds what entails it.

VII

KANT'S ATTACK ON METAPHYSICS

Kant agreed with many recent philosophers in having achieved to his own satisfaction a refutation of all metaphysics, and it may be instructive at the present juncture to compare his methods and conclusions with theirs. Firstly, Kant does not rest his argument at all, consciously at least, on any special study of language. I think he would, unlike many contemporary English philosophers, have considered it completely wrong to suppose that we could reach any philosophical conclusions of importance by merely studying how words are used in ordinary speech. Secondly, his contention is rather that metaphysical[1] statements are incapable of theoretical justification than that they are meaningless. Traces of the latter view may indeed be discovered in Kant. Metaphysical statements would have presumably to involve the categories, and he repeatedly denies that the latter have any 'meaning' except as applied to phenomena,[2] but this is not consistent with his subsequent use of the categories in making metaphysical statements of a theological kind, and his admission that, although we cannot 'know' transcendent objects according to the categories, we can 'think' them.[3] Kant indeed makes a distinction between theoretical and practical reason, but even if we cannot prove the existence of God or understand his nature theoretically, we must be able to form some concept of God even to accept or understand the practical ethical argument which Kant gives, and such a concept involves categories, at least that of cause,[4] which is required indeed not only by the practical concept of God as creator and ruler of the universe, but even by the theoretical concept of thing-in-itself, since we can only think

[1] In this article I am using 'metaphysics' in the sense of transcendent metaphysics, not in the other sense of the word in which Kant admits it as an analytic account of the nature of human experience.

[2] *Kritik der Reinen Vernunft*, B 149, 178, 308. (B is used to signify the original second edition paging commonly reproduced in texts and commentaries.)

[3] E.g. *ibid.*, B 166 n., Proleg., Section 58.

[4] In B 344, he makes an unexplained distinction between cause and the other categories, and says that things in themselves can be thought as causes but not in accordance with any of the other categories.

of things-in-themselves at all in distinction from appearances by thinking of them as cause of the appearances. At least one of the two chief British commentators on Kant, Professor Paton, thinks that, when he denies 'meaning' to categories applied beyond the realm of experience, he is only denying their objective validity, and this is supported by his identification of '*Bedeutung*' with 'relation to the object' in at least one passage.[1] And Kant's arguments in general are not very like those of most modern antimetaphysical philosophers: yet there is a certain degree of affinity, and at a time when the very possibility of the existence of metaphysics is once more one of the leading issues in philosophical circles, it is well worth while considering the attitude of the greatest of the hostile critics of this subject. It seems to me that the modern school of positivistically inclined philosophers, although successful in a good deal of their detailed logical criticism of the arguments of past metaphysicians, have not themselves managed to produce anything of the nature of a successful argument to rule out the possibility of metaphysics in general. Has Kant succeeded better? What are, precisely, his main arguments?

There is, first, the argument from the possibility of synthetic *a priori* judgements. As is well known, Kant distinguished analytic judgements in which the predicate is contained in the concept of the subject from synthetic judgments in which it is not, and claimed that a reference to experience is necessary to make the latter possible at all. Since particular experiences cannot yield *a priori* judgements and some synthetic judgements are *a priori*, he argued that these must depend on the form of our experience in general. Kant is noted for having explicitly introduced the concept of synthetic in opposition to analytic *a priori* propositions (though he is anticipated here, except in terminology, by Locke[2]), but it is less frequently realized that his particular views depend to a large extent on the assumption that pure thought cannot of itself advance to anything new not already contained in the concept with which it started, an assumption which he nowhere tries to justify. It is because of this assumption, which he shares with modern positivists, while disagreeing with them in asserting the possibility of synthetic *a priori* judgements, that he finds it necessary to suppose that synthetic judgements,

---

[1] B 300 (*Beziehung aufs Objekt*).
[2] *Essay on the Human Understanding*, IV, 8.

even when *a priori*, must depend at least on the sensuous form of our perceptions and therefore cannot advance beyond actual and possible experience. There is not space to go into his detailed argument, but I think its inadequacy as an attempt to refute metaphysics may be shown in purely general terms. The problem of synthetic *a priori* propositions is essentially the problem how thought can advance from S to P, P being not already included in our concept of S. Kant holds that pure thought by itself can yield only analytic judgements, and he holds that synthetic *a priori* judgements are only rendered possible by the presence of a sensuous element, but just how does the latter element help? Suppose S is a sensuous concept and P another sensuous concept not included in the former, and S entails P, there is still a transition of thought from one to the other and *a priori* thinking has after all yielded something new. Kant is ordinarily, and no doubt rightly, understood as having maintained that Euclidean geometry and the categories are valid of phenomena because we could not experience the latter without applying our forms of intuition and our categories, and therefore we know *a priori* that they must conform to these. But, leaving aside the new difficulties raised by modern advances in non-Euclidean geometry and physics, which cannot affect arithmetic or the categories, this would at the best only solve half the problem. In Kant's day at least it might be very plausibly regarded as an explanation why geometry can be applied to physical objects, but it would not explain how the inferences within geometry itself or in any other sphere of thought are possible. If we can assume, as Kant did, that Euclid's axioms are true of space as such, and that physical phenomena can only exist in Euclidean space, it follows that they and all theorems which follow from them are true of the physical world, but this does not explain how it is that the theorems can follow from their premises. In one passage[1] Kant may be interpreted as saying that, granted the axioms, all the rest of mathematics follows analytically, but if, as he insists directly afterwards, even $5 + 7$ and 12 are different concepts neither of which is analytically contained in the other, this must *a fortiori* apply to most inferences in geometry. Kant tries to explain our ability validly to infer synthetic *a priori* propositions in geometry by reference to our ability to construct figures,[2] but I do not see how this could possibly help him with

---

[1] B 14. This disagrees with the whole spirit of the account given in B 741 ff., the only passage of any length on geometrical reasoning.   [2] B 744.

arithmetic, or indeed even with geometry, unless all non-analytic geometrical proofs were effected not by inference at all but by mere observation of the figure drawn. Either Kant must maintain that it is merely a case of sensuous intuition, i.e. of sensually seeing the new properties in the figures we have drawn or some ideal figure, in which case it is not an inference at all, and certainly neither *a priori* nor necessary, or he must admit that over and above the sensuous intuition there is an inference, in which case the inference can be valid only if it is possible for a premiss by its own nature to imply something beyond itself, and this, like all implications, cannot be intuited sensuously and, if it leads to anything new, is incompatible with his view of pure thought as analytic. The conclusion from all this is that Kant has not succeeded in explaining the possibility of synthetic *a priori* judgements by a reference to experience and is therefore not entitled to argue that we cannot have them in metaphysics on the ground that they cannot be explained without a reference to experience. My own view is that they must be accepted as a fact not requiring explanation and that all useful inference is invalidated if we cannot thus accept them.

Yet I think Kant has made a great contribution here in laying the foundations of the doctrine that all factual judgements include both an empirical and an *a priori* element, the former being needed to supply the content and the latter the form or organization. (I should indeed say that this is the case with all judgements. Pure logic does indeed itself deal with form, not content. But even formal logic presupposes at least previous experience of what thought and judgements are; without this we should not understand any of the statements of logic books. And this experience can only be obtained in particular instances, from which the forms and relations treated in logic are abstracted. It would, however, be misleading to call the empirical element here 'sensuous'.)

The presence of an empirical element in all our judgements does not necessarily rule out the possibility of reaching metaphysical conclusions by inference. We may accept another contribution of Kant and admit that we cannot establish any affirmative existential propositions without some empirical premiss, but we may still be able to argue to new conclusions from the empirical premiss, if synthetic *a priori* propositions are possible at all. The inference that we draw to the effect that $5 + 7$ is equal to 12 is certainly valid also of non-experienced objects, if there are any such, and though it does not by itself prove any affirmative existential proposition, *a priori* propositions combined with an empirical premiss may do so even in metaphysics, as they do in geography when we infer the height of a mountain from *a priori* propositions of trigonometry plus certain empirical facts about its angle of projection and the distance of the base. Many metaphysicians have thought that our experience implies something beyond itself and can only be rendered intelligible and coherent if we go beyond it to transcendent entities such as God or the Absolute. There may be other objections to these arguments, but they are not ruled out at once by the mere fact that we need an empirical premiss. The empirical premiss is present, though it is only a very general one.

Kant, however, also argues that we cannot have theoretical metaphysics because all our thought presupposes the categories and the specific proofs of the categories given by him are valid only for the realm of experience. I am again prevented by limitations of space from discussing Kant's detailed arguments, but this is the less urgent because they have commanded very little assent among subsequent philosophers. I myself believe Kant to have successfully established that physical object propositions can be analysed in terms of experience only if we introduce the concept of causal laws, a point which modern phenomenalists[1] have often ignored, but this will not appeal to a person who has not accepted a phenomenalist analysis, and we cannot accept phenomenalism merely on the ground that, if it were true, we could prove something we should like to prove. I think also that the argument of the first Analogy, if valid at all, supports a realist and not a phenomenalist view of the physical world. But what has been very widely accepted in Kant's teaching here is not his set of specific proofs, but his belief that to know anything involves putting it in a system, and that the ultimate guarantee of the objectivity of our thought is its systematic coherent character and not any correspondence with an external entity, or, to put it more moderately and more in accordance with my own beliefs, that the ultimate criterion of the truth of our judgements, if not the definition of

---

[1] I am using 'phenomenalism' in its usual sense today in my country to stand for the view that propositions about physical objects can only be justifiably asserted if they are understood as propositions about the experiences or sense-data human beings have or would have under certain conditions.

truth and knowledge, lies in their ability to organize our imme-diately given data into a coherent system. This principle of coherence the post-Kantian 'idealists' then extended beyond the realm of phenomena on the ground that the concept of the thing-in-itself which Kant had used to limit human knowledge must be rejected as meaningless.

The absolute rejection of the doctrine of the thing-in-itself I think to have been over-hasty, though I certainly do not hold the distinction between appearance and reality tenable in the form asserted by Kant. The three principal objections urged against things-in-themselves have been: (1) If we cannot know anything about them, the concept becomes a mere blank and we cannot intelligibly assert their existence even as a possibility. (2) Kant had repeatedly asserted that the categories could only be validly applied to phenomena, yet he often inconsistently applied them to things-in-themselves, and this inconsistency was inevi-table since without using the categories we cannot think anything at all. (3) It is inconsistent to say that we cannot know things-in-themselves but only phenomena, because we could not know that the nature of things was such as to impose an absolute limit on our knowledge without knowing something, however little, of what lay beyond these limits. It seems to me that all these objec-tions can be met by Kant's distinction between knowledge and thought.[1] We can have no definite concept of what things-in-themselves are like or as to how the categories are to be applied to them, but we can have a vague schematic idea of them as ground of phenomena, and to have even this much we must *think* them in terms of categories, or at least, of the category of causation, although we cannot *prove* that they conform to the categories and although there is admittedly not much meaning in a pure category unschematized by reference to our form of intuition, time, which does not apply to things-in-themselves. We may add that Kant was bound to introduce the concept of the thing-in-itself at least as a possibility if he was to avoid 'dogmatic idealism', although it may be objected that he was not entitled to assert its existence as an actual fact. He had not proved that there was anything in the world besides human beings and the content of their experiences, but neither had he proved that there was not.

Kant's agnosticism as to metaphysics was bound up with his doctrine that we can know only appearances and not reality, but

[1] E.g. B XXVI n., XXVIII, 166 n.

at this point there seems to me to arise an inconsistency in his work which has been too little noticed. He insists on maintaining, and it is indeed essential to his philosophy to maintain, that though we cannot know reality, we have real knowledge of appearances. But by 'appearances' is meant what we experience under given conditions: to say that something is an 'appearance' is to say at least that we really experience it under these conditions. But in that case, if we have knowledge of appearances, we know something real, namely, our experience, and our experience is in time. Therefore time is real, contrary to Kant's teaching. Kant had to maintain that we can have real knowledge of appearances, otherwise he could not defend science, and he had also to maintain that we can have knowledge only of appearances, otherwise he could not refute metaphysics. But the two positions are incompatible. What is from one point of view an appearance as 'our representation' is *per se* a reality equally with the physical objects of the realist, for even mere representations are real. We cannot rid ourselves of anything by calling it an appearance; if it is anything at all, even only an experience, it as such still falls within the real. In view of this Kant's position about appearances seems to me an untenable halfway house. As long as he accepted his arguments against the reality of time, his only consistent course would have been to give up the view that we had real knowledge even of phenomena, and to maintain that we are under an illusion not only in supposing that there are things independently existing in time but in supposing that we really experience anything temporal at all. At least this applies if we are to take the arguments of the section on the antinomies at their face value; the argument of the Aesthetic is less destructive in character. Such a position would have been as destructive to science as to metaphysics; even a modern scientist imbued with philosophical scepticism must admit that certain observations really take place, and if we do not know this we are not in a position to have science. Yet if nothing is really in time but only seems to be, this cannot be known. It is not a mere irrelevant accident but essential to the nature of the observations that they occur as part of a temporal sequence of events: our whole experience would be rendered unrecognizably and unintelligibly different if time were taken away. Here is an objection which does not arise if we take a phenomenalist view merely of the physical world, but only if we extend our phenomenalism to the self we observe and call this too merely appearance. We can without such an inconsistency say that physical objects do not exist independently of human experience and that our judgments about them are true but true only of appearances, i.e. of our experiences of them, but if we then say the same thing about our experiences themselves we do fall into an inconsistency. And if time is not real in the sense in which Kant pronounces it not real, we must say this about our experiences. Of course to say that time is real is not to say that its nature is just as we are apt to think of it as being, nor that it is an entity over and above temporal events and processes, nor is it necessarily to reject the applicability of the concept of degrees of reality (a concept however apparently foreign to Kant). There are other points besides this, quite apart from theology, where Kant seems to break through the barrier he set up between appearance and reality, e.g. he assumes knowledge of the existence of other human minds and not merely of their appearances to himself, and his epistemology seems to presuppose some knowledge of his real self.

Obviously, if we admit that we have some knowledge of reality and not only of appearances, we cannot locate the barrier excluding metaphysics at the point where Kant located it, and some of his arguments against metaphysics disappear altogether. In practice the opponents of metaphysics from Kant to the contemporary positivists have accepted what we may roughly call coherence as a criterion in science but have refused to admit this criterion as a ground for any conclusions in metaphysics; they have not, however, as far as I know, succeeded in proving either that its use is justifiable in science or that it is unjustifiable in metaphysics. The argument for the validity of the criterion which post-Kantian 'idealists' have used is that it is a necessary presupposition of all rational thought, and it may seem that if we are claiming to know reality and not merely appearances we are not entitled to use an argument of this sort. That was the view of Kant. His arguments were mainly epistemological, or as he called them, 'trancendental',[1] that is, they were arguments to the effect that certain principles must hold because without them all knowledge, or at least all knowledge of the kind we have, would be impossible, and for this very reason he held that they could not apply to reality but only to appearances. For, he thought, it does not matter to thing-in-themselves a bit whether we can know them or not, but it does matter very much to appearances, because if we could not know

---

[1] This should of course be sharply distinguished from 'transcendent'.

them, they would not be appearances. But this cannot, I think, be used as an independent argument for the view that it is impossible for us to know reality, only appearances. A transcendental argument is an argument that a proposition p is true because, if it were not true, we could not know something which we admittedly do know, and I contend that such arguments can on principle be used about reality as well as about appearances. Of course this is not so if there are other valid arguments establishing the conclusion that we can know only appearances, but suppose that there are not and that we do know some propositions about the real world. In that case we can still equally well argue—we know them, we could not know them if certain principles were not true, therefore these principles are true. Kant said: Physical things could not exist without being known by us since they are only phenomena, they could not be known by us unless they conformed to the categories, but they are known by us and so exist in the only way in which they are capable of existing, therefore they do conform to the categories. The realist could say: Physical things existing independently of human beings are known by us in fact or at least are objects of justified probable judgements, they could not be objects of knowledge or of such judgements unless they did conform to the categories, but, to repeat, they are objects either of knowledge or of such justified probable judgements, therefore they do conform to the categories. For even if physical objects may exist without being known by human beings, they assuredly cannot be known without being known or justifiably judged probable existents without being so judged, and therefore any conditions which epistemology may show to be presupposed in knowledge and rational probable judgement will hold of them.

Unfortunately Kant did not realize this and assumed that the categories could only be proved if his system of idealism were accepted. He assumed, I think wrongly, that the transcendental method necessarily involved transcendental idealism, and that it was only if we made the objects we cognized that we could argue from the principles governing our cognition to the nature of these objects. In making this assumption he was influenced by the idea that to apply the categories to real things independent of us was equivalent to an arrogant assertion that reality must conform to the laws governing our minds, but is not this to confuse psychological and logical necessity? If the categories are known at all, they are surely known primarily not as laws of our thought but as laws of the objects about which we think. The way to discover what categories are valid is indeed to see what categories are involved in those judgements which we really cannot help being convinced are true. But, if true at all, a judgement is true of something real, if only of human experience, and I do not see that Kant has succeeded in justifying the view that we can make true judgements only about human sensuous experience and its immediate objects and not about any other part of reality. There is indeed a valid distinction between judgements about one's own experience and judgements about anything else including the experiences of other men, since the latter judgements (unless purely *a priori*) have to be derivative from the former, but Kant was no solipsist and took it for granted without discussion that we can make the transition in question. Where he wants to draw the line (apart from a reservation about ethics) is where all positivists have wanted to draw it, i.e. between science and metaphysics.

Kant, however, speaks rather of denying the possibility of knowledge in metaphysics than of denying that of rational belief, and it is indeed a much more plausible proposition that we cannot have knowledge in the realm of metaphysics than that we cannot have in that realm rational belief. Kant admits such rational belief in some metaphysical propositions on the strength of ethical premises, but he sets his face against it elsewhere, i.e. in the field of theoretical reason. He denies that we can have opinions or hypotheses in this field, and insists that here the only possible two alternatives are on the one hand to have *knowledge* and on the other not to be entitled to assert anything whatever.[1] He admits no intermediate grade between certainty and mere groundless fallacy. Now I should certainly agree with Kant that we do not *know* the things metaphysicians of the time said they knew, and although I am not clear how to fix precisely the boundary between metaphysics and other studies I should be even prepared to say that we have no certain knowledge at our disposal in the sphere of what is usually called metaphysics. But this is not to say that we cannot have rational grounds for holding one view rather than another, as Kant admitted we could in the case of some religious beliefs based on ethics. Kant gives as a ground for holding the contrary with theoretical reason that metaphysics, since it goes beyond experience, must be *a priori* and an *a priori* judgement cannot be only probable

[1] E.g. B 803.

but must either be certain or a mere fallacy, as in mathematics. Now he is no doubt right in holding that *a priori* judgements cannot have the same kind of probability as that attributable to inductive judgements, but it does not follow that they need be certain. The relevant difference between them and inductive judgements here is that, while probable inductive judgements would still be only probable even if made by a perfect reasoner, provided he had only our data, *a priori* judgements can fall short of certainty only because of a risk of error on the part of the person who makes them. In mathematics the possibility of error can usually be eliminated easily and then the judgement is certain, but the persistent disagreement of metaphysicians shows that it cannot be so eliminated in metaphysics, at any rate in our present state of development. In this subject it is too hard to make our concepts sufficiently clear for us to be *certain* what they do or do not entail. But this does not mean that we may not reasonably think they entail something rather like *a* and not something rather like *b*. We may readily grant that metaphysical conclusions are less certain not only than those of mathematics but also than the better established results of the natural sciences, but we need not therefore rule them out altogether. We may still be able to rejoice in conclusions which are as well founded as we can make them: half a loaf is better than no bread at all. Incidentally, if Kant's argument against non-certain judgements in metaphysics were valid, it would destroy all justification for the metaphysical propositions which he admits we can accept on the strength of ethics, though they are not objectively certain.

Kant's craving for certainty may well have been the chief reason why he rejected a form of cognition for which strong claims have been advanced by many people and which, if valid, is undoubtedly of great metaphysical import, I mean mystic or religious intuition. To admit such intuition as valid would have been to admit non-sensuous cognition and so to make a big breach in Kant's scheme of epistemology. He had indeed made one such big breach in the interests of ethics, where he claims that we can have pure *a priori* knowledge independently of experience, but he was not prepared to make another in the interests of theology. He saw that we could not attain objective *certainty* on these lines and was very alive to the danger of accepting mere subjective fancies as communications from God. He has however produced no epistemological arguments which would prove the impossibility of such valid cognition. If its validity is to be admitted, we obviously have a source of metaphysical insight for which Kant left no place whatever, without giving any at all conclusive grounds for excluding it.

But it would not be doing justice to the points Kant and others have made to say that all they have brought out is that metaphysics is less certain than natural science. There is another difference which Kant was perhaps the first well-known philosopher adequately to realize and on which we must now dwell. I shall start with the sharpest and most drastic formulation of the point, which comes from modern positivists. They have argued that all metaphysical statements must be, strictly speaking, meaningless because they have to use everyday terms, yet use them apart from the everyday contexts which alone give these terms meaning. This strikes me as the only at all plausible argument in favour of the view that metaphysical statements have no factual meaning. It is easy to see that, when a metaphysician speaks of God as 'first cause', still more as 'his own cause', he is not using 'cause' in the ordinary sense in which we use it when we ask, e.g. about the causes of the Conservative victory at the last general election, or speak of arsenic as causing death, and so it may be asked what right we have to use it at all. Or if we speak of God as a mind, we have to admit that he is so vastly above human minds that we can have very little idea of what his states of consciousness are like or how his mind works, and so it may be asked how we can then be entitled to refer to him as a mind. Similarly Kant's difficulty about applying the categories to reality is not only that we cannot prove them except of phenomena, but that they have little meaning outside the phenomenal world. (As I have remarked above,[1] Kant sometimes inconsistently said that as thus applied they had no meaning at all.) Similarly Kant insists that we cannot form a proper theoretical concept of God or freedom, although we can treat these as *practically* known. His distinctions between constitutive and regulative principles, categories and ideas of reason, knowledge and thought, theoretical knowledge and merely practical knowledge or faith are, in the main, distinctions between concepts which we understand in the clear definite fashion necessary for science and concepts which, to put it colloquially, we can only 'think in a sort of way'. And these distinctions also provide the answer to the positivist argu-

[1] P. 4.

ment just given, which is to be found only in the recognition of different degrees of clarity and meaningfulness. The fact that metaphysics has to use words in a way very different from that in which they are used in ordinary speech does not prove that it is meaningless, but it does necessarily involve a loss of some of the fullness and clarity of meaning which the words can have in science and common life. At least the definite core of meaning decreases, although the indefinite aura, so to speak, surrounding it, may increase. The concepts of cause and mind as applied to God may in a sense mean more, for the religious man at least, than they do as applied to human beings, but the element of the meaning which even he can hold clearly in mind must shrink. Kant indeed only distinguishes explicitly two degrees of meaningfulness, that which belongs to scientific terms and that which is present with those metaphysical ideas to which he is prepared to assign a limited validity, but it seems to me that he should rather have admitted an indefinite number of different degrees shading into each other in a continuous series. All useful scientific terms are not equally clear and meaningful, nor are all terms used in everyday non-scientific speech. Yet he might well say that the distinction between the meaning of terms in metaphysics and the meaning of the same terms outside it is much more important than the distinction between any of the intermediate degrees to which I have referred. And within metaphysics itself he is clearly prepared to assign more meaning to those concepts of God which he holds to be needed for ethics such as that of just ruler than he does to the concept of *causa sui* or necessary being. In that he is surely right: there are metaphysical terms which we might reasonably sacrifice to the positivist, but our decision, I should hold, must be made on the merits of each particular case and cannot be settled in advance by a single sweeping argument against all metaphysics.

The part of metaphysics which Kant is prepared to defend, though not as strict knowledge, is of course the part relating to the ideas of God, freedom and immortality, which have an important bearing on ethics. He held that, from the ethical point of view, we must think of the world as if it were directed by a completely good intelligence, since otherwise it would not be directed in such a way as to make the *summum bonum* attainable. He thought that this was practically certain but denied that it amounted to theoretical knowledge. He did not call our cognitive attitude to it that of holding an opinion (*Meinen*), even a rational one, but assigned to it a term intermediate between knowledge and opinion or hypothesis, calling it believing (*Glauben*).[1] A belief is distinguished from knowledge in not being objectively certain nor involving theoretical understanding of the nature of what we are talking about. As compared with an opinion or hypothesis, it is superior in one respect but inferior in another. It is superior in that it is at least subjectively certain, but inferior in that to speak of the belief in God as a hypothesis would imply a concept of the nature of God which we do not possess. For to form an opinion or hypothesis already presupposes some knowledge of the kind of being we are putting forward as a hypothesis and of the possibilities in the field, Kant insists.

Kant's clearest explanation of the nature of our concept of God is perhaps given in the *Prolegomena*.[2] The difficulty that I have just mentioned is there forcibly stated. 'Let us suppose for example that I were to attribute to it [the supreme being] understanding: but I have no concept of an understanding except of one that is like mine, namely such that intuitions have to be given to it through senses. . . . But then the elements of my concept would still lie in appearance; but it was the inadequacy of appearances that compelled me to go beyond them to the concept of a being not dependent on appearances or involved with them as conditions of its determination. Yet if I separate the understanding from sensibility in order to have a pure understanding, nothing is left over but the mere form of thought without intuition, through which alone I can know nothing determinate and thus no object. To this end I should have to think a different understanding which intuited objects, but of this I cannot in the least conceive, because the human understanding is discursive and can only know through universal concepts.' What is Kant's remedy? It is that our judgements should be limited to the relation between this being and ourselves and should make no attempt to assert what the supreme being is in itself. Of the relations between ourselves and God Kant holds we can have a clear concept because the relations are like those holding between beings in the phenomenal world. He even rashly implies that it is here not merely a case of a metaphor but of complete likeness. For he calls this 'knowledge by analogy' and defines 'analogy' as a 'perfect

---

[1] B 850, 855.
[2] Section 57–58. I am using Mr Lucas's translation in quoting.

similarity of two relations between quite dissimilar things'. Thus 'when I say we are compelled to regard the world *as if* it were the work of a highest understanding and will, I am really saying nothing more than: as a clock, a ship, a regiment is related to the artisan, architect, commander, so the world of the senses . . . is related to the unknown'. He adds in a footnote: 'For example as promotion of the happiness of children $= a$ is related to parental love $= b$, so the well-being of the human species $= c$ is related to the unknown in God $= x$, which we call love, not as if it had the least similarity with any human inclination, but because we can posit its relation to the world as similar to that which things in the world have among themselves'. Kant indeed may fairly be accused of inconsistency here: since God was not conceived as in time, the causal relation between him and us could not be *quite* similar to any relation known in the phenomenal world, and in any case it is difficult to admit that we can have so clear an idea of the relation as to say that it is *exactly* like another if we have no idea of the related term itself. But this conception of our idea of God as essentially relative and analogous strikes me as at least a valuable line of approach to the problem of reconciling due intellectual modesty with firm religious belief and of meeting worthily the attacks of the sceptic. Since relations hold objectively, it is not of course equivalent to saying that God is a merely subjective idea, as the word 'relative' might to an unwary reader suggest. It is rather to say that we must suppose God to be really related to us in action as a loving parent etc., i.e. really to pursue our welfare as an end in itself, without being able to say what God feels like in relation to us, as we could with a human parent, since God's manner of thought and feeling (if we can speak about God's feelings at all) must be so immensely different from ours.

In the *Critique of Pure Reason* Kant brings out the more negative side of his doctrine, but throughout his work Kant maintains that the concept of God is to be derived mainly from ethics, which leads us to view the supreme being as a just judge and ruler and a loving father. It is not indeed correct to say that for Kant there would be nothing positive left in our idea of God if we took away the ethical elements. We could still think of God as cause of the world, a statement which tells us little since 'cause' is here only an unschematized category and therefore empty and formal, but is certainly regarded as telling us something. And, since Kant contends that the argument from design has a considerable, though not a conclusive, weight of its own, and that even the scientist must look on the universe as if it were designed by a mind, he must have supposed that we could even apart from ethics have some, though a very poor, idea of God as a mind.

The comparatively negative attitude which Kant adopts on this topic must be regarded as a salutary reaction against most philosophers who lived prior to his day. They had treated the idea of God as they might a concept of mathematics, to be defined precisely, established by a formal proof and then used to help them in their theories of the universe, even in their scientific theories. It comes with a shock to modern readers to observe the crudity with which the concept of God was used even by such a greater thinker as Leibniz, who boasted of his doctrine of the pre-established harmony as his own finest contribution to philosophy, and even by the best scientists, who argued that everything must be explained in terms of circular or rectilinear motion respectively because the one or the other (according to the particular scientist's views) was the most perfect type of motion and therefore the one most worthy of God. It was one of Kant's great achievements that he brought it about that the concept of God ceased to be used within science as an explanation even by theists. One great philosopher, St Thomas, had indeed, long before Kant, adopted a theory in which positive knowledge of God is possible only by analogy, but it is difficult to reconcile this with St Thomas's dogmatic conviction that his 'proofs' justified not merely reasonable belief but absolute certainty and with the way in which he indulges in statements which come at least perilously near falling justly under the charge of meaninglessness which positivists have unjustly brought against all metaphysics. I am thinking of doctrines such as that the existence of God is the same as his essence, a very good example of the sort of metaphysical statement which Kant wished to condemn about things we cannot know or understand. And from Descartes on the best known philosophers at least had dropped the Thomist qualifications embodied in the doctrine of analogy and spoken with dogmatic confidence as though they knew exactly what they were saying. The Cartesians expressly claimed to have perfectly clear and distinct ideas of God (as far as they went, not of course, be it said in fairness to them, of the whole nature of God). It was no doubt with this background in mind as well as in opposition to the cruder views of popular religion that Kant put forward his negative criticism.

We must remember, however, that according to his own account he removed knowledge in these matters only to make room for belief, and we may conjecture that, if he had written at the present day when the more sceptical and secularist side of thought has the advantage, he would have emphasized the positive features of his teaching more than the negative.

The full significance of Kant's contribution is veiled because he refused to admit anything short of knowledge as tolerable in theoretical metaphysics. Since it was for him a matter of certainty or nothing, he had then to deny the possibility of such metaphysics altogether, and the subsequent revolt against this in the post-Kantian idealist school obscured the fact that Kant at least had definitely shown that metaphysics could not give certain knowledge or really clear, definite ideas. But room is still left for a more tentative metaphysics which will admit the obscurity and only partial adequacy of its ideas. Kant indeed made an attempt to found such a metaphysics, but only in a limited though very important portion of its field, the field of those metaphysical doctrines which can be regarded as required by ethics. But there is no reason on principle which I can see why the same thing might not be done in other departments of the subject. Further, the realization of the tentative and obscure nature of metaphysics may enable one to give a place to non-sensuous intuitions, for example in religious experience, which are worthy of some credence and yet cannot be said to give complete certainty (except subjectively for a few exceptional people) or fully clear and distinct ideas.

What has been, I think, psychologically at least, the main objection to metaphysics for almost all its critics, including Kant himself, indeed remains, namely the great and apparently irremovable differences of opinion between metaphysicians, but at least such differences become less inexplicable and more tolerable if we no longer claim knowledge where knowledge obviously cannot be attained. Further, if we recognize that all our ideas in this field are partial and more or less erroneous, we can see that both of two conflicting schools may be needed to bring out different sides of one more comprehensive truth. When two metaphysicians are disputing, what often seems to happen is this. One asserts the truth of p and another the truth of q, p and q being apparently quite incompatible with each other. Now presumably the facts are likely to be such that *some* of the criteria

F

required if we are to assert p are really present and also *some* of
the criteria required if we are to assert q, and it is in consequence
of this that there will be both a tendency to assert p and a tendency
to assert q. What I have said will hardly be true of all metaphysical
controversies, but my remark is no doubt true of some, and where
it is not true there will presumably be some definite fallacy, *on
principle* discoverable, thus settling the dispute. Now if there are
some facts which go towards making p true and others which go
towards making q true, it may well be that it cannot be said that
either of the contending parties is wrong. It may even not matter
much whether we say p or q provided we make the necessary
reservations. Both sides may be right, provided we look on them
not as giving arguments to prove p or q, but on the q-side as
stating the reservations which have to be made if we say p, and
on the p-side as stating the reservations which have to be made if
we say q. The rival philosophies can then be regarded as both
making a positive contribution to the truth, and as supplementing
rather than contradicting each other. This point has been brought
out very effectively in recent years (at least orally) by some of the
positivistically inclined philosophers themselves[1] in dealing with
critical or analytical philosophy, and I do not see why it should
not be extended to speculative philosophy. To give an example,
philosophers have often disputed whether reality is one or many,
but we obviously cannot say that it is either without qualification.
The pluralist however may be regarded as giving the reservations
which we still have to make if we decide after all to say that
reality is one, and the monist the reservations we have to make if
we decide to say that it is many. In that case, if we insert all the
appropriate reservations correctly, it will only be a matter of
emphasis whether we say reality is one or many.

[1] Especially Prof. Wisdom at Cambridge.

VIII

THE RELATION BETWEEN MIND
AND BODY AS A PROBLEM FOR
THE PHILOSOPHER[1]

This article must open with a warning. In face of the positive information which the sciences supply, the philosophical contribution to this problem will seem disappointingly negative, or at least mine will do so. For I shall insist, and I think we can only rightly insist, that the philosopher is not yet in a position to produce a satisfactory positive theory of the relation between mind and body. And I shall annoy many of you further by insisting that the old-fashioned 'dualism' has not really been disproved. However, even if you do not agree with me, it is at any rate a good general piece of advice that, when we are confronted with a philosophical view which has maintained its ground for a very long time but seems to ourselves or to our generation very unreasonable, we should look specially carefully to find the positive grounds which have made so apparently unplausible a doctrine seem true to so many competent thinkers.

Modern science rightly insists very much indeed on the intimate connexion between body and mind, but we must remember something else too, which is apt to be forgotten, I mean their qualitative diversity. A thought may be causally connected with a change in the grey matter of the brain or a pain with an impulse in the nerves, but this does not alter the fact that there is a tremendous difference between a thought or a pain as it appears to the person who has it and anything in the brain that the physiologist can possibly observe. If you doubt this, hold a red-hot iron in your hand and read a physiological text-book giving an account of what happens when you feel pain. The two, the actual pain and the physiological phenomenon observable, are at least as different from each other as are a sight and a sound. And the pain is equally different from the reactions of withdrawing the hand and exclaiming to which the

[1] Given to the Royal Institute of Philosophy as the concluding lecture in the series *Mind and its Place in Nature* (November 21, 1952). There is not intended any specific reference in this article to preceding lectures in the series, since in fact I was completely unaware of their contents.

behaviourist will try to reduce it. The mental side of our nature is made up of experiences which are thus intrinsically different from anything that could exist in the physical world or figure in textbooks of physiology as observable phenomena. This is not an *a priori* philosophical assumption, it is a given empirical difference which we are no more justified in explaining away than the difference between a sight and a sound. This of course does not prove that the mind and the body are different substances, as the dualists put it, but it suggests this dualism and at any rate refutes the extreme materialism which denies that there is 'anything but matter'.

We may add that, despite the advance of brain physiology, it is still true that we can know a great deal more about the psychological antecedents of mental events than we can about their physiological antecedents or concomitants in the brain. Any detailed predictions from brain-states are in fact quite impossible for us today—I do not say they will necessarily always remain so— while on the other hand we can quite easily predict from psychological data to a very considerable extent and we are constantly doing so. Such predictions are in fact an absolute necessity of daily life, even if *all* psychological events are not predictable, as they are not on the indeterminist view. We can indeed arrive at psychological data about people other than ourselves only through their behaviour, provided we include in the latter their reports as to their own experience: this we must grant the behaviourist. But we can only pass from past to future behaviour *indirectly* by assuming that the behaviour is a sign of certain mental states and dispositions. It is not a case of just arguing from similar behaviour to other similar behaviour; the same kind of mental disposition or state may display itself under different circumstances in quite different physical behaviour, and so we can only predict the latter by passing to it from the first kind of behaviour via a posited mental state or disposition. Only in this way can we pass from the friendly behaviour of *A* towards *B* to the belief that he will probably show sorrow in the event of *B*'s defeat, help him in misfortune, etc. One has still to appeal to psychological factors like desires rather than to brain states, if one is to give an intelligible and useful account of the development of a person's character and the causation of his experience and actions. Even the postulate of complete correlation between body and mind is only an ideal of physiology, not a proved fact, and if it is true it may be explained just as well by supposing them to interact, so that every mind-state affects the brain in a particular way and every brain state the mind, as it can be by supposing them to belong to one thing of which they are parallel manifestations.

The difference between psychological and physical phenomena is indeed *prima facie* so great that it is no matter for surprise that a dualist philosophy has been widely adopted. Dualist in one sense philosophy must be if this signifies that it must recognize the great difference between the two kinds of phenomena. But the philosophy of the body-mind relation has commonly been dualist in a further sense, in that it has insisted that body and mind were not merely different but different substances, whereas they might be held to be different qualities of the same substance. It was, however, only natural to suppose that, since the qualities were so different, they must belong to different substances. An especially marked difference is that the mental is not extended in the way in which the physical is. It is nonsense to talk of a thought as being 4 inches square or moving at 0·6 feet a second or being 7·9 inches distant from another person's thoughts. It is not that we do not know the size, shape, velocity, mutual distance of thoughts: it is that nobody could know these things, any more than they could know the width in inches of A's broadmindedness or the area of a square deal. They could not know them because the very question the expressions presuppose is absurd. And it was thought that attributes of an extended substance must themselves be extended, so that mental attributes could not possibly qualify the body or brain.

There is another set of arguments which has been used to support the view of the self as a separate substance. For, it has been argued—there are thoughts, therefore there must be a thinker (substance) to do the thinking; there is knowledge, therefore there must be a knower (substance) to do the knowing, etc. A mere series of events could not know that it is a series of events. It has further been argued, knowledge is always of a multiplicity, a, b, c, but to compare or connect a, b and c, the same single entity that is aware of a must be aware of b and c. One entity aware of wolves, another of lambs, and a third aware of eating cannot give us the proposition, wolves eat lambs. Again, if there is to be consciousness of a connected argument, the same single entity which recognizes the premises must recognize the conclusion. But the body, or even the brain, is not a single entity but a plurality of cells. Further, memory tells me that the same 'I' which does so-and-so now, did so-and-so in the past, and this entity is not my body, since I very rarely remember what my body felt or looked like on a particular occasion, though I may remember what I did or experienced very well indeed. I do not say that these arguments are decisive, but they seem to me to possess very considerable force and to have not yet been adequately met.

I do not see that this dualist view has been refuted, and it certainly possesses a considerable plausibility. The principal objection to it is the extent to which it separates mind and body and the odd relation it leaves between them. Most people today have a strong feeling that the theory does not do adequate justice to the unity of body and mind. Incidentally that feeling must have been shared by Descartes himself, who is regarded as the classical type of the dualist, for after having said that the body and soul are separate substances (strictly speaking, the body is for him, and other philosophers generally, a group of substances), he said they still together make a sort of composite substance. But he does not make it clear what he means by this, what makes them more of a unity than are two different physical objects. However, the worst difficulty, namely, that relating to the interaction between body and mind, seems to me only to arise from mistaken reasoning. In order to account for what happens in human life it seems necessary or at least natural to suppose a causal connexion between body and mind, but it was supposed there could not possibly be a causal connexion between two such quite different things. From this objection a number of theories have taken their rise. In order to account for the appearance of interaction between things which could not really interact the Occasionalists, who followed after Descartes, supposed that God intervenes every moment to make them happen in due correspondence. Leibniz thought it more worthy of the deity to suppose that he created body and mind in the beginning in such a way that the changes in one would always correspond to the changes in the other, like two self-winding clocks devised by a watch-maker, when they are made, so as to keep perfect time with each other without mutual interaction. Later thinkers who denied the reality of interaction have preferred to account for the appearance of it by supposing that body (or brain) and mind correspond because they are just different attributes of the same substance, and I agree that if interaction is not a fact, this is a much better explanation, indeed the only plausible explanation, of what it will then be most urgent to explain, namely, the continual correspondence between mental and physical states. We therefore have a very good case for the one substance view if interaction is proved impossible.[1]

But it is not at all clear to me that there is any valid objection against interaction. It is true, body and mind are very different, but we cannot know *a priori* what degree of difference is incompatible with causal connexion. The fact that we cannot see why the connexion holds is no good ground for supposing that it does not hold. Even in the case of two ordinary physical things which are generally admitted to interact we cannot see *why* they should do so. The case would be much stronger if we still maintained the original Cartesian point of view. Descartes held (*a*) that there is a necessary logical connexion between cause and effect, (*b*) that we know the essence of matter to be extension and nothing else, and that of mind to be thought and nothing else, and can see no connexion between extension and thought. That did raise a serious difficulty, but the difficulty disappears if either of the premises is dropped. In particular if, as is generally held nowadays, we cannot know anything about the internal nature of matter, it is difficult to see how we can know what it can or cannot cause. Further, if mental and bodily attributes are really so different that they cannot interact causally, they must surely *a fortiori* be too different to be attributes of the same substance.

The other main old objection to interaction has also been invalidated by modern developments. It used to be regarded as a most potent argument against interaction that it violated the principle of conservation of energy and so was incompatible with the physical world being a closed mechanical system in which there was no causation except through the laws of motion. Modern scientists, however, are more doubtful about the principle of conservation of energy being universal, even in its modern amended form, and are finding reason to think that mechanism conceived in the sort of way in which Newton conceived it does not hold universally even in the inorganic world. If the path of electrons is, for all we know, not completely determined by physical causes, how are we to deny that it might in some cases be determined by psychological causes operating on the human body?

[1] Everything that I say in what follows will hold whether we take mind to be one substance with the body as a whole or only with the brain or part of the brain.

All we can say is that it remains odd, and not what we should have expected, that two such different substances should stand in such a close connexion, but oddness is not sufficient to refute a theory. On the other hand I am not prepared to say that the theory is established: in particular I feel very dubious about the concept of substance. What is the substantial self over and above its experiences? This question is one that has never been satisfactorily answered yet, but on the other hand I am not at all satisfied with what seems the only alternative, namely the theory that the self is a series of events, and I must add that there are at lest equal difficulties about the notion of the substance of matter. But this difficult conception of substance is presupposed not only by the dualist but by the opposing monist view. It seems very plausible to argue: The body is admittedly a substance (or group of substances), so we do not need to posit a different substance to account for mental events; but the theory cannot be adequately founded or even discussed unless we have decided what is meant by substance, and this its proponents seem generally to neglect to consider. Now it seems to me that there are four alternative types of theory about substance.

1. On the 'phenomenalist' view to talk about physical objects is simply to talk about human sense-data, but in this case the one-substance doctrine obviously collapses. My mind is certainly not a collection of the sense-data perceived by those who observe my body, nor is such a collection a substance of which the mind is an attribute. My mind cannot even be regarded as an attribute of my own sense-data of my body, for I observe many other things besides my body. This is not for me an objection to the one-substance theory, because I prefer realism to phenomenalism, but I mention it as very many modern thinkers including philosophically-minded scientists have accepted some kind of phenomenalism.

But what can be meant by substance on a realist view?

2. On the common-sense and older philosophical view substance is regarded as something over and above the attributes, itself unchanging, to which the attributes belong. But can we form any idea of such a thing? When we have taken away the attributes, it seems that there is nothing left of which to form an idea. Substance becomes an unknowable x. But how can we possibly tell whether there are one or two such unknowable xs involved in the relation of body and mind? What is the use and sense of asking such a question as whether there are one or two unknowables? It

may indeed be said that in the case of mind, though not of matter, we have a positive idea of what this substance is, since while we cannot be aware of matter apart from its attributes we can directly perceive an 'I' distinct from its experiences; but this would be no argument to support a philosopher who made the body the primary substance. If it were accepted and the one-substance theory retained, its effect would be, on the contrary, to make the mind the real substance and its body the appearance.

3. This older view of substance is commonly rejected today and replaced by a theory according to which a substance is simply a series of events grouped together. We must ask then how one substance is to be differentiated from another, and it can only be in terms of a relation such that all events inter-connected with each other by this relation may be said to belong to the same substance and all events not connected by it with them to a different sub-stance. We may call this the defining relation of the substance. The difficulty then is to find a relation which can serve both as the defining relation of the body as substance and as the defining relation of the mind. The relation must be the same, otherwise the term substance will be used in a different sense when applied to body and when applied to mind, and it will be nonsense to speak of them as the same substance. Yet the alternative relations which have been proposed as constituting the defining relation of the mind are all of them such that they could not possibly constitute the defining relation of the body. It has been suggested, for instance, that what constitutes self-identity is memory, but memory is not a relation between physical events but a relation of consciousness. No doubt there is some physical relation corres-ponding in the brain, but it is very different from the relation of consciously recalling. Felt continuity of experience is another relation that has been suggested, but that again obviously is a relation between mental events and not physical. To say that what is meant by saying that two mental events belong to the same self is that they are attached to the same body will not help, for the whole problem is in what sense they are attached to the body.

4. It may be said that it is a mere matter of degree and con-venience whether two events or attributes are said to belong to the same substance or different substances, but in that case it will not be of much philosophical importance which answer we give to the question. In particular, to say that body and mind are one substance will not logically exclude the possibility of the mind

F*

surviving bodily death, as would the view that the body or brain is the substance of the mind understood in any ordinary realist sense. The question whether we are to regard body and mind as one or two substances will then be the question whether we can more conveniently treat them together or separately, and the answer is obviously—for some purposes the former, for some the latter. Neither can be treated quite adequately without reference to the other, but there are a great many cases of what we should admittedly call quite separate things neither of which can be adequately treated without any reference to the other. We cannot understand a man's nature adequately without considering his relation to his parents, yet we should not therefore say that he and they were the same substance. There are in fact many circumstances which incline one to think of body and mind as different substances. I refer to the great qualitative difference between bodily and mental states, the differences in the causal laws which govern them, the fact that bodily states can be observed by anyone and mental states only by a single individual, our ability to predict facts about a man's state of mind from our psychological knowledge of him when we cannot predict them from his brain-states. And if for certain scientific purposes such as those envisaged by the physiological psychologists it is better to treat them as if they were one substance, this on the view of substance before us now becomes only a relative matter, a matter of degree of emphasis and convenience of arrangement. We could not longer even say that one of the views was right and the other wrong, only that one terminology was more convenient than the other. And obviously convenience of terminology can be no adequate ground for excluding the view that the mind is existentially independent of the body, even if for certain purposes it is more useful to treat them as one substance than as two.

Consequently the view that the mind is a mere attribute of the body or brain, so plausible at first sight, turns out to be a theory to which no intelligible meaning has been given. I must add that it seems to me that I can see that, e.g. 'having an experience' and 'having a shape' are not only different sorts of attributes but incapable of being attributes of the same thing in the same sense of 'attribute'.

It does not follow, however, that we are entitled to adopt the two substance theory. If a mind cannot be a substance in the same sense as the body is, it must be almost equally misleading to refer to them as two different substances. The fact is that we are not yet in a position to frame a satisfactory philosophical theory of the relation between body and mind. But at any rate the view that the mind, whether just a closely related series of events or a substance in some deeper sense, comprises what is not merely a set of qualities of the body and therefore does not necessarily perish with it has not been overthrown. I do not see any strong positive argument against it, and there is a science in process of birth, psychical research, which at least in some degree, to what degree opinions will vary very much, supports it.

There has recently been a more subtle attack on mind as distinct from body, that launched by Professor Ryle,[1] and I cannot conclude this article without mentioning it, though I have obviously not the time to deal with it with any approach to adequacy. Ryle's chief point is that the words we ordinarily understand as psychological terms do not refer to actual states of mind identifiable by introspection but to dispositions, and that statements about these dispositions must in turn be understood as referring to the outward behaviour in which they manifest themselves. A disposition is after all nothing beyond its manifestations. To say a man is bad tempered is to say that he will behave in an angry way more often, more violently, and with less provocation than most men, not that there is some mysterious quality, bad-temperedness, residing in his nature all the time even when he is not angry at all. Again, Ryle points out that a man's intelligence may be expressed as truly and directly in his physical movements as in what he says 'mentally' when he is 'thinking'. But this may be granted without removing the 'dualism' he deplores, if we grant that the dispositions are sometimes translatable in terms of the mental states and not only of the physical states in which they are manifested. To say truly that a person desires something is not necessarily to say that he is having any thoughts or feelings relating to it at the moment you speak, but it is to say that he has a disposition that manifests itself not only in physical behaviour but at times in definite experienced emotions and thought. To say that a person believes something is not indeed necessarily to say that he has had a specific experience of coming to believe it, but it is not only to say that he acts as if he believed it. It is to say also that if it were challenged he would feel disagreement, if it were refuted he would

[1] In his book, *The Concept of Mind*. For a fuller treatment v. my article *Professor Ryle's Attack on Dualism* in *Clarity is not Enough*.

feel surprise, etc. Without the mental, not publicly observable, side, life would indeed be valueless. Who would see any point or value in going on existing without any experience or feeling (if it indeed could be called existing)? Objections are brought about the difficulty of observing mental states or acts introspectively, but this difficulty may be explained by the fact that our mental acts or states of apprehending, observing, willing, considering, never can be observed by themselves because they never occur by themselves but only in conjunction with what is apprehended, observed, willed, considered. As Ryle has pointed out, many psychological terms stand not for a single state but for a variety of processes and dispositions. It would be a mistake to think that we could never use the word 'know' truly of anyone unless he had performed a specific act of knowing relatively to the thing said to be known, but it is still the case that there certainly are introspective experiences of coming to know something, seeing something to be true, etc. What introspective psychology suffers from is not inability to know when such things happen, but inability to analyse or adequately describe them. We must not, however, I think, go to the other extreme to Ryle and maintain the infallibility of introspection.

I must therefore conclude that so far no intelligible theory which makes our mind inseparably united to our body as a physical object has been stated, let alone proved. This at any rate leaves it an open question for philosophy whether the mind can survive bodily death. No doubt the mind, in the present life at least, is dependent on the brain for its ability to think at all and not only for its outward expression of the thought in words and action, but as McTaggart said, to argue that because under present conditions we cannot think without the brain, we shall be unable to think when we have no brain might be like arguing that, because I cannot see the sky in my study without looking through the window, I shall be unable to see it when I have gone out of the house because I shall have no windows to look through. In general I should confront those who say that body and mind are so closely connected that we cannot survive bodily death with this dilemma. Either they must maintain that they can see a logically necessary connexion between bodily and mental events, and it surely cannot be claimed that we see this. It is just our inability to see it that makes us feel their connection is a problem, and in any case few philosophers now, least of all those of the type inclined to materialism, would claim to see logically necessary connexions in nature. Or, if they cannot maintain this, they must admit they have no real grounds for their view. The connection is not *a priori*, and inductive grounds there obviously cannot be. We have never observed a mind being annihilated at death: no one could observe this but the mind in question itself, and even that could not because it was annihilated, so if a phenomenon it is certainly an unobservable one. This negative conclusion at any rate leaves the field open for any empirical evidence drawn from 'psychic research' and any arguments for survival there may be based on ethics and religion.

IX

PSEUDO-SOLUTIONS

A way of solving philosophical problems has lately come into
fashion in this country—to which it may even be largely peculiar—
that consists in rejecting unheard any philosophical theory which
conflicts with 'common sense'. I want to argue that the solutions
to which I am referring are pseudo-solutions and leave the
problems just where they were. I do not mean to maintain that
'common sense' is necessarily to be adjudged wrong in these
matters or even that the fact that a philosophical theory conflicts
with common sense is not a powerful argument against the theory,
but I do wish to protest against the manner in which the dismissal
of the theories is effected and the grounds given for it, and I wish
to trace the way of approach I am criticizing to an ungrounded
assumption derived from the verificationists at the height of their
dogmatism and still not eradicated from the minds of many
thinkers.

Philosophers have made such statements as: Time is unreal.
I do not know that physical objects, or that other minds than my
own, exist. We do not perceive physical objects but only sense-
data. Body and mind do not interact. There are no substances
but only events. There are no universals but only particulars.
And the reply is made that of course these propositions are false
(or meaningless). I do know such things as that the table in front
of me exists or that I was at such and such a place yesterday or
that when I burn my finger I feel pain, and I do know many true
sentences including substance terms and names for general
qualities. The philosophers in question contradict common-
sense propositions, and we know common-sense propositions to
be true. This is the line G. E. Moore took as regards at least some
of the propositions I have mentioned, but he has given no reason
for taking this line. He has merely said that he knew certain
common-sense propositions to be true. His *Proof of an External
World* consisted merely in arguing: I know that my hand exists.
My hand is an external thing. Therefore, some external things
exist. For holding the vital first premiss no reason whatever is

given. I am not saying this by way of criticism: for us to know anything to be true by means of reasons, there must be something we know without a reason, otherwise there will be a vicious infinite regress, and it is at least very plausible to say that one of the things I know without a reason is the existence of my hand. There are however also *prima facie* very grave objections to saying that I can know this and know it without the help of reasons, and I cannot help thinking that Moore would have done better if in the paper in question he had discussed these objections and also tried to say something further about what we do exactly know when we know that our hand exists and how we know it. However in this article I am not disputing with Moore, but with those younger philosophers who provide an argument for the view which Moore does not provide. I think the argument they give very bad and philosophically very dangerous, whether what it was supposed to prove be in fact true or not. As regards Moore's view, apart from the later argument for it, I can only say that I am in a dilemma. I agree with Moore that it is very hard to resist the conviction that we know with certainty the things which he says we know, but while thinking this I also think that the arguments against saying we know these things with certainty are much stronger than they were held to be by Moore.

The argument which I am going to discuss is put forward, for instance, by Malcolm, who however claimed it to be an interpretation of Moore. He says 'the essence of Moore's technique of refuting philosophical statements consists in pointing out that these statements go against ordinary language.'[1] Moore has not said whether this is a correct interpretation of his view: I hope it is not. Certainly it seems to me that Moore was falling back on the immediate underived certainty of commonsense, while Malcolm instead bases his defence of commonsense on an appeal to an argument that must have occurred to few people and is therefore certainly not an argument of commonsense. The argument is not therefore necessarily the worse—that of which we are convinced without argument may later be justified by argument— but I shall contend that it happens in fact to be a bad argument, though one which is exceedingly popular in England at the present time. It is to the following effect. According to the ordinary use of language we 'know' that material objects exist, etc., and that a

[1] *The Philosophy of G. E. Moore* in The Library of Living Philosophers, p. 349.

philosopher who questions these statements is therefore saying or at least suggesting that in stating them language is being used in a wrong way. But the only criterion of the correctness or incorrectness of language is whether most (or at least most educated) people use words in a particular way or not, and therefore to object that statements which would be universally accepted as correct are incorrectly phrased is absurd. I have heard similar things said about propositions such as that body and mind interact, and about the propositions that there are substances and universals, on the ground that there undoubtedly are substance-words and general words. Or, when it is admitted that the procedure of the sceptic is not quite absurd, it is said that he is merely altering language in an inconvenient way to call attention to the difference between physical object propositions and some other propositions which are said to be certain in another sense of 'certain'.

Now it may of course be replied that we must draw a distinction between false statements and statements incorrectly worded, and that the sceptic is doubting not whether the language in which the statements are put expresses correctly what is meant, but whether the statements are true. He is not in the position of a man who wants to use the word 'tiger' instead of 'cat', but only of a man who should on account of certain pecularities question whether his cat was not really a tiger-cub smuggled in by an enemy or escaped from the zoo. We might regard the suggestion of the latter as extremely unreasonable, but this would certainly not be because it was a suggestion that ordinary language was incorrect. The man would admit that we were expressing correctly what we meant when we called it a cat but would be suggesting that to say it was a cat was untrue. However Malcolm and no doubt most other philosophers who have used such arguments are aware of this distinction and would be prepared to admit it in the case of ordinary empirical judgments, but they think that the philosophical disputes in question must be disputes about language because they are not capable of settlement by empirical evidence. This argument is used or assumed again and again by contemporary British thinkers: Philosophers are not disputing about what can be settled empirically, therefore they are disputing about language. But plainly the argument is only valid if the dichotomy is exhaustive, and on its exhaustiveness I wish to cast doubt.

Why do modern philosophers assume that there can only be

these two alternatives and say that a dispute must either be about empirical facts or be about language (or in some cases partly about the one and partly about the other)? I cannot see any ground for this rigid dichotomy, and it seems to be just a legacy of the old dogmatic verificationist view, which has admittedly never been proved true. Certainly it is clear that what the people who denied or doubted the commonsense propositions I have mentioned meant to say was not that the language in which they were phrased was or possibly was incorrect, but that what these asserted to be true was not or possibly was not true. Similarly metaphysicians in general would have perfectly readily admitted that there was no difference between themselves and their opponents as to empirically ascertainable facts, but would have claimed to be dealing with a kind of facts which were not empirically ascertainable in at least an ordinary sense. Of course it may be said that they had a mistaken idea of what they were doing, but the alternative that metaphysicians were right at least in their admission of the meaningfulness of asserting such facts, even if wrong as to what these were, should at least be treated as requiring serious discussion. For the argument that philosophers who question commonsense propositions must be talking about language because they are not talking about empirical facts lacks any foundation till this alternative is disproved.

But whatever sort of things would facts not empirically ascertainable be? Their fancied inability to answer this question is one of the chief causes that make people inclined to say that if a statement is not an ordinary empirical statement it must be a statement about language. In one sense of the words 'not empirically ascertainable' there is of course no difficulty at all. It is perfectly intelligible to say that we are not in a position to ascertain whether there is life on Mars, but then though we cannot in fact find this out, it is quite *conceivable* that we might be able to do so. This will of course apply even to cases where it might look (though we can never be sure of this) as if owing to inconvenient causal laws the knowledge will be for ever beyond human power. The criterion is whether or not we can form an idea of an empirical test which, if it *could* be applied, would settle the issue. But philosophers seem often to have disputed over alleged facts where no empirical test could possibly decide between them. Can such alleged facts conceivably be facts?

Now it seems to me that there has been a great deal of confusion here. On the one hand even metaphysicians have commonly put forward their conclusions as supported by experience. With one notorious exception which I do not wish to defend, namely, the ontological proof as usually understood, even the most abstract proofs of a metaphysician include some empirical premiss, at least the premiss that he exists, and he would usually defend a metaphysical view by maintaining that it is the only view which adequately explains or makes sense of experience. On the other hand if we limit establishment by experience to direct establishment, we shall have to say goodbye to most of science and for that matter to most of the ordinary assumptions of practical life. What then is the difference between a metaphysical and a scientific theory? They both are established by inference from experience. The chief difference, or at least the one most relevant to our discussion, is that in the case of a scientific theory there is usually agreement both as to the empirical facts and as to the validity of the inferences from them, while in the case of a metaphysical theory there is agreement as to the empirical facts but persistent disagreement even among experts as to the inferences to be drawn from these. Similarly, the philosophical sceptic, when he casts doubts on the existence of physical objects, usually backs his doubts by empirical evidence about perceptions, and the difference between him and his opponents is not as to whether these empirical facts he cites are facts but about the conclusions to be inferred from them, i.e. as to whether they do or do not cast doubt on commonsense physical object propositions. But why should disputes about the inferences we are entitled to draw from facts be called disputes as to language? The only justification for this would be if all inference had been shown to be verbal in character. Now I certainly do not think that even all deductive inferences are verbal and should still be prepared to support the opposite view strongly, but even if they were, this would not have disposed of metaphysics as transcending experience. Deductive formal arguments can with some plausibility, though not, I think with truth, be described as verbal, but most metaphysics does not depend on such arguments. Metaphysics has commonly consisted in the putting forward of theories which seem plausible as explaining and rendering coherent the facts of experience we seem to know, backed perhaps, explicitly or implicitly, by some synthetic non-formal propositions supposed to be intuitively known, and this is certainly much the more usual type today, though a metaphysician will commonly understand experience less narrowly than does an 'empiricist'. Now I do not see how such inferences, any more than the inferences by which people establish or support scientific hypotheses, can possibly be regarded as verbal (except where they are shown to be due to definite verbal fallacies, which can only be done by a special argument in each case).

People have spoken as though there were something strange and incredible about supposing non-empirical facts, but is there anything odd about there being facts, not themselves experienced, which can be inferred from facts that have been experienced? Are not many physical facts, if not all, in this position? Are not all general laws of science? No doubt we have better hopes of agreement in science than in philosophy, and the arguments are different in kind, but we must remember that scientists very often disagree as to which theory is more strongly supported by the evidence, and the disagreement often becomes acute, widespread and without any promising prospect of settlement when we pass to a science like astronomy as an account of the history of stars and planets or the social sciences.

But it is not only on the ground that the alleged facts are incapable of being empirically established that metaphysical have been sharply differentiated from scientific doctrines. The alleged facts seem themselves also to be of a peculiar kind, quite different from those of ordinary experience. It is not only that they are said to be incapable of being inferred from experience, but that they are supposed to be the sort of thing of which nobody could have an experience, and it is plausible to raise doubts as to whether we can form any idea of things of which nobody could have any possible experience. But the opponents of metaphysics have here certainly neglected important distinctions which require making.

The alleged trans-empirical facts fall into several widely different classes. First, there are some alleged facts about conscious non-human beings, e.g. God. Such facts cannot be experienced by us, but if the being that they characterize experiences them, they do not form a class of quite unexperienced facts. Secondly, there are facts about experiencing beings which are not themselves experienced by these beings but knowable by thought. My experiences and elements in my experience stand in many mathematical, causal and logical relations of which I am not sensibly aware, and in many cases prior to their discovery was not aware at all, though the relation existed all right, and the same will no doubt be true of any other conscious being except an omniscient God. A person who denies the meaningfulness of trans-empirical assertions can hardly wish to exclude the possibility of knowing propositions of this nature. It is surely statements of this kind which a philosopher is usually making when he talks about e.g. causality or the mind-body problem. No doubt some statements made by metaphysicians and purporting to be of this class, e.g. some statements about substance or being and not-being, can rightly be rejected as meaningless, but each one must be tried on its merits. Thirdly, it seems to me perfectly meaningful to assert that some properties of which we have only known by experiencing them exist also without being experienced by anyone because they belong to entities which are not capable of experiencing. Such properties are ascribed by 'realists' to physical objects. It should be noted that we may ascribe both to non-experiencing and experiencing beings properties which are not identical with any properties we experience, provided they are such that a concept of them can be constructed in terms of what we have experienced. This is done if we think of the real world as different in quality from the world as experienced but yet similar in structure to it, or if we think of something as having a property more or less similar in quality to one we experience but much less in degree, as with the spatial properties of atoms, or much greater in degree, as when a philosopher talks about the properties of God, or again if we suppose to exist combined in one thing properties which we have only experienced separately.

I cannot see any reason whatever why we should not be able in any of these ways to form ideas which go beyond what is given in experience. 'Similar to p' is of course a concept constructed from p. This is not altered by the fact that it is much poorer in content than the original concept p unless we have some further knowledge of the property similar to p. How we can be justified philosophically in applying the concepts thus formed to anything is another question which I do not propose to discuss here. But at any rate the argument that the metaphysician must be disputing about language because he is not talking about what can be directly established by sense-experience seems to break down altogether. He may be significantly claiming to apply concepts reached in any of the above-mentioned ways, and if so he is talking neither about what can be directly established by sense-experience nor about language, except in a sense in which anybody who says anything is talking about language. (He may of course also discuss the logic of arguments which do not lead to the postulation of trans-empirical facts or entities but throw new light on what is experienced, although such enquiries would be described more often as belonging to general philosophy than to metaphysics.)

The position is this. Some propositions in the truth of which we all believe we find on philosophical investigation not to be capable either of strict logical proof or of direct establishment by experience. In addition to these are a number of other alleged facts which most people, not having thought about the matter, do not believe to be facts, but which some of those who have thought about it (metaphysicians) do. And there is an intermediate class of alleged facts, e.g. the freedom of the will or the existence of God, which very many people believe to be facts, but the conviction in which is not, as with the first class, common to practically everybody and is inferior in subjective certainty with most who hold it to that possessed by the belief in, say, physical objects. A person who questions the first kind of facts is called a philosophical sceptic, a person who asserts the second kind a dogmatic metaphysician. The terms we apply to a person who asserts the intermediate third kind will vary very much according to our philosophical position. But all these people differ from their respective opponents not, or not only, as to empirical facts and language but as to the validity of certain arguments. I do not see why there should be supposed to be anything particularly mysterious about this kind of difference. We all know from painful experience that it is difficult to think philosophically and so that it is difficult to see whether a philosophical argument is valid or not, and this being so it is easy enough to understand that people should differ about these matters.

However, to return to the discussion of commonsense propositions about physical objects, in view of the collapse of the argument that the philosophical sceptic as to commonsense propositions is denying the correctness of ordinary language, the person who dismisses his objections unheard can only be falling back on an intuitive certainty that physical objects exist. If so, it is not very clear what the difference is in this respect between his attitude and the attitude of a person who asserts that he has an inexpugnable intuitive conviction of the existence of God without considering objections. Is it simply that more people agree with the former than with the latter? This seems a superficial ground, and though certainly true of almost all parts of the world today, it is perhaps not true of e.g. the Indians, at least in certain periods of their history. In any case, once we dismiss the argument from language, to say that commonsense is perhaps wrong is plainly not self-contradictory or meaningless. The most that can be claimed is that the sceptical position here, though not logically or linguistically absurd, is incredible. However, even if it is incredible that the physical objects I seem to see around me, should not exist at all, is it incredible that our commonsense propositions about them should be just a little wrong, i.e. that physical objects should not have exactly the properties we mean in our ordinary conversation to ascribe to them? The scientist has no doubt that they have not.[1] And what degree of difference between the reality and our notion of a physical object would there have to be for us to say that, e.g. the table in front of us did not exist at all? If an attitude like that of Moore is adopted, these questions will call urgently for consideration.

To sum up the arguments so far, philosophers agree with each other and with non-philosophers as to the empirical facts observable in the ordinary sense but differ from each other in the inferences they draw from them and not only in the language they use in describing them. With mathematics and straightforward logical arguments differences, if any, can quickly be resolved and certainty attained, but this has, presumably owing to the greater difficulty of the subject-matter, proved impracticable in philosophy. But there need not be anything to excite particular comment or puzzlement in the fact that two people who agree as to the empirical facts differ as to the inferences to be made from them, unless we think that to draw inferences is always child's play too simple to admit of error. If one thing is a matter for agreement among all philosophers, it is that the concepts with which they deal are difficult to grasp, and if so we need not wonder at the occurrence of errors and at differences of view as to what constitutes an error. And it is the inferences to be drawn from them, the logic of the concepts, not the nature of language, that constitutes the main subject-matter of philosophy.

[1] I am well aware that such remarks have been very much criticized, and I have not space to defend them. They are only made here to suggest problems. My own view is that the conflict between commonsense and science could be removed wholly only by accepting a phenomenalist analysis of physical object propositions, and this I cannot do.

This does not of course mean that linguistic questions may not be indirectly of great philosophical importance. An instance of this is provided as regards the physical object problem by a consideration of the meaning of the word 'know' on lines which had occurred to me independently but have also been suggested by writers of the school I am criticizing. I do not think that the word 'know' as ordinarily used commits one to the complete and absolute theoretical certainty which it has been generally supposed by philosophers to connote, and therefore it seems to me that we might still agree with commonsense language in saying that we 'know' the truth of physical object propositions even if a consideration of philosophical argument does show the knowledge not to amount to absolute certainty. Unfortunately, however, the philosophical arguments in question seem to me to show not merely that no physical object propositions have absolute certainty but that at the best they have only a degree of probability below any that would warrant us in speaking of 'certainty' even in the commonsense sense. I think the realist arguments good up to a point, but only as probable arguments. Hence I am in a dilemma between the case in favour of doubt and my natural instinctive conviction, which still remains, despite what is to be said against it. I do not think it relevant to point out that even philosophers do not act as if they doubted the existence of physical objects. 'Doubt' here means 'recognize intellectually the uncertainty of', not 'act as if it were uncertain': it is a commonplace that in practice it is often wise to act as if uncertain things were certain, where we cannot get certainty.

I have discussed the question of this article especially in relation to our knowledge of the existence of physical objects, but of course it is wider than that. The same sort of answer which Malcolm gave about physical objects may be and is given in answer also to a number of other questions. It may be and sometimes is said: Of course, time is real: we are constantly applying temporal predicates to things. Substantive words do not function as adjectives, therefore of course there are substances not reducible to qualities. It is correct to speak in causal terms of the relation between body and mind, therefore of course body and mind interact. It would be very bad English to say you do not perceive the paper in front of you, therefore of course we perceive physical objects and not only sense-data. The method has been used also to avoid the difficulties about justifying induction. It is said that a 'justified induction' *means* an inductive argument which is accepted itself or is at least of a kind accepted by accredited experts, and in that case to suggest that an inductive argument of a kind generally accepted by scientists might be invalid is self-contradictory unless the intention be to appeal from present to future scientists. I am not intending to discuss induction as such in this article, and there might of course conceivably be peculiarities about induction which made this kind of answer a good answer in the case of induction without its being a good answer in the other cases I have mentioned, but it is quite clear at any rate that the main motive for such a solution of the problem of induction is similar. It is to avoid having to admit any other source of knowledge or reasonable inference besides experience and language. An attempt is made to represent inductive, as well as deductive, inference as a matter of linguistics, and the sceptic about induction, like the other sceptics we have encountered, is represented either as contradicting himself or as proposing a revision of language.

It is admitted indeed that the points philosophers make are not *merely* about language but also relate to facts, especially to the resemblances and differences between different kinds of facts. Philosophers, it is said, propose to alter language, reasonably or unreasonably, in order to bring out certain resemblances and differences which hold between the propositions they are discussing and certain other propositions, and to which they think insufficient attention has been paid. Thus it is said that philosophers who say we do not know physical object propositions or inductive propositions with certainty are thereby bringing out the difference between these propositions and propositions of mathematics or propositions such as 'I have a pain'. It is not that they differ from other philosophers as to what the empirical facts are, but merely that they think that sufficient attention has not been paid to certain empirical facts and that language is misleading in that it tends to direct attention away from these facts.

Now this may be all that philosophers are doing sometimes but it is certainly not all they are always doing, and there is no reason to think it is but for the fallacious dichotomy to which I have referred. If it had been shown that all significant assertions that people can make were really either about facts established directly by experience or about language, this would be the least unsatisfactory line to take, but the premiss is quite unfounded. Language is only misleading because it gives a misleading account of the facts, and no general reason has been given to show why 'facts' should not include facts that are trans-empirical of any of the kinds I have mentioned earlier. *Prima facie* one would certainly think that a philosopher who said we did not know physical object propositions did so because he thought that the logical relation between any proposition he did know and a physical object proposition could never be such as to prove the latter and that we were not justified in claiming certainty for them without proof. These are propositions about logical relations, not primarily about language or empirical facts. And they are not propositions as to the truth or falsity of which all philosophers are agreed. It is not therefore merely a question of revising language in order to direct our attention to relations which we all know are there but may overlook. Similarly, it is useless to inform a philosopher who is disputing about interaction between body and mind that common-sense language admits it; he wants to know whether there really is interaction. If commmonsense speech admits it because we really know it as an objective fact at the common-sense level, so much the better. But to say this is no longer to appeal to the nature of language; it is to claim a veridical immediate cognition.

It is, I think, a major misfortune for contemporary philosophy in England that there has arisen such a strong tendency to make out that what philosophy does is to talk about language. To say this is not to overlook the extremely important part which the use of the same language by different people in different senses plays in causing philosophical disputes. It is certainly very common indeed for a dispute in philosophy to be greatly intensified and obscured by different uses of language giving rise to verbal misunderstandings, but just as disputes in science may be both linguistic and factual in the empirical sense, so disputes in philosophy may be, and indeed usually are, both linguistic and factual in the sense of relating to one of the kinds of trans-empirical facts of which I spoke a little while ago.

The question of physical objects provides a good illustration of the large rôle which empirical evidence can play in philosophy. The sceptic rarely just contents himself with saying negatively in general that sense-experience does not prove their existence; he brings forward detailed arguments ultimately based on empirical facts in favour of his view. And his opponent will usually act similarly. Nothing is plainer than that they agree as to these empirical facts but differ as to the inferences to be drawn from them. Even if it be true that no empirical evidence can establish physical object propositions with certainty, it can at least be used to support or throw doubt on them. It may be said, however, that this is not enough. In order to say significantly that physical object propositions are either certain or uncertain we must have an idea of what certainty in this connexion means, and it has been argued against the sceptic that without an idea of certainty it is meaningless even to suggest that they are uncertain. But if no physical object judgment is certain and no empirical evidence could conceivably remove his doubts, how could such an idea be obtained? If it cannot be obtained, is not scepticism about physical objects nonsensical after all? The notion of certainty may indeed be derived from pure logic or from propositions about one's immediate experience and sense-data, but the reply is made that it would be self-contradictory for physical object propositions to be certain in that sense and to say they are uncertain thus becomes merely to say that they are what they are and not *a priori* propositions or propositions about one's own sense-data. But this argument again assumes that the only way of settling a dispute about any matter of fact is by empirical evidence. May it not be by *argument* based on empirical evidence? And is it not at least conceivable that some time in the future through a new insight into the arguments now used or, more probably, through a discovery of fresh arguments the issue may be completely settled so that everybody who has studied the subject will agree with complete certainty on the conclusion? This may be very unlikely indeed, but it is at least not an inconceivable or meaningless supposition, and our ability even to entertain this as a possibility is sufficient to give meaning to the notion of certainty here, even if we should come to the conclusion that we must at the present stage of thought admit the existence of physical objects to be, strictly speaking, uncertain. A person who disagrees with Moore can at least conceive the possibility that he might some day be completely convinced by what Moore has written. Even if he is sure now that he has arguments which disprove Moore's views absolutely, he must remember that philosophers often make mistakes and are sure of things which are not really true, and he can envisage the possibility that he will some day be forced to admit that he has himself made a mistake in this matter. In all this I am not arguing that the existence of physical objects is uncertain, but that we cannot dismiss the statements of those who question it as self-contradictory or meaningless.

Another, allied method of solving philosophical problems on linguistic lines is not to dismiss one particular theory as meaningless but to take two contending philosophical theories and say that, since they agree as to the empirical facts, they must really be saying the same thing in different words. This may indeed be followed by an expression of a preference for one theory over the other, but only because its language is less misleading, not because one is true and the other false. The best example of this method to take is perhaps the treatment of the question of sense-data. It is maintained that the man who says a penny is round but appears elliptical, and the man who says it is round but our sense-data of it are elliptical, both mean the same thing and only express themselves in different words. This conclusion indeed seems often to be regarded as directly established by the mere fact that they agree as to the empirical evidence. Since they cannot be disputing about this, it is concluded that they must be disputing about language, in complete disregard of the possibility that the dispute may be neither about the emprical data nor about language, but about the inferences to be drawn from the empirical data. Then, the difference being regarded as linguistic, it is pointed out that the sense-data language, though admittedly useful for certain purposes, is misleading because the substantival form employed suggests the existence of sense-data as actual entities, and that it is therefore better to talk in terms of 'appearing' and say that the penny appears elliptical to us but is really round. This way of putting it will not suggest that the elliptical appearance is another thing outside the physical object somewhere in the observer's brain or a mysterious non-spatial entity dependent on his mind. This solution is certainly tempting: few philosophers nowadays are very anxious to assert that we do not perceive physical objects directly but only sense-data. But whatever its philosophical merits, it cannot be claimed that the appearing theory means just the same as the sense-data theory and therefore that the difference between them is merely a matter of language which is more or less misleading in suggesting what the holder of either does not really believe.

The people who have asserted a sense-data theory (or 'representative theory' as they used to call it), and for two centuries at least the theory had almost a monopoly, were certainly maintaining the actual existence of sense-data as our immediate objects of perception distinct from any part of the physical object said to be perceived, and did not merely against their will slip into the use of language which suggested such a view. When they did not recognize the sense-data as distinct entities, it was because they refused to separate them, not from physical objects, but from the state of the mind when perceiving. Or are we to say that the assertion of sense-data as distinct entities is really meaningless, though people thought they meant something by it? I do not see how this could possibly be established without assuming the verificationist dogma that a sentence cannot have any meaning unless what it says is empirically verifiable, and this dogma seems generally to have been discarded, at least nominally, even by 'advanced thinkers', though in practice it still covertly exercises a very great influence on them, as I have tried to show in this article.

That the people who hold the difference between the sense-data theory and the opposing theory of perception to be merely a matter of language are not right may, I think, be shown in the following way. Suppose A to be directly perceiving a physical object, and B not perceiving it but having a mental image of it without looking in its direction. Everybody will admit that there is a factual difference between that situation and a situation in which A is perceiving it and B neither perceiving it nor having the image. To add the words 'B is having an image of it' to 'A is perceiving it' is not merely to repeat in different language all or part of what one has already said, but to say something fresh. B's image is a different existent over and above anything mentioned in the other sentence. Now the sense-data theory asserts that besides A and the thing he is said to perceive there exists also a sort of image in A's mind. (Even if a sense-datum be always qualitatively different from any mental image, which is extremely doubtful, it is conceived as the same kind of thing, though caused in a very different way.) But we have seen that the situation A + the physical object without the image in B's mind differs factually from the situation A + the physical object + image in B's mind. Therefore it must differ factually also from the situation A + the physical object + image in A's mind. Professor Ryle has indeed to the great surprise of most readers denied images as existents, but in any case all that is needed to make my point is that it should be admitted that it is not *meaningless* to talk of images as existents. If this is admitted—and I do not see how it can possibly be denied, it is *meaningful* also to admit sense-data as existents. I should say I can directly verify the proposition that images exist by observing them, and even those who think they cannot verify it must surely admit that it is conceivable that it could be verified. To say that there are sense-data is to say that there is something like an image besides the physical object, and this is to assert, rightly or wrongly, the presence of an additional existent.

Yet, if so, it seems peculiar that the existence of sense-data is not even conceivably capable of an absolutely conclusive empirical proof. The position seems *prima facie* quite different from what it is as regards alleged transcendent entities like God. If these exist, we cannot expect their existence to be provable by sense-experience, therefore the fact that it cannot be need not worry us. But surely such a proof should be possible of what are, if they exist, the very objects of sensation itself? The answer to this question, I think, is that when we discuss whether sense-data exist, what we are discussing is not whether there are sense-data if this means 'immediate objects of sense-perception', for everybody except through a misunderstanding must agree that there are. What we are discussing is whether besides these there are also independent physical things in the realist sense, and if so, whether the immediate objects of perception are part of these independent physical things or only caused by the latter acting on our body and mind.

The realist who holds a representative theory of perception does indeed admit additional entities beyond those admitted by a 'direct realist' or a 'phenomenalist', but that is because, having admitted independent physical objects and denied that we experience them immediately, he, being still bound to leave a place for the immediate objects of perception, has to treat them as another class of beings distinct from physical things. That there are immediate objects of perception is empirically established, though there is much philosophical doubt as to the characterization of these. In particular are those that I perceive also perceived by other human beings and do they exist independently of being perceived? A realist who holds a direct theory of perception will answer these two questions in the affirmative, and will therefore usually object to speaking of ourselves as perceiving sense-data (at least in all cases of perception), because the phrase 'sense-data' unlike 'immediate objects of perception' has usually implied dependence for their existence on being perceived.

Another question is how far what we immediately perceive is due to the senses and how far to the activity of the mind in systematizing and interpreting? An important motive for denying 'sense-data' has been a belief that what we perceive immediately is largely due to the work of the mind and that we cannot sort out a distinct element to be ascribed to sensation and to sensation alone, but even those who deny sense-data on such grounds would hardly say that when we perceive we perceive nothing at all. The question is of the nature of our immediate object of perception, not whether there is any such object (unless indeed 'immediate' is being used in a different sense to mean 'given apart from any interpretation or systematization', in which sense it may be a legitimate object of dispute whether there is anything given immediately at all).

I have perhaps already spoken more about the tricky problem of sense-data than is in place in this article. It does however illustrate well the more general point that where philosophers differ is not about the empirical facts or primarily about language but about the kind of arguments they think warranted by the empirical facts. Philosophers agree as to our experience and as to the established scientific facts but some think these provide the basis of a good causal argument to make the existence of physical objects, realistically conceived, highly probable as the only means of explaining our experience and the success of our predictions, others think this argument quite lacking in cogency. Some philosophers think that the occurrence of 'illusions' and the physiological facts connected with sense-perception force us to admit that the only reasonable theory of perception is a representative one, others think the same empirical facts can equally well be explained in terms of a direct one. That physical objects exist in a particular sense is a factual and not an *a priori* proposition, but though a factual proposition it cannot be established directly by sense-experience, and of course all the established scientific hypotheses and common-sense beliefs to which we refer as 'the empirical facts' are in the same position. Even if interpreted phenomenalistically they would be, for as thus interpreted they are statements about future possible experiences of human beings. And the same is true of the proposition that we perceive sense-data, for as usually understood this is a statement about causal and other relations of immediate objects of perception. But that there are immediate objects of perception is established directly by experience, so if we use sense-data in that sense as Moore does, there may be disputes as to their nature, but their existence cannot be questioned. It is not because philosophical disputes are about language but because of the greater difficulty of agreeing about their logic than about the logic of scientific arguments that philosophical disputes are very peculiar and never seem to end.

The problem of the existence of God is more analogous to that of the existence of physical objects than might be expected. God, like physical objects, realistically conceived, is a trans-empirical being. Some claim to be immediately aware of God, as some claim to be immediately aware of physical objects, but on neither point has agreement among philosophers been obtained. There are indirect arguments for the existence of God as for that of physical objects, but philosophers are again not agreed on their logic even when agreed on the empirical facts. And both with God and physical objects, even if it is admitted that their existence can be established by the arguments, it must also be admitted that we have at the best a very slight knowledge of their properties. I say this in reaction to those who speak as if to assert the existence of God were merely to take up a certain emotional attitude towards the universe (and practical attitude towards life) and not commit oneself to any beliefs in trans-empirical facts, as though it had been proved there could not be any such facts and as though the emotional attitude of the religious man did not depend on a conviction about the objective character of Reality. Yet of course the parallel does not bring out the valuational and emotional sides inseparable from genuinely religious belief and is therefore misleading. It is misleading in just the opposite way to that in which I think Wisdom's account in *Gods* is misleading and is therefore needed to supplement the latter. I give it as a corrective to the view that religion can do without belief in any trans-empirical facts.

The solution of philosophical problems which I have examined and rejected, is a solution which is effected by laying it down that philosophical theories cannot assert or contradict any facts or supposed facts and must therefore be regarded merely as suggestions about language to make it less misleading than it is. How we can decide whether a particular use of language is misleading or not without having some idea of a metaphysical kind in a more objective sense, is not clear in the least. For instance, how can we decide that sense-data language is misleading unless we have already decided that the direct theory of perception is true and that there are no such entities as sense-data? How can we say that a language which suggests the existence of trans-empirical beings is meaningless unless we assume that nothing exists but sense-experience? How can we say that it is misleading to speak of God (or the State for that matter) as a person unless we have already rejected the metaphysical theory that God (or the State) is a person? The view which I am discussing owes all its philosophical merits, which I do not deny, to not being carried out consistently, for it presupposes that there are no *facts* to be discovered besides those of science, and therefore is at bottom a solution of philosophical problems by forbidding us to do philosophy. It is fortunate indeed that the prohibition has not been obeyed even by those who issued it.

X

THE CORRESPONDENCE THEORY
OF TRUTH

Professor Woozley has described the topic of this article as one of the bitterest and bloodiest battlegrounds of philosophical theories. While not wishing to engage in bitter or bloody battles, I do think that the question I shall discuss is very important philosophically, both in itself and in its bearing on other questions, e.g. the epistemological character of ethical judgments. As has been remarked, the first impression which the correspondence theory gives is one of extreme obviousness. Truth does consist surely in corresponding to the facts. Why is it a true judgment that I am in America? Is it not just because it corresponds to the facts? Why is it a false one that I am in Australia? Surely just because it does not correspond to the facts. But if the first impression given by the theory is one of great obviousness, the next is usually one of great puzzlement. We are used to what is obvious raising philosophical difficulties, but, surely, few apparently obvious propositions have raised more difficulties than the doctrine that truth consists in correspondence with facts.

In the first place, what corresponds? It is not the judgment as a psychological event (or as a behaviour disposition). Psychological events or behaviour dispositions are not true or false. We must say that *what* is judged or believed is true, not the judging or believing of it. Now, what is judged or believed is what is called a proposition. It is commonly said that only propositions can be called true or false and statements or sentences indirectly according as they express true or false propositions. So the question is raised, What are these odd entities, propositions? I cannot pick out introspectively entities in my mind, propositions, as I can images, distinct from the experience of thinking of or believing propositions, and I do not wish to maintain the queer view according to which all the propositions that can be asserted have a kind of being or subsistence other than existence, whether it be held that they have this only when asserted or considered or that they always have it whether asserted or considered by anyone or not. Neither

G

do I want, however, to say that, when we are talking about propositions, we are to be understood as talking about words. I think that statements about propositions must somehow be translated either as statements about states of mind (or dispositions) or about the reality to which these refer, or about both together. No doubt, which way of translation is correct will vary with the context; neither method is universally the right one. On the psychological side, I think, to talk about the proposition S is P is to talk about what there is in common between A's believing that S is P, B's disbelieving that S is P, C's doubting whether S is P, D's hoping that S is P, etc. Mind, I do not say that the proposition *is* the common element in all these; I say that, when we are talking about it, we are talking about that element. The proposition that it rained yesterday is not a quality or a part of my state of believing or of my disposition to believe that it did rain. The common element could not be described as the proposition itself but as the property of 'having the proposition as its object'. I think this is a case where language is definitely misleading. Because 'believe' is a transitive verb and we cannot 'believe 'without 'believing something', the suggestion is conveyed that what we believe is an entity distinct from the believing to which we do something when we believe it, as 'hitting somebody' implies a being who is hit distinct from the hitting. In fact, however, there is in the case of the believing no such distinct object except the reality toward which the believing is directed and it is not this reality that we believe. One does not 'believe the rain which fell yesterday' but one 'believes that it fell'. But to add to the word 'believes' the words 'that rain fell' is not to introduce a new thing which is believed distinct both from the physical event and the believing that it occurred, it is merely to specify more in detail the mental state or the disposition of the person who believes. (Of course, in the first person present it also claims that what the belief refers to exists or existed, otherwise I should not now be holding the belief.) There are other cases where the grammatical object of a verb does not stand for a thing distinct from the activity expressed by the verb. A sack of coal is, but a sigh is not, something distinct from the 'heaving' of it; a life is not anything distinct from the living it; a crime is not anything distinct from the committing of it, a proposal from the making of it, a wish from the wishing of it. I am convinced that it is on lines like this that the problem of what propositions are is to be solved, but I must admit that I am distinctly puzzled as to why it should be that we can only talk of truth in terms of such fictitious entities. It is not our state or disposition of believing as such, but only the 'proposition' which is believed, that is said to be true or false. Certainly, if truth is constituted by a relation of correspondence, this relation holds not between the real and the state of believing as a whole but only in respect of a certain aspect of the latter which is described in terms of propositions.

The next difficulty arises when we attempt to define correspondence. We cannot define it as copying or likeness or one-to-one correlation. Another type of definition is given by Russell in *Problems of Philosophy*, pp. 200–1. 'If Othello believes truly that Desdemona loves Cassio, then there is a complex unity, "Desdemona's love for Cassio," which is composed exclusively of the *objects* of the belief, in the same order as they had in the belief.' But does this as a definition of truth tell us anything more than that my belief *A r B* is true whenever *r* really relates *A* and *B* in the order in which they are related in my belief, i.e. that a belief is true wherever what is believed is in fact the case? And does this answer the question the philosopher wants to ask when he inquires about the definition of truth? What he wants to find out is surely just what the relation is between truly believing and what is in fact the case.

There must be such a relation and it does seem as though truth must consist in it. A theory has recently been put forward according to which 'true' does not stand for any objective relation at all but is merely a word used to convey additional emphasis. On this view, to say '*S* is *P*' is true is only to repeat *S* is *P* more emphatically. We might call this the emotive or the interjectional theory of truth. (For some reason, obscure to me, its usual name is the semantic theory.) I do not wish to deny that this theory gives an approximately correct account of the way in which 'true' is often used. But it surely remains the case that a belief-state or belief-disposition—even if it be only a behaviour-disposition as Ryle says—is distinct from the objective facts to which it relates, and the question of the definition of truth is the inquiry about the relation between these two. This question is not settled by saying that to call something true is just a question of emphasizing it more. My judgment that it rains is distinct from the raining and yet refers to it; it is further obvious that the judgment is related in a different way to the external events when it is true and when it is false, and that on this relation its truth depends.

When we try to say, further, what the relation is, we are involved in difficulties, but there clearly is a relation and a legitimate question about what the relation is. I think the theory to which I am referring appears plausible as a final account only because the notion of truth is already assumed when we first make a judgment, even if we do not use the word 'true'. To make a judgment is not just to recite the words; it is to believe them true, and this is why nothing is added except emphasis to a judgment by saying that it is true.

Are we, then, to say that the relation of correspondence is indefinable? But, if we admit this, why not say outright that truth is indefinable and give up all 'theories of truth'? Is anything gained by a mock definition which merely substitutes for 'true' a technical term, 'corresponding', that itself has to be admitted to be indefinable? Some concepts must be indefinable in the sense of unanalysable, or we have a vicious infinite regress; and truth is such a fundamental concept that it is one of the most likely to be so. But let us not then pretend that we have defined it. It now seems as though the correspondence theory has nothing to tell one; but this is not quite correct. It does make one important assertion, namely, that truth depends on a relation to an objective reality beyond any set of judgements or beliefs. This may seem so obvious as to be hardly worth saying, but, after all, there have been many philosophers who in their theory of truth have ignored or at least not done justice to this simple fact. For instance, no adequate place for it is given in the coherence theory of truth. Further, the mere fact that the correspondence theory has appealed to people and initially strikes one as all too obvious is evidence that there must be some analogy which the theory brings out between the truth relation and the relation of correspondence in other cases where we should use the word. Otherwise it would hardly appear obvious at all.

But a difficulty now arises about the other term of the relation, facts. The theory maintains that a true proposition always corresponds to a fact. But is this the case? At first sight at least it seems plausible enough as regards affirmative descriptive propositions such as 'there is a man here' or 'it is raining'. But even here it may be agreed that there is also a series of possible true propositions, more or less definite, referring to each single fact. Instead of saying 'there is a man here', we might say 'there is a Cambridge graduate here' or we might say 'there is Tom

Jones'. Yet, are not all these three propositions and an indefinite number of others made true by one fact, the presence of Tom Jones? And are there negative facts over and above positive? Is there a distinct objective fact that there are no lions in this room, another that there are no tigers, and so on? Even with affirmative propositions which look straightforwardly descriptive difficulties arise as soon as dispositional properties are ascribed to something. It is by no means clear that, if I say this lump of sugar is soluble, I am asserting the existence in the lump of an actual quality, solubility, which is there even when the sugar is not exposed to water. This brings one to hypothetical propositions. To what do they correspond? Where the hypothetical proposition just links two categorical propositions both of which correctly describe something, the difficulty may be met, I think, by saying that the hypothetical proposition asserts a logical or causal connexion existing in the real world. It must be remembered that relations as well as qualities are objective. But where the protasis of the hypothetical does not by itself constitute a true proposition, i.e. where we have a 'contrafactual conditional', to what fact does the proposition then correspond? An advocate of the correspondence theory seems driven at this point to admit, besides existents, a strange realm of subsistent entities for his propositions to correspond to. He seems to have to say either that besides existents and facts about them there are subsistent hypothetical facts or that universals subsist independently of the existent world and hypothetical propositions assert connexions between these subsistent universals. Only so could we have a fact corresponding to each true proposition that we assert.

All this strongly suggests that we should replace the notion of correspondence as a necessary condition of truth by something more general. As I have said, the strong point of the theory is that it insists that the truth of a proposition is dependent on its relation to reality, not to other propositions—a point to which some theories of knowledge fail conspicuously to do justice; but the formula is dangerous unless by 'reality' is meant 'whatever exists', thus not admitting subsistent entities; and this dependence need not involve any likeness or one-to-one correlation with facts. It might still be said that all true propositions 'correspond' to the real in an extremely wide sense of 'correspond', but I think the sense has now become so wide as to make the word inappropriate. All we can say is that they always depend in some way for their truth on the nature of what is, the way in which they depend varying with the kind of proposition in question. Categorical affirmative straightforwardly descriptive propositions depend on the real in a way which at any rate is such as to suggest and not make wholly inapposite the analogy of copying, though even here this analogy is not very strong. They are at any rate directly rendered true by the possession of a quality or relation on the part of the thing or things to which it is attributed in the proposition. But even here different descriptive propositions may well be said to be rendered true by the same fact; for each 'fact' can be described more or less definitely. We may say, 'It rained yesterday here,' or 'It rained in the evening,' or 'It rained from 6:16 to 7:30,' or 'Half an inch of rain fell between 6:15 and 7:30 p.m.,' etc.; and there is scope also for many varying degrees of precision as regards place. We might, of course, speak here of 'different facts', and, in a sense, we should be right; for any one of the propositions might be true without any one later in the series being so. But it seems more appropriate to speak here of vaguer and more precise ways of describing the same fact.

However, it is better not to talk as if facts were definite objective entities the number of which could be unequivocally fixed as can the population of a town. The truth of beliefs certainly depends on a reference to things or events, but there are not entities, facts, besides things and events or, indeed, existing as parts of things or events. To talk about facts is a way of talking about things and events. An attempt has been made to solve the problem of the definition of truth by identifying a fact with a true proposition.[1] But this identification cannot be carried out quite literally. We can say that the fact that an atom bomb was dropped accelerated the Japanese surrender but not that the proposition that an atom bomb was dropped accelerated it. But apart from this, surely, even if facts are reduced to true propositions, there will remain the problem of the relation between these true propositions and the reality to which they refer. But I still think that we could eliminate the word 'fact' from language altogether. Instead of talking of facts we could then talk either of the qualities and relations of things or events, or of true or false propositions.

If we do not regard every true proposition as corresponding to some one fact, we should admit that the exact nature of the relation to reality which makes a proposition true may be very different

[1] A. D. Woozley, *Theory of Knowledge*, p. 169 ff.

according to the kind of proposition. Straightforward affirmative descriptive propositions, as I have suggested, may be said to be true when the qualities or relations ascribed by them are actually present in the object or event to which they refer. But I do not want to talk of negative qualities or negative facts as though they were ultimate entities. I do not want to say that I have, besides the actual positive quality of being a man, also in the same sense the actual negative properties of not being a bird, an ant, a hippopotamus, and so on. But if we think it unsatisfactory to talk of negative qualities or negative facts, we may say that what makes a negative proposition true of something need not be itself a negative property; it had better be regarded as the positive qualities of the thing referred to, which exclude the qualities or relations denied by the negative proposition. This is not incompatible with our being able often to know a negative proposition without knowing the corresponding positive qualities which make this proposition true. That may be for two reasons. (1) We may have a vague idea of these sufficient to negate some propositions but not sufficient to describe them at all determinately, e.g. I may see that a mountain is not less than a mile away without being at all clear how far away it is. I need not be able to describe all the objects in this room in order to know that it does not contain an elephant. (2) In very many cases we deny an affirmative proposition (i.e. assert a negative) because we have very good reason to think that, if the proposition denied had been true, we should have known it. I do not remember all my experiences of yesterday, but there are a lot of things which I should confidently deny happened to me yesterday on the ground that, if they had happened, I should have remembered them.

Universal propositions, at least if they are neither logically necessary nor express causal laws, must be understood as including a negative to the effect that there are, e.g. no Ss which are not Ps. Here, however, it is not a single proposition which is denied but any one of a whole class which is expressed by the use of the word 'anyone'. 'All the people in this room are over 20' is not made true by the presence here of Mr A who is 35, Mrs B who is 29, etc., etc., unless the list is complete, but by the fact that we should have to assert at the end of our list that there is not anyone in the room who is not included in the list. But the proposition denied by this negative might have been rendered true in millions of ways: there are millions of people under 20 who are not in this room and any one of them might conceivably have been in the room. However, since few propositions which we utter describe anything with complete precision, this is by no means peculiar. Almost all our negative propositions might be falsified in various ways, e.g. 'Churchill did not die yesterday' would be falsified alike if he had been beheaded, burnt at the stake, or died from any one of hundreds of different diseases, and if he had died at any of the 1440 minutes of the 24 hours. But in any case, my explanation of negative propositions does entail that for their truth they are as much as affirmative propositions dependent on the nature of the real, only not in quite the same direct fashion.

With hypothetical propositions, at least where their protasis would not be true as a separate proposition, the relation to the real is somewhat more indirect. But even here their truth may be held to depend on the nature of the real. Take the true hypothetical proposition that, if the Nazis had won the war, they would have subjected the inhabitants of England to tyranny. They did not win the war and therefore this proposition does not correspond directly to anything in events which actually occurred, but the real nature of the existent Nazis was still such as to imply the truth of the proposition. Or take the proposition that, if I jumped from the top floor of the Woolworth Building in New York, and my fall was unbroken, I should, to put it mildly, be damaged. I hope the truth of this proposition will never be put to a direct test in actual fact, but I can still assert it to be true because it has an adequate basis in my knowledge of the law of gravitation and the height of skyscrapers. We can assert contrafactual conditionals, as this kind of proposition is usually called by philosophers nowadays, because, though they do not (like many categorical propositions) actually describe the real, the nature of the real is such as to make them true; for they must be based either on the causal or on the logical relations of elements in reality. What other grounds could there possibly be for holding the hypotheticals to be true? This is not to be regarded as contradicting the generally accepted view that there can be no affirmative existential *a priori* propositions. I am saying only that the truth of the hypothetical propositions depends on the nature of some properties or relations in the real world, not that they themselves assert that anything exists. They may even make statements about relations or properties which are not exemplified in reality provided these statements are derivable from properties or relations that are exemplified as the most ultimate properties or relations surely must be. It is the person who refers hypothetical propositions to subsistent entities who really treats them as existential because subsistence can only be understood as a kind of shadowy existence. Many philosophers today would deny that there are logical connexions in the real world, but if they are to defend this, they must say either that logically necessary propositions do not tell one anything and therefore cannot, strictly speaking, be true, or that they tell us something about language and its meaning, in which case they will depend on linguistic facts. The use of language itself consists of a series of events in the objective world.

This way of approach throws light, I think, on the nature of ethical judgements. These also are clearly made true by the nature of the real. Whether something is good or an action right or obligatory depends on its factual nature plus, in the case of an action at least, the actual nature of its circumstances. But it does not follow that ethical and evaluative judgements are just factual statements about the empirical nature of the objects concerning which the judgements are made. That is the mistake of naturalism. Yet, they are surely dependent for their truth on 'natural properties'. What makes very many actions wrong is just their natural property of giving pain; and it is clear that, if an action is really right or an experience or state of mind intrinsically good, it could not fail to be so, its natural properties being what they are. Suppose a man who wanted very much to do something but also realized that it was wrong. Now suppose he said, Well, I want to do this but I do not want to act wrongly, so I shall solve my problem by doing just the thing I want to do in all other respects but seeing that my act does not have the quality of wrongness which is the one quality I dislike in it. It is plain that such a suggestion would be absurd. At the same time, it is not the kind of absurdity that would be committed by a man who ignored or forgot well-established causal connexions. This shows that ethical and evaluative propositions depend necessarily for their truth on the factual nature of the actions and experiences with which they are concerned. I do not say that it is the same kind of necessity as occurs in logic. At the same time, it shows that they do not assert the presence of some additional empirical quality, for no empirical quality can be seen by us to be necessarily connected with the others in that way. Ethical and evaluative judgements may thus be said to correspond to reality in a very

G*

wide sense. There is clearly a sense in which, for a valuation to be correct, it must correspond to the real nature of what is valued. But an ethical or an evaluative judgement, I now realize, is better regarded as saying something dependent for its truth on the nature of the real than as describing the real or informing us about the nature of anything.

This has an important bearing on the controversy as to non-natural properties in ethics. From the premisses that ethical and evaluative judgements are true and that they do not ascribe empirical properties to anything, it was concluded that they must ascribe other, 'non-natural', properties. And of those who thought this very unplausible, some then argued that ethical judgements could not be objectively true because there were no non-natural properties, while others tried to make out that ethical judgements did, after all, ascribe empirical, natural qualities. Now, it may be contended that all three views make the mistaken assumption that, if value judgements are true at all, they must correspond to reality in such a way that the concept of good must be regarded as referring to a property actually present in reality (I do not, of course, mean purely physical reality). From this assumption some philosophers argue that good must be a 'natural property', others that, since good is not a natural property, it must be another, peculiar kind of property, a non-natural one; still others refuse to admit that value-judgements are objectively true at all because, if they admitted that the judgements were true, they think that they would have to admit non-natural properties. But all three lines of argument presuppose that, if value-judgements are objectively true, they must be treated as corresponding to reality in the way in which plain descriptive judgements correspond. It is clear that with ordinary descriptive judgements truth consists in ascribing to things qualities (and relations) which they really have; but if ethical judgements are not descriptive judgements, this is not so clear; and is evaluating or deciding on obligations a way of describing? We might therefore retain an objective view of ethics and yet drop non-natural properties. I still do not see how the concepts of 'good' and 'ought' can be reduced to any empirical concepts or concepts of causal properties. But even if we therefore call them non-natural concepts, it does not follow that we need conclude to the existence of non-natural properties in the objects to which they refer. That would be like saying that, because there are true hypothetical propositions, there must be, besides actual events, another set of peculiar events, hypothetical events, to which true hypothetical propositions refer.

Are all these different propositions true in the same sense of 'true'? It is a difficult question, which has hardly been discussed by philosophers at all, by what criteria we are to settle when a word is being used in different senses and when it is only being applied to different kinds of things. It does seem as though the different true propositions must have something in common in their relation to reality, otherwise we should not be so strongly tempted to call them all true; and we may use 'true' to signify this very wide (as yet not successfully defined and perhaps indefinable) relation. In that case they will all be true in the same sense of 'true'. Or we may argue that different kinds of propositions are true only in different senses of 'true' when they depend for their truth on the real in different ways. We may thus distinguish a general meaning of the word and a set of more special meanings which can all be regarded as applications of the general. To illustrate by an analogy, we might ask whether Churchill is clever in the same sense as Kant. Now to say that somebody is clever is to say that he has outstanding mental ability, and no doubt both Churchill and Kant have this; so we can well justify ourselves in answering Yes. Yet the way in which the two manifested their cleverness was so different that it would be more natural to say, No, they are clever only in different senses. Similarly the different kinds of judgement can all be said to be true in the same sense because they can all be successful cognitively, but what they succeed in doing is sufficiently different for us to hesitate after all to call them true in the same sense of the word. Whether we used the word 'correspond' for the wider sense of true or for the narrower sense applying only to descriptive propositions is a matter of choice, but I think it would be wisest not to use it at all.

I have discussed correspondence only as a proposed definition and not as a criterion of truth. It is difficult to see how it could be regarded as a criterion of truth except where we are concerned with judgments about our own experience or its immediate objects. It has been objected against the correspondence theory even here that nothing is immediately given without an element of interpretation, thus raising questions of great difficulty. However, there can be no interpretation without something to interpret. The rival view that coherence is the test of truth can only be made plausible if coherence is interpreted not as mere internal coherence but as coherence with our experience, and it is difficult to see what that can mean except coherence with judgements seen to describe truly or correspond to our experience. It does seem to me that we may see immediately that some judgements are true of our experience, e.g. I have a toothache, that, in fact, we must do so if we are to know their truth at all, and that these judgements must be the ultimate starting-point for all empirical inferences. And, if we like, we can call being true of our experience 'corresponding to our experience.' I should be prepared to include here judgements of memory, which are also empirical and not based on inference. But, when we go beyond these judgements, I do not see what could be meant by saying that correspondence is the criterion of truth.

XI

MAY CAN-STATEMENTS BE ANALYSED DETERMINISTICALLY?

In recent years a number of very original approaches have been made to the old problem of 'the freedom of the will' of a type which support an indeterminist rather than a determinist view. What might perhaps almost be called the orthodox linguistic approach tries to reconcile determinism with responsibility (while admitting that determinism is not known to be true). It insists that there are criteria for using and good purposes to be served by using moral predicates even if determinism is true, but I do not regard this approach as particularly original, though I should not reject it as far as it goes. A different line is however adopted by one who might be regarded as the linguistic philosopher *par excellence*, Prof. Austin in *Ifs and Cans*. His argument admittedly does not show that determinism is false, but it is certainly intended to incline one in the direction of adopting indeterminism, and it is his argument primarily that I intend to discuss.

In the first place however I should like to say something in general about the relevance to the free will controversy of this type of argument. Austin seems to make the relevance of his argument to the controversy centre on the support it gives to the view that determinism is inconsistent with what we ordinarily say and presumably think.[1] That determinism is inconsistent with what we think can indeed hardly be denied, if he means by 'we' most people. Most people are not determinists (though it may be doubted whether they are either *consistently* indeterminists). This is not to be wondered at, for whether determinism is true or false, it is certain that there are very plausible and obvious arguments against it which are, superficially at least, quite intelligible to the man in the street and have a very wide appeal. But determinist philosophers have frequently contended that these plausible arguments are really fallacious and that determinism can be reconciled with ethics and with our having

[1] P. 131 BA, 179 PP (BA signifies the page numbers of the original British Academy lecture, PP its page numbers as reprinted in *Philosophical Papers*).

freedom in the only senses of this word which are intelligible and express anything worth having at all. In that case it may be argued that if the arguments against determinism are valid the indeterminist philosopher does not need to help himself by appealing to the authority of common sense, while, if the arguments are invalid, he cannot rightly invoke it since the attitude of common sense seems to be due only to these same invalid arguments. So I was induced to take the view that, even if Austin's linguistic analysis were quite irrefutable, it could have little relevance to the question whether determinism is true. But on second thoughts it seems to me that this is a mistake: it would, I think, be an independent objection to determinism if it could be shown that no intelligible analysis of can- and could- propositions in determinist terms is possible, and this is plainly what Austin has ultimately in mind. Admittedly he has at the most only refuted certain ways of analysing them, but he does seem to think that there is no intelligible mode of analysis compatible with determinism, and it seems incumbent on the determinist to provide such an analysis.

There is however a further point which should be noticed here. In most determinist accounts indeterminism is only asserted in a small minority of cases, namely, in those where a proposed course of behaviour is *both* thought by the agent to be his duty and also goes against his 'strongest desire' at the time. This is the view of e.g. both Professor C. A. Campbell and Professor H. D. Lewis, the chief recent exponents in this country of indeterminism on ethical grounds. Yet they would have to admit that it was still quite correct to say, e.g. that I could have walked a mile in cases where there was no question of its being my duty to do so. They are bound therefore at least to admit besides the indeterminist a determinist sense of 'could', and the argument that no such sense can be intelligibly stated would tell against them as well as against the determinist. If the term 'could' cannot be analysed deterministically, they must either hold that it is untrue that I *can* go for a walk now when it is not my duty and I do not want to do so, or admit that I am free in the indeterminist sense to perform motiveless acts. Unless we make the latter admission— and few indeterminists would make it—we have at least to admit a relative sense of 'can' and 'could' as well as an absolute one, and the interpretation of 'could' in a relative sense is being assailed by Austin. It is also a fact that the distinction between the past indicative and the conditional sense of 'could' on which Austin lays such great stress occurs both in these cases and even in statements about inanimate objects.

I shall not discuss in this article whether the determinists are right or even whether their view can be reconciled with ethics and real freedom. Philosophers have at any rate so far not succeeded in proving determinism to be anything more than at most a possibility which cannot be refuted. Instead of discussing the problem in general on its own merits I shall enter into the linguistic field with Austin. I am at least enough of a linguist to think that it is of some philosophical importance to discuss the logic of 'could' and 'can'. At the same time I, like the contributors to the book, *Freedom and the Will*, recently edited by Pears, hope without here making a frontal attack on the free will problem, to contribute to those connected questions which must be tackled before the problem can be adequately solved. Certainly determinism will not be in a strong position unless it can produce a tenable analysis of the crucial cases of 'could' on which the indeterminist philosopher relies, and if the determinist analysis breaks down the indeterminist in order to understand his own position needs to know just how that happens.

Austin criticizes the view suggested by Moore[1] that 'I could have done A' is to be analysed as 'I should have done A if I had chosen'. I should like first to say a word about Moore's substitution of 'I should have done A if I had chosen' for 'I could have done A if I had chosen'. I do not know why Moore thus changed his analysis, but I can give what seems to me a good reason for rejecting the former analysis, viz. that it defines 'could' in terms of itself. The objection could only be met if it were maintained that there were two different senses of 'could' and we were defining one in terms of the other, but this would leave the second, which might just be the absolute sense of the indeterminist, undefined. Yet the propositions which result from the alternative modes of analysis, though different, entail each other. If it is the case that 'I should have done something if *p*', I obviously 'could have done it if *p*', and 'I could have done it if I had chosen' would ordinarily be understood as entailing that 'I should have done it if I had chosen', since the phrase implies the absence of fatal external obstacles. Austin indeed points out that 'I should have

---

[1] I am not going to discuss Austin's criticism of Nowell-Smith later in the article because I am much more inclined to agree here with Austin's criticisms.

done it if I had chosen' might be used to mean that I should have carried out my decision and not changed my mind,[1] in which case its negation would be in a sense compatible with my having chosen, but it is plain that this usage is not the one involved in the analysis of 'I could' in terms of 'I should if I had chosen'. We plainly should not deny that a man *could* have done something merely because we knew that he was very liable not to carry out his decisions.

Of Moore's view I shall say more later. Austin is concerned rather with examining the alternative analysis of 'could' as 'could if he had chosen'. He points out two very peculiar logical features of this type of ostensible hypothetical.[2] One is that we can infer 'I could' understood categorically, which is certainly very different from the logic of an ordinary hypothetical. We cannot indeed infer that I could have done what I did without choosing to, but we can infer that 'I could' (past indicative, not conditional) have done it without any condition at all being specified. The other logical peculiarity is that from the proposition in question together with the proposition 'I could not' we could not infer that I had not chosen. These pecularities do not affect the proposition 'I should if I had chosen,' for this certainly does not entail 'I did,' while 'I should if I had chosen' together with 'I did not' entails 'I had not chosen.' The peculiarities mentioned are taken to show that the most plausible way of analysing can or could propositions deterministically break down. Austin's explanation of them is that the 'if' in the sentence is not the conditional 'if' at all but expresses doubt or hesitation. This explanation does not seem to me satisfactory. In many cases where the condition given is a presupposition of blame there is no doubt in the speaker's mind that the person did not choose to do what was required and that is why he is blamed for his inaction. Further, the introduction of the protasis even as a subject of doubt would not be to the point if there were no causal or logical connexion between protasis and apodosis such as the ordinary hypothetical expresses. What would be the relevance of doubting whether A had chosen or would choose to do B if his ability to do B or at least his doing B did not depend on his choosing?

Nor can I accept the suggestion made by Prof. O'Connor in his inaugural address to the Joint Session of 1960[3] that 'if'

[1] P. 112 BA, 157 ff PP.   [2] PP. 113 ff BA, 157 ff PP.
[3] *Aristotelian Society Supp.*, Vol. 34 (1960), pp. 5 ff.

here expresses a necessary, though not a sufficient, condition. If it expressed merely a necessary condition, then it would be correct to say that I 'could do' any action which could only be done voluntarily if at all, even in cases where external circumstances or my lack of capacity rendered this quite impossible. It would be one necessary condition of my performing certain surgical operations too complicated to be performed by accident that I should choose to do so, but no one would therefore say that I could perform them or even that I could do so if I chose. I have not the requisite capacity, and if I were mad enough to volunteer to try I should not be allowed. O'Connor argues that the 'if' of sufficient condition cannot be meant because it does not follow that, if I choose to do something, I shall or presumably, that I can do it, as I may be prevented by external circumstances, but in that case the original proposition too that I can or could do it, which we are supposed to be analysing, would be false. It is no objection to a proposed analysans that it may be false if it is false only in cases where the analysandum is false.

It is well to note here a circumstance which ought to serve as a warning against too readily interpreting Austin's account as a victory for indeterminism. It is that the words 'can' and 'could' are also used of inanimate objects and of events which are not conceived as in any way dependent on free will and that as thus used they display the very same logical features which were noticed in Austin's lecture. It may indeed be retorted that this is a different use of 'can' more properly rendered by 'may' or 'might',[1] but at any rate he is debarred from using these logical peculiarities as an argument for undetermined free will if they are also present in cases where the presupposition of free will is never made. And they are so present. I can infer 'this piece of paper can burn' from 'it can burn if exposed to a naked flame' or 'the hurricane could have wrecked the town' from 'the hurricane could have wrecked it if it had diverged from its path by a mile'. (I cannot indeed infer that these things could have happened whether or not the specified conditions were fulfilled, but neither can I infer from: 'he could if he had chosen' that: 'he could whether he had chosen or not.') And I think the second peculiarity is present also, as we shall see, in this kind of propositions.

[1] What Austin says on p. 111 BA, 155 PP and 120 BA, 166 PP suggests that he would have made this retort.

I shall now suggest an alternative explanation of the peculiarities in question. It is an explanation perfectly compatible with 'could' being understood deterministically, though it does not in itself entail determinism. As I have said, 'could' is frequently applied in cases where free will would never be seriously ascribed. I might well say 'the weather this winter could have been better' or 'the car could have gone faster' or 'petrol can explode,' yet if I did, nobody would think that I was ascribing free will to the weather or the car or the petrol. Plainly 'could' here does not mean 'would if it had chosen', but it seems reasonable to say that it means 'would under unspecified conditions of some sort'.[1] Now if 'could' is used in this way, it provides a good explanation why I can do what seems so peculiar, namely, infer '*A* could' from '*A* could if'. If '*A* could' be understood as meaning '*A* would under some conditions or other (unspecified),' this is justified if you show that you are entitled to say that it could under certain partially specified conditions. From 'petrol can explode if a flame is applied to it' we may infer without qualification that it can explode, if '*A* can' means '*A* will under some conditions or other.' It is still right to say 'can' in the second sentence and not 'will', as even under the conditions specified we are only justified in saying that the event happens sometimes and not that it does so always. Where the subject term of the proposition is singular, the analysis would be somewhat different, although in principle similar. 'This car could go faster' might be interpreted as meaning that under some conditions sometimes realized with cars (a better or at least more daring driver, better or less crowded roads) it would go faster. And we can infer from the fact that the car or the winter weather could do better under some specified conditions that 'it could do better' without specifying any conditions. But Austin overlooked one very important assumption without which what he said does not hold, namely the conditions must be assumed possible. We cannot infer from the proposition that 'the average winter temperature would have been over 80 degrees if the sun had shone here with the same directness as in equatorial regions' that therefore 'the winter temperature in England could have been over 80 degrees.' This condition is necessary also in the case of 'I could if I had chosen.' There are many things which I could do if I chose but which it

---

[1] I do not maintain that all 'can' and 'could' propositions are hypothetical but that some are.

is impossible for me to choose to do because it requires more intelligence than I possess to think of them, and those things it would be untrue to say that I could do. The form of the argument is not therefore simply: 'A can if p. ∴ A can,' but 'A can if p. p is possible. ∴ A can.' This brings it nearer to the ordinary hypothetical: 'A has property x if p is true. p is true. ∴ A has property x.'

The foregoing discussion is relevant to Austin's argument that a language cannot contain a verb which can only occur with an if-clause appended to it.[1] (He should surely have said 'understood to be appended', for nobody says that the verb 'can' in all correct uses must have an if-clause actually appended). Austin's argument was that 'I can if y' plus 'y' according to the ordinary logic of hypothetical syllogisms entails 'I can' unqualified by any if-clause. I think O'Connor[2] is right in saying in reply that the sense of 'can' is different in 'I can if y' and 'I can,' the difference being that it is relative in the one case to a more and in the other to a less fully specified set of conditions. When we infer 'A can' from 'A can if y,' we are inferring that since A can under conditions y, A can under some conditions or other. But it does not necessarily follow from this that we could significantly say 'can' as distinct from 'will' without reference to any conditions or that such a 'can' would have any application. On the determinist view proposed 'can' means 'will under certain conditions', and 'can' would then coincide with 'will' in cases where it could be asserted without limitation by any unknown or unspecified conditions. The distinction between the past indicative and the conditional 'could' on which Austin insists would then depend on the relative remoteness or unlikelihood of the conditions with the reservation that where the conditions are thought impossible, the past indicative 'could' must not, but the conditional 'could' with an if-clause might be used.

I think I can also explain why we cannot infer 'not y' from 'A could be B if y' and 'A could not be B.' We have just seen that from 'A can' or 'could be B if y' it follows that 'A can or could be B' (provided y is at all possible). Therefore to say that A could not be B would if, as usually, y is assumed possible, contradict the other premiss in the suggested inference, i.e. the original hypothetical, and so make the inference null and void.

[1] P. 118 BA, 164 PP.   [2] *Loc. cit.*, p. 10.

This would obviously apply equally if A was inanimate. I cannot say consistently both 'This could catch fire if a flame were applied to it' and 'This could not catch fire' as long as it is assumed possible for a flame to be applied to it. If however the assumption is not made, we might be able to infer that y is impossible. If it was true that a particular drug-addict could stop taking the drug if he chose and it was also true that he could not stop taking the drug, it would be a legitimate inference that he could not choose to stop taking the drug. But such inference would be liable to be precarious because new conditions not envisaged in the original statement may be relative to the 'could'. If a doctor said, 'The patient could survive if his temperature were brought down' and later, after the temperature had been brought down, said 'The case is hopeless,' it would not necessarily follow that he was contradicting his original statement. Whether this was so or not would depend largely on the tone of voice in which the doctor said 'could'. If it were said in such a way as to imply dogmatically that there would then be nothing to prevent his surviving, the doctor would have been wrong in one of his two statements, but in that case he might just as well have said 'would'. If however it merely meant that there was a chance of his surviving, this would not be incompatible with dircumstances other than those mentioned rendering survival impossible. Suppose I said to a motorist 'You can get to B in time for lunch if you leave A at 10,' I could not be pronounced wrong if he left A at 10 but could not reach B in time for lunch because he had a collision with another car, but if he had had no delays on the route and affirmed that he had left A at the earliest possible moment, I could rightly infer, if I believed him, that the earliest possible moment was later than 10.

If I am right, Austin's view requires amendment in three respects: (1) The logical characteristics he ascribes to certain can- or could- propositions can only be admitted subject to a reservation which he does not mention, i.e. the condition must be itself possible. (2) Subject to this reservation they apply equally to many can- or could- propositions which have no relation to free will because they deal with inanimate things. In these cases at least they certainly may express causal conditions e.g. 'the petrol can explode if exposed to a naked flame.' (3) The peculiarities depend not on the 'if' being other than the hypothetical 'if' but on the nature of the verb 'can'. The peculiarity of 'can' is that it is relative to unspecified or not fully specified conditions. If all the conditions were specified—and they never can be—it should be on the determinist view still correct but pointless to use the word 'can' because the distinction between 'can' and 'will' would have disappeared.

But how is it that, as Austin points out,[1] there are sentences including 'could or 'can' which do not exhibit the logical peculiarities he mentions but function as ordinary hypotheticals. His example is, 'I can squeeze through if I am thin enough.' From this proposition alone we obviously cannot infer 'I can squeeze through,' and we can infer from it together with the proposition 'I cannot squeeze through' that 'I am not thin enough.' I think the difference between the cases where hypothetical statements including the verb 'can' behave in the normal way and the cases where they do not is that in the latter the protasis gives a condition of the occurrence but not of the ability, while in the former it gives a condition of the ability itself. My choice to do something may be a condition of my doing it, but it is not a condition of my ability to do it as a dispositional property of mine. And the application of a flame to a piece of wood is a condition of its actually catching fire, but not of its having the dispositional property of being liable to catch fire when a flame is applied. The difference between the two kinds of propositions may be expressed by saying that in the latter kind the if-clause is included in the statement defining the ability itself, while in the former kind it gives a condition of possessing the ability. Where the ability itself is defined as the ability to do so-and-so if p, p is not a condition of the possession of the ability expressed by the can-clause but of its exercise. Even an ability 'to do A if one chooses' might figure in the apodosis of a hypothetical which admits the ordinary inferences. Suppose there were a treatment 100% efficacious which would give confirmed drug-addicts the ability to stop taking the drugs if they chose. We could then infer that a drug-addict who had not this ability had not had the treatment. And it would not be permissible to infer that all drug-addicts could stop taking drugs if they chose. (The treatment, even if it were one hundred per cent effective, might be too expensive for some to take it or some might not have heard of it.) This way of talking of course presupposes that abilities are properties which can themselves be acquired (or lost) and are thus subject to causal conditions.

It is easy to see how the general meaning of 'can' leaves the field open for various distinctions of meaning according to the different conditions we have in view when using the verb. I have spoken so far as if '*A* can' or 'could' meant that *A* actually would occur under certain conditions, but this is not adequate, although true so far as it goes, for at least one additional statement is normally implied, namely, that the conditions in question are themselves possible. Now there might seem to be a vicious regress here, since 'possible' is itself a derivative of the Latin verb *posse* which is merely a translation of the verb 'can'. But the regress need not be infinite. I *can* get home tomorrow? How do I know this? The movements concerned are ones which I have constantly made without difficulty, and I have no reason whatever to suspect that I shall be unable to make them tomorrow. The regress thus has a finite terminus in certain categorical propositions positive and negative, i.e. *A* has occurred many times in the past and there are no causes of which we know that will prevent *A* happening tomorrow. The ultimate logical reason why it can so end in a categorical proposition without 'can' or 'could' is that such a proposition always entails one with 'can' or 'could'—'*S* is *P*' entails '*S* can be *P*,' '*S* was *P*' entails '*S* could be *P*' (past indicative, not conditional could). This last 'can' is not hypothetical. There is usually not much point in saying that *S* can be P when we already know that *S* is *P*, so we do not say it, but it is none the less true, and it is an inductive basis for arguments that *S* can again be *P*. I walked on the 1st, 2nd . . . 31st of last month, therefore I was able to walk then, this is an inductive ground for saying I am still able unless conditions have changed in a relevant way, and there is a total absence of evidence in support of the view that conditions have changed or will change by tomorrow in such a way that when I try to walk I shall fail.

I have above used both the phrase '*A* can do *B*' and '*B* can happen.' What is the significance of the difference between the two phrases? It seems to be that the former makes the occurrence or non-occurrence of *B* dependent on *A*. This usage is specially associated with those actions in human beings which are called free but is not limited to those. Austin indeed speaks as if we ought never to use 'can' or 'could', only 'may' or 'might', of inanimate things, but although this usage is more common, I cannot see that the other is wrong, and there are some cases where it is much more appropriate to say 'can' even of things than to say 'may' or 'might'. An example would be 'the car can get me to London in two hours.' Actually something different would be meant here if we said 'may' or 'might', since these words connote an uncertainty not connoted by 'can'.[1] But now we come to a feature of the logic of 'can' and 'could' which is different in cases where we should be inclined to speak of human freedom and in cases where we should not. Nobody would say that a certain car could not get him to London in two hours if the reasons why he did not get there in that time, though quite compelling, were unconnected with the nature of the car. It would still be said that the car could have got him to London in the time if the reason why it did not get him there was that there was nobody to drive it (or drive it really efficiently) or that he was detained on the way by an appointment. But it would be said that the car could not get him there if its engine was in such a condition that it broke down on the way without an externally caused accident. With human beings, however, we should be much more inclined to say that they could have done something which they did not do if whether or not they did it depended on them and to say that they could not have done it if external circumstances prevented them. There thus exists a diametrical opposition between the way in which we sometimes use 'could' of human beings and the way in which we use it of inanimate things. We must note however that this does not hold in all cases. We sometimes use 'could' of men in a similar sense to that in which we use it of things. That occurs when the reference is to abilities or inabilities. It is correct to say that A 'could' or even 'can' beat B at tennis even when external circumstances make a game between the two impossible, but one certainly would not say that he could have beaten B if what prevented him was relative lack of ability in the game. On the other hand we should say that he could have beaten him if he lost because for some reason, not externally compelling, he did not try or did not try hard enough to win. This supports the view that there is a special sense of 'can' and 'could' connected with voluntary action such as the indeterminists have fastened on, though I think even a determinist can make a distinction between this and other senses of the verb can.

[1] Such uncertainty might or might not be connoted if I said 'could'.

Now for us to be able to speak of 'can' or 'could' in the sense which is especially relevant to human freedom, it is certainly not sufficient that the negative condition of there being no causes outside us, let alone no causes known by us, to prevent us from acting should be fulfilled. This would not be enough either for the determinist or the indeterminist. For us to be free what we do must not merely not be prevented from outside, it must be positively produced by ourselves. For this reason it seems to me quite wrong to describe free acts as uncaused. If my acts are not caused by anything at all, they are not caused by me, and therefore I am no more to blame for them than if somebody else had done them and I had had no share in influencing his actions. It has been argued that determinism is incompatible with responsibility, but whether this is true or not it is quite certain that *indeterminism* thus understood is incompatible with responsibility. What I think the indeterminists really want to say (and sometimes, but not always, succeed in saying) is that our free actions are caused (by ourselves) but caused in such a way that their nature is not completely fixed by any preceding events or any pre-existing qualities in ourselves or in anything else. This would be sufficient to escape the conclusion they dread and not altogether unplausibly think incompatible with moral responsibility, namely, that everything that happens is fixed in advance so that it could have been predicted from any earlier state of the universe by a being who knew fully the state of affairs at that earlier time and the relevant causal laws and was intelligent enough at causal prediction. It should be noted here that causation must come in at three points on any tenable view of free action. (1) Our physical acts must be determinable by our choices in order to be free. (2) Our choices must be determined by ourselves. (3) The choices (or the states of mind in which we choose) obviously are determined partly at least, though not necessarily wholly, by previous events.

I should now like to give a definition of a relevant sense of 'can' or 'could' which might be accepted by the determinist and then consider very briefly what could be meant by the unconditional 'could' of the indeterminist. If we think of 'could' positively in terms of production by causes, the sense of 'could' will still vary according to the causes to which we think it relative. This being so it is reasonable to say that an action cannot be free unless it is at least immediately dependent on the agent whether the action is done or not. (Without this it would not even be called an action—it would not be an action of mine to be hit by a rock the fall of which I had not anticipated.) This minimum condition of freedom is however of course insufficient. Nor need even the determinist admit that it is sufficient. What even he wants to say is not that an act is free in so far as it depends on *any* qualities in the agent but in so far as it depends on certain qualities, which might be summed up under the heading of 'volitional'. Hence Moore's suggested analysis of an act which I was free to do as 'an act which I should have done if I had chosen'. Moore did not, as Austin seems to think,[1] put forward the view that 'I could have if I had chosen 'means the same as 'I should have if I had chosen' but only the different view that 'I could have' (unqualified), in the sense in which it is specially relevant to ethics, means the same as 'I should have if I had chosen.'[2]

It has been objected to any definition of Moore's type that choice is too closely connected with action to be regarded as a cause which produces the action. But: (*a*) the conditions to which 'can' is relevant, though usually causal, need not always be so. A conditional may well signify not causation but inclusion. If *A* includes *B*, *A* certainly cannot occur without *B* any more than if *B* is a necessary causal condition. (*b*) While it is at least plausible to maintain that choice is not a cause but a constituent of the mental state which is the counterpart of the physical act a man chooses to do, I cannot see any good reason for saying that choice as part of a mental state may not be a cause of a physical action, and mostly the 'can' or 'could' in these cases refers to a physical action. And (*c*) where what we choose to do is to engage in a purely mental activity, e.g. to think about the next sentence before writing it down, it seems to me that the mental activity in question is distinct from and subsequent to the decision to engage in it. It seems to me clear that an analysis more or less on the lines of Moore's gives one important meaning of 'can' or 'could'. For the determinist it will be the meaning in which moral action can be said to presuppose the freedom expressed by the verb 'can'.

But the indeterminists are of course not satisfied with this. Some, though not all or even most, go so far as to deplore the use of the word 'cause' at all in connection with free actions, but even if these are not determined by causes in all their features

[1] P. 119 BA, 165 PP.   [2] *Ethics*, p. 131.

I do not see how anybody can deny that causation plays a considerable part. Melden[1] argues that the concept of causation cannot be applied to the operation of a volition, because causation is not a logical relation and a volition is logically related to its alleged effects. A volition can only be defined as a volition to do something and therefore there is a logical relation and not a causal relation between it and what we do. This argument assumes the rejection of a view of causation which was generally accepted by philosophers at one time and is not without its supporters even today, i.e. the view which assimilates causation to a logical relation between cause and effect. I have defended this view of causation elsewhere,[2] but even if I was wrong and it is a quite mistaken view, I do not see that Melden's argument would carry us very far. It seems to me that he has confused the statement that the notion of a volition logically entails a reference to the notion of the action willed with the statement that the notion of a volition logically entails the occurrence of the action willed. The latter is plainly false since the volition may occur without the action. As far as I can see, the same confusion has affected Melden's account of desires and motives. I can describe a desire specifically only in terms of what is desired, but it certainly does not logically entail the occurrence of what is desired. If it did all desires would be satisfied. Therefore it can still act as a cause even if a cause never logically entails the existence of its effect.

My argument about volition here has not assumed that all voluntary actions are preceded by a specific act of volition, only that some are. That I sometimes decide to do something and then do it just because I have decided to do so surely cannot be denied by anybody except a sheer behaviourist or one who thinks that mental events have no effect on physical, and if it is false it will be futile for me to try to think any more about what I shall write in this paper because my decisions will in that case have no effect whatever on what I do write. I think that a determinist at any rate will do well to adopt a definition at least rather like Moore's of 'could' in the sense in which it is regarded as the prerequisite of moral responsibility and that even an indeterminist should regard such a sense as one important sense of 'can' or 'could'. It does seem as if such a sense must be the

---

[1] *Free Action.*   [2] No. 6 above.

sense to go on at any rate in computing legal responsibility, since, even if one's acts of choice are 'undetermined', we can hardly verify scientifically whether a particular act of choice is undetermined. Even with those blameworthy acts which are not preceded by a volition or decision, I think we could always say as Moore suggests, that if the agent had chosen to act differently he would have done so. A man might fly into a rage and assault somebody or be grossly careless with his car without making any definite choice to act in such a way, but in that case we should still deem him responsible because he would have acted differently if he had chosen, and this is covered by Moore's account. Whether it would be better to have recourse here to the verb *try* than to the verb *choose*, as has been suggested, is a question of detail. I should prefer 'choose' because not all choices involve effort. The notion of trying is covered by that of choice if we include under the latter persisting in our choice even when circumstances and our desires make it hard to persist.

But if we are said to be free when we do what we choose to do or at any rate what we should have avoided doing if we had chosen, the question presents itself—Are we free to choose? This question leads up to the rift between determinists and indeterminists. Is it any good saying 'we are free' means 'we can do what we choose' if we are not free to choose, and on a determinist view can we ever be said to be free to choose? The best course for the determinist in face of this difficulty is, I think, to reply that choices are free at any rate in the sense of depending on us. It does not follow, because the freedom of an act has been defined in terms of choice, that therefore the freedom of choice will have to be defined in terms of another choice. The indeterminist of course will then object that my nature on the determinist view is ultimately determined not by myself but by my ancestors, matter or God, and that therefore on this view I can never really be free. But I am not trying to settle this wider issue in my paper, my aim is simply to give modes of analysis of could-propositions both in determinist and in indeterminist terms. Now, proceeding with our study of the determinist mode of definition, I must point out that there is at least one strangely overlooked kind of case where the determinist himself would have to admit that there was something which it was not possible to say we could have done, although we should have done it if we had chosen and although even the immediate reason why we did not do it lay in our own nature and not in external circumstances. This is the case where a person could have done something if he had chosen but did not choose to do it because it did not occur to him, though it would have occurred to a more intelligent, or differently constituted, person. Here at any rate Moore's definition breaks down. It cannot be said that the man could have done A. Yet he would have done A if he had chosen. Further, it is not that he was prevented by external circumstances from choosing. It was his own nature which prevented him from thinking of the best thing to do, but it was his intellectual, not his volitional nature, and it need not even have been ultimately due (though it may have been) to bad choices in the past involving a voluntary misuse of or voluntary neglect to make the best of his intellectual powers.

Of the determinist sense of 'could' I have elsewhere[1] suggested an alternative analysis not very dissimilar from Moore's. I suggested that the determinist might say that A could have acted differently when and only when a certain difference in his volition without any other difference in the situation not consequent causally on the difference in his volition would have resulted in a different act. It is not intended to suggest that this is the only sense of 'could' in which a determinist may use the term, but at any rate it is the sense bound up with praise- or blame-worthiness and moral responsibility. The term 'difference in volition' was intended to cover (1) deciding to do something else, (2) deciding instead of not making any decision at all or vice versa, (3) exercising more or less effort in carrying out the decision. This analysis would cover the case I have just mentioned because for a person to choose to do something which had not occurred to him the situation would have had to be different otherwise than in respect of volition, i.e. thoughts which were not in his mind would have had to be present, and as a condition not as an effect, of his volition.

If we define the determinist 'could' in this way, we can see how it connects with moral responsibility. It is generally agreed that we can only blame somebody for volitional faults or for what results from these, and the determinist can easily explain this by saying that the purpose of blame is to discourage repetition, and it obviously can succeed in this purpose only by affecting

[1] *Second Thoughts in Moral Philosophy*, p. 160 ff.

the agent's volition. It is also the case that volitional faults are commonly held to be intrinsically evil, whereas merely intellectual defects are not, and I do not see why a determinist should not hold this view. Something might be intrinsically evil although it was caused. If he does hold the view, he can also justify blame as an appropriate recognition of the evil in the man blamed. In either case it is right to say that 'A is to blame (morally) for an act' entails that the quality of the act is due to and therefore displays a volitional fault, and it could not be due to or give any indication of such a fault if no difference in the agent's volition would have produced a preferable act. Now in the case where a man could and would have done A if he had chosen but did not choose to do A because he did not think of it, his omission to do A, however unfortunate, was not due to a volitional but to an intellectual defect, and therefore he is not liable to moral blame for it in itself, though he might in some cases be blamed on the ground e.g. that it would have occurred to him to do A if he had not been a habitually selfish person who hardly ever bothered to think about the interests of anybody else. Suppose again the man thought of doing A but did not do it because, through a factual mistake, he thought A to be wrong and not the right thing to do. In that case it would be correct to say that he could have done A, at least in the determinist and perhaps even in the indeterminist sense. But he would not be liable to blame, though he had done a wrong act, because his doing so was due to an intellectual and not to a volitional defect. But suppose his error was not factual but ethical. In that case it would be a disputed question whether he was to blame or not. Certainly for the grosser kinds of moral errors such as those of sincere Nazis I should find it very difficult to refuse to admit blameworthiness. However if moral errors were held blameworthy, they could still be brought under the heading of volitional rather than of intellectual faults on the ground that the moral error consisted in directing one's will to wrong ends and not merely in a mistake as to the means.

What about an indeterminist analysis of 'can' and 'could'? We cannot say that such an analysis makes it relative to no causal conditions at all in the sense of holding that 'can' means that we may do what we choose whatever our previous circumstances and external environment. It must envisage a limited number of alternatives and can only imply (if applicable at all) that it is not determined by antecedent causes which of these possible

things we shall choose to do. But it may still be absolute in the
sense that 'can' does not now mean we 'could or should do if . . .'.
The indeterminist conception indeed shares with the determinist
the positive conception of our determining our actions by choice,
but it adds the negative conception that this choice is not itself
determined completely (though influenced) by antecedent events.

XII

RELIGIOUS ASSERTIONS IN THE LIGHT OF CONTEMPORARY PHILOSOPHY

Today the questions most commonly asked by philosophical critics of religion, at least in this country, relate not to the truth or falsity of religious assertions but to their meaning. To be fair to the philosophers, however, we must of course realize that very few, if any, of those who have denied 'meaningfulness' to religious statements were using 'meaning' in other than a technical sense. They did not mean that the sentence 'God loves us' conveys nothing at all, that it is like 'schwarzibarshinee'. What they meant was that it *expresses* an attitude of mind but *states* nothing that can be true or false. This is often expressed by saying that these sentences have no *factual* meaning or no objective meaning. All sincerely uttered sentences express an attitude of mind, if only that of theoretical belief, but not all state anything. Questions, exclamations and commands do not, and neither, it is claimed, do religious sentences properly understood, the reason usually given for saying this being that no possible experience can establish or refute them. Of the two functions, expressing an attitude and stating a fact, it is held they fulfil only the former, or at least in so far as they make a factual assertion it is only about the experience of the speaker. A possible way of putting this would be indeed to say that they are not statements or assertions at all but merely appear to be so on a superficial view.

Now there is no doubt that a sentence which verbally appears like a statement of fact may be emotive or practical and not informative. The former is the case with most poetry. Again, if I say 'I want you to go,' this is a form of words which ostensibly gives information about the condition of my desires but is fundamentally an exhortation to go (practical function). It is something of this kind that is being said of religious assertions except that emotive and practical functions are here combined in a very much more complicated way than in at least my second example. Only, while in the cases I have just given the sentences were presumably not intended as information by the persons who uttered them, there can be no doubt that most religious people have always held that when speaking religiously they did assert facts. So what is meant can hardly be that religious assertions have no objective meaning in the sense that they are not intended to assert anything objective but only in the sense that they somehow fail of their intention, though not in the way in which does a factually false assertion supposed by the asserter to be true. What is claimed is that, owing to the lack of reference to ordinary experience by which the assertions could be tested, there is nothing in the mind of the person who makes them which could *conceivably* be objectively true (except of course for any ordinary empirical propositions which have their place in a religious context). He thinks there is something more but he is mistaken, having taken what is really a subjective expression of his emotions and moral principles to be an objective assertion about a trans-empirical reality. In regard to this view of religious assertions I shall maintain both that it is groundless and that, if true, it would leave very little of value in religion.

To take the second point first, it has been suggested that what religion does is, like poetry, just express certain more or less emotional states of mind which need have no more objective or intellectual basis than the poet's delight at kinship with nature on a sunny day or the awe he may feel at the sight of storm-capped mountains. I have been told that Wittgenstein once admitted that he would be prepared to say that God created the world but that he meant by this simply that he had a feeling of security about the course of the world. If this is a correct report, it provides an admirable example of the simpler form of the view of religion in question. But surely any such view is open to the gravest objections from the point of view of the religious man. Emotion, at least except in pathological cases and perhaps even then, requires some objective belief, true or false, about the real to support it for long, and if it exists without knowledge or a rationally founded objective belief with which it is in agreement, it is to be condemned as irrational and unfitting. The emotion of fear is irrational (though for some people psychologically inevitable) in cases where there is no reason to anticipate harm from the feared object, the emotion of admiration in cases where there is nothing worth admiring. Similarly if there is no warrant for thinking that the world is really controlled for the best, the feeling of security and peace which a religious man has can only be described as the enjoyment of a fool's paradise. It is comparable to the attitude of a student who should feel blissfully confident of getting a first when according to his teachers there was no good reason to suppose that he would even pass. That is not religion. And similarly with any other emotions which depend on religion.

It will be said indeed that religion is not merely a feeling but a much more complex mental attitude, but all mental attitudes require some objective conditions if they are to be appropriate. If we have no ground for thinking these conditions fulfilled, still more presumably if it is meaningless to suppose they could be, the attitude is as unfitting as it is unfitting to rejoice at something hateful or be angry with an inanimate thing. It might be argued on purely utilitarian grounds that it is worth having the benefits of religion for its effects in the way of increased happiness and goodness even if from an objective point of view there is no warrant for it and the attitude involved is therefore only in one respect unfitting, but it is certainly an essential part of religion to regard the attitudes it inculcates as intrinsically and supremely fitting. According to all highly developed religions it is very evil to worship what is not worthy of worship. Yet if there is thought to be no objective justification for belief in God all worship of God becomes idolatry. Nor is it easy to see how a religious attitude could long survive the conviction that reality is not such as to warrant it.

But besides the emotional and the intellectual there is the conative practical side, and it has been held that religion can be reduced mainly to this. The clearest and, at the moment at least, the most familiar exposition of this view is provided by Professor R. B. Braithwaite in *An Empiricist's View of the Nature of Religious Belief*,[1] and I shall deal with this as a straightforward, clear, brief exposition with which a number of you will be already familiar. Braithwaite maintains that religious assertions are primarily declarations of adherence to a policy of action, declarations of commitment to a way of life. I agree that this brings one nearer to the heart of religion than any view which discusses it primarily in terms of emotional attitudes and even that such commitment to a way of life is the most important feature of religion, but it still seems to me that one must urge against this view the same type of argument as I used against the emotional interpretation of religion.

[1] The Ninth Arthur Stanley Eddington Memorial Lecture, Cambridge University Press, 1955.

H

For just as an emotion is irrational and unfitting unless objectively founded, so is a policy of action wrong unless objectively justified. In saying this I am not just asserting the 'objective' theory of ethics. I hold such a theory, but this is not the topic for discussion here. What I mean is that any theory of ethics, whether objective or not, must recognize that there are certain factual conditions which make us say something is good and something else bad, one act right and another wrong, and justify these statements in whatever sense of justification is admitted by one's ethical philosophy, while in their absence the ethical judgements become wrong in whatever sense an ethical judgement can be so. Thus even on a thoroughly subjective theory of ethics, if a person has condemned A because he thought A killed B and then finds that A did not even try to do so, he must withdraw his condemnation of A. This may or may not involve saying that A's action or state of mind has not, while on the former view it had, the non-natural quality of badness, but at least it must be admitted that whether one ethical judgement is to be preferred to another or not depends on the actual situation and therefore on objective facts, including under this heading facts about the states of mind of the persons concerned. Braithwaite himself says, quoting Hare, that 'an ultimate decision to accept a way of life "far from being arbitrary . . . would be the most well-founded of decisions because it would be based upon a consideration of everything upon which it could possibly be founded".'[1] This implies that on his view ethical decisions are in this sense objectively founded: if so, religion as an ethical policy should be objectively founded, and I shall contend that the ways in which religion is commonly used to give reinforcement to ethics all presuppose that religion is objectively founded.

In what way can religion function as a basis of ethical policy on Braithwaite's view? For him ethical and religious assertions are both declarations of behaviour policy, and the fundamental difference between them is that in religion behaviour policies are associated with the thinking of certain 'stories'.[2] That these stories help many people to carry out their ethical policy is a matter, he claims, of empirical fact, and the different religions are distinguished chiefly by the different stories used to help their adherents to live a good life. He insists that to be a Christian one must

---

[1] op. cit., p. 34; Hare, Language of Morals, p. 69.

[2] The term 'stories' is preferred by Braithwaite as 'neutral', implying neither that the story is believed nor that it is disbelieved (p. 26).

entertain (bear in mind) the Christian stories but that one need not believe them to be true, and that even without this belief they can have their ethical effect.

Now we need not deny that 'stories', even if not accepted as true, may still psychologically help a man to lead a good ethical life, but what I do deny is that they can provide a reason (or additional reason) for living ethically, and I shall further insist that by far the greater part of any efficacy they have depends on an objective grounding of some kind. It seems to me that the stories fall into two main classes, not always sharply separable (especially in Christianity). First, there are stories of noble deeds done by human beings and, more generally, stories of human actions which in various ways illustrated ethical laws. The efficacy of these is not necessarily impaired or at least much impaired if they are not thought to be a correct account of actual happenings. They are often, as in the parables, not even put forward as such. But in two ways the stories, if apposite at all, will be objectively founded, and their value depends largely on that. (*a*) It does not matter greatly whether any particular such story is true or false, but if it were thought that a particular height of e.g. fortitude or unselfish love illustrated in a story had never been attained by any human being, this would lessen the influence of the story on anybody except a person who could aspire to rise altogether above the level of other men. (*b*) Quite fictitious stories may exercise a great ethical influence because through a fictitious medium they bring out the nature of certain factors present in real life.[1] The most potent way of getting a person to do right is to make him love goodness when he sees it, and a man of great literary power may make a person see and love goodness when he would not otherwise have seen or loved it. The same, *mutatis mutandis*, with badness. But then, in so far as the influence is ethically satisfactory, it is effected by bringing out the real factual nature of certain qualities, so that we, seeing them to be what they really are, see them to be good (or bad). Only that is a point that can appeal to the thorough secularist as much as to the most devout believer. So far we are wholly in the realm of ethics without any specific reference to religion.

[1] Incidentally when Braithwaite (p. 27) cites the *Pilgrim's Progress* as an example of a work of fiction which has had a great religious influence, he seems to be forgetting that the work was admittedly intended as an allegory, i.e. it claims to be picturing by fictitious characters just what the author regards as objectively true, as with Christ's parables.

Secondly, there are stories about God. To give a complete account one would have to deal with intermediate cases, but I do not think that these raise any additional points of principle. Now it can hardly be doubted that a religious person may be very much helped to lead a better life by stories about God. He may be prompted to be much more careful than he otherwise would be as to what he does and even what he thinks by thinking of God as knowing everything he does and thinks. He may refrain from sins he would otherwise have committed because he feels they would offend God and he is unwilling to offend a being whom he loves and regards as loving him. He may be encouraged to persevere courageously through adversity because he believes that God will see that everything works out for good in the end or even because he believes it to be God's will, though this story can be used in a less edifying fashion. He may be more disposed to be charitable and forgiving to other men because he thinks of them as all God's children and so his brothers and sisters. At a lower level he may try more to do right and avoid doing wrong because he thinks he will be rewarded or punished by God according to what he does, though the appeal to this motive is not without its moral disadvantages. But why do these stories help? Is it not only or mainly because they are regarded as objectively true or at least as symbolizing an objective truth? Two accounts may be given here. It may be said (and this is certainly true, though it is not the whole truth) that what a person who speaks like this is doing is telling the stories to himself and others as additional *reasons* for doing his duty over and above those which a secularist has. If we believe in ethics, there is no doubt at all that a secularist has also good reason for doing his duty, and indeed if we see something to be our duty this ought to be sufficient without other reasons to make us do it. But when doing one's duty is hard, additional reasons why a man should do it may be badly needed to increase the likelihood of his doing it and the religious man may by his stories supply these. A story, however, certainly cannot provide a good reason for doing anything unless the story is true. If it is not true, no conclusion as to action can be drawn from it whatever. If I believe that I shall hurt somebody I love by doing *A*, this is a reason against doing it, but if I now discover that I shall not hurt him in the least, the reason just disappears and it is no use repeating the story as a fiction. Similarly surely with the stories about God. Secondly, it may, however, be urged that to talk in terms of reasons for acting rightly is an inadequate account of the influence of religion, though true as far as it goes. It may be not so much that the man who has acquired an effective religion is given new reasons for doing right but that his whole emotional attitude to life is altered by religion so that what would have been impossible or very difficult for him before is now relatively easy. This brings us back to the emotional aspect of religion again, though only as a means to the ethical, and I can only repeat what I have said before that, unless certain propositions of a metaphysical kind are objectively true, the religious emotions felt in contemplating the universe are totally unfitting to their object and it is difficult to see how they could long survive the thorough conviction that these propositions could not possibly be true. I do not wish to maintain that the function of religion is simply to provide extra reasons for doing one's duty. If its object is real, it is also an end in itself and the highest kind of life is impossible without it, but I do not see how the entertaining of the idea of God by a person who believes that God could not possibly exist objectively could be the foundation of these values. A man may be at peace because he believes he is in the hands of God, but he will not be at peace because he imagines a God who he believes could not possibly exist. The same I should have thought applies to any other values besides peace that can be obtained from religion.

I have argued that the stories, unless true, provide no reason for any course of action based on them. But it would be objected by some philosophers, of whom I much fear Braithwaite is one, that 'reasons' in ethics does not mean 'arguments to justify a certain course' but only 'considerations which in fact make people inclined to act in a certain way'. It may then be claimed that as an empirical fact the stories do have this effect even when not believed and there is no more to be said on the matter. But how is this known? It would have to be a purely empirical question, and nobody can claim that there are sufficient data for giving even a probable answer to it. For the people who use the stories habitually and do not believe them are as yet far too rare for a generalization to be possible. Even if it can be shown empirically that people who think habitually in terms of the stories are on the average better than people who do not, this will not help, for the vast majority of the people who have thought in terms of the stories up to the present have believed them to be true either literally or at least symbolically and so their conduct can provide no evidence that these are ethically efficacious when not believed. Braithwaite would say that he is ethically benefited himself, but different people may be benefited by different psychological techniques, and there is no evidence that his medicine is helpful at least to more than a very small minority. The universal claim of religion has disappeared.

Further, even if it should turn out empirically that religious stories could be very helpful to many people who intellectually repudiated their truth this might easily be explained in two ways. (1) Religious stories, like many secular stories, commonly depict ethical actions of an exalted kind and so focus one's attention on an ideal. (2) It is not true that a person must either believe all the time or not believe all the time, and I suggest that, in so far as a person who denies that he believes in these stories is helped by them otherwise than in the purely ethical way just mentioned, it may be because, when he thinks of them in a religious way, he is really believing them 'at the bottom of his heart' or at least half-believing them, though at other times he can quite honestly and correctly say that he does not believe them. The effect on his emotions and actions produced by the stories at the times he believed them might persist even at times when he explicitly disbelieved them, as it admittedly can at times when he is not explicitly thinking of them.

We must not assume that all symbolic use of religious statements is of the kind Braithwaite has in mind when he talks about stories. He quotes a report of the Commission on Doctrine in the Church of England as supporting the symbolic use of religious language,[1] but the reason given in the quotation is that the statements are 'pictorial expressions of spiritual truths', not that they are ethically effective without expressing any truth. For all of us expressions which are not taken to be literally true can be of value as symbolizing some truth which we cannot express at all or realize vividly enough without the help of symbols, but this is not to say that the symbolical expressions can be profitably used without caring or reflecting whether they are true or false as regards their ultimate meaning, though this may be the case as regards their literal meaning.

The view of religion I have criticized would destroy any universal claim of religion on all men, and make it merely a psychological technique for benefiting some; it would deprive the religious man

[1] *op. cit.*, p. 28.

of the comfort, happiness, serenity, incentive which come from believing that things are ultimately ordered for the best; it would deprive him of the conviction that he was in touch with the fundamental nature of reality when he was at his best, and it would make the experience of those who are convinced they are an illusion. I cannot see that it would, if carried out logically, leave much of religion that was worth having at all. Yet, if the arguments commonly used by the school of philosophers to which Braithwaite belongs are valid, he can only be congratulated on the courage and skill with which he has carried out the desperate salvage operation needed to recover a small fraction of what the sceptics have destroyed. However, it does not seem to me that there is the slightest need for the salvage operation, for I do not think that any good arguments at all have been produced for saying that religious assertions have no factual meaning. I do not, of course, think there are no difficulties about them or that their justification is a simple matter; what I do say is that there is no case at all for ruling them out *en masse* as devoid of factual meaning and so incapable on principle of being true. The remainder of this lecture will be devoted to trying to show this to be so.

A word is necessary first about the meaning of 'factual'. The terms 'facts' is by modern philosophers commonly limited to empirical facts such as could be the object of observation and natural science, and in that sense the existence of God is not a fact. This is not, however, the usual meaning of the word outside the books and lectures of these philosophers. The proposition that nothing can exist except the type of object we know in science and ordinary sense-experience is certainly not known to be true, and if other things do exist there will certainly be facts about them (in a well-recognized sense of 'fact'). The metaphysician who claims to have discovered something about them may therefore sensibly claim that he is giving 'factual information', though not about the empirical facts of ordinary life. The modern philosophers I am criticizing are those who have dismissed this claim as on principle meaningless.

Arguments to the effect that religious assertions cannot have factual meaning have commonly been based on the verification principle. According to this a sentence can only have factual meaning, i.e. meaning of a kind which admits of its being informative, if it is capable in principle of verification by sense-experience, and it seems plain that specifically religious sentences are not so capable. If so it follows at once that they have no factual meaning. The verification principle is however itself in by no means such a flourishing condition as it was twenty years ago, even among the philosophers who are sympathetic to this way of thinking. As has been repeatedly pointed out, even the most respectable scientific propositions are not capable of direct verification by sense-experience, and the principle, if carried out strictly, would result in the denial of all natural laws and the reduction of the world to one's own sense-data, surely a *reductio ad absurdum*. Further, the verification principle is itself not verifiable. The reply is made that it is not a factual statement and therefore does not on its own terms need verification, but certainly if it is to be used as a premiss for any conclusion it must need some justification. It is not claimed that it is self-evident, and it is most difficult to see what the justification could be. In fact the principle is now commonly defended rather as a methodological assumption than as a true proposition, but a method cannot be regarded as a premiss to prove anything. If the verification principle is to be used to prove that religious assertions cannot be true, it must be itself true, as must any premiss if it is to justify a conclusion.

In order to see how the verification principle is used as an argument against the view that religious assertions can have factual meaning, I shall again fall back on Braithwaite's book as presenting the argument clearly and simply.[1] He divides statements into three classes according to their method of verification and then denies that religious statements can properly be included in any of the three. From this he concludes that, though they have an important function, they can have no factual meaning, and there is no doubt that his argument would be accepted in general by a great many other contemporary philosophers. While I realize that we cannot just identify religion with belief in God, it will be most convenient to discuss this question, as Braithwaite does, in terms of evidence for or against the existence of God.

(1) The first of the three classes into which statements are divided consists of those which are testable by direct observation, by sense-experience. Obviously we cannot justify religious statements in this simple fashion and so I shall not go further into this class of statements.

(2) The second class is that consisting of explanatory hypotheses. These need not be directly verifiable by a single sense-experience

[1] p. 4 ff.

and may introduce concepts which are validated only by the fact that they serve to explain and predict experiences without themselves standing for anything observable. Now propositions introducing God have no doubt been put forward as providing an explanation of our experience and so far they bear a resemblance to scientific hypotheses. But Braithwaite argues that, if the belief in God is to be like a scientific hypothesis, there must be certain possible experiences which, if they occurred, would constitute a refutation of it, yet the religious man will insist that we ought to hold on to our faith whatever happens. But it may well be replied that, if the cosmic process as a whole through its entire duration could be known to be of a certain character, this would really constitute a refutation of the belief in God, only that it is of such a kind cannot be known by us since, however bad the part which we experience here and now may be, it is always possible that later parts will redeem the badness (either for us if we survive bodily death or at least for humanity as a whole). Provided the belief in God is justified as things stand, it might then be justifiable to say that we should hold to the faith whatever happened, simply because nothing that could happen in the very limited part of the whole in space and time which we can know could constitute a refutation of the existence of God. But I do not see that the religious believer, unless he thinks that God's existence can be known intuitively with certainty or proved quite conclusively *a priori*, need mind admitting that, if certain empirical conditions had been fulfilled up to the present, this would have made the belief in an omnipotent good God unreasonable. Suppose everybody in the world were in intense pain all the time, and suppose nobody ever helped anybody else or did anything at all because they thought it their duty, but everybody maliciously desired that everybody else except himself should continue to be in pain, then I think *this* belief would be unreasonable, whether it is reasonable as things are or not. But what precise degree of evil and what diminution in the amount of good would make the belief unreasonable if it is now reasonable, it might still be impossible to specify. The situation is not so totally different from that of certain scientific hypotheses as one might think. For many hypotheses in science are justified as the explanation of a whole extremely complex set of facts, and it would be impossible, I imagine, to obtain an agreed account as to precisely how much evidence to the contrary would require the abandonment of the hypothesis.

H*

(3) We now turn to *a priori* arguments. I accept the view mentioned in this connexion by Braithwaite that a logically necessary proposition cannot assert existence, but of the arguments for God only the so-called ontological proof is committed to claiming that it can. The ontological argument I certainly reject, but in doing so I am in the company of very many, perhaps the majority of, metaphysical theologians, including St Thomas himself. The cosmological argument is not purely *a priori* but has an empirical premiss, though a very general one, namely that something exists, and though it implies that in one sense God's existence is necessary, it does not like the ontological argument imply that there would be a formal logical contradiction in denying God. It does not in the least follow because they cannot prove existential propositions without the help of an empirical premiss that therefore *a priori* arguments cannot give new information not included in their premisses. This is often asserted,[1] but I do not see how it can be reconciled with even such a fact as that we can infer the height of a mountain by mathematics from the distance between the foot of the mountain and a given point and the angle of projection from that point of the summit. I do not see how scientific inferences of this kind can be reconciled with the view now commonly held that the necessity of *a priori* propositions and arguments is dependent on the way in which we use language any more than the *a priori* arguments of philosophical theology. I therefore do not see that modern logic has refuted in principle the possibility even of a logically certain demonstration of the existence of God provided one of the premisses for the demonstration is empirical. However, in common with most philosophers today, religious and otherwise, I do not myself think that this is the sort of thing that could be logically proved, even with the help of an empirical premiss.

I do think, however, that the threefold classification given is far from constituting an exhaustive classification of the ways of testing and establishing propositions. For one thing the classification does not cover ethical propositions, but I shall not go into that now, though it should be noted that those religious assertions which are value judgements such as that God is good can only be objective if ethical judgements are so, as I believe they are. Secondly, a synthesis is possible of the second and third method of proof. *A*

---

[1] Braithwaite does not base his argument on this, but attacks on metaphysics have certainly been based on it.

priori arguments give certainty in mathematics because we can, either immediately or after a process of checking, get quite clear as to the argument, but this is not the case with philosophical arguments (whether metaphysical or non-metaphysical). Philosophical arguments depend on concepts in regard to which the course of controversy has shown that it is impossible or at least has so far proved impossible for the human mind to become so completely clear as to arrive at universally agreed conclusions as in mathematics. But an argument may not give certainty and yet support a conclusion strongly. So in the absence of certainty the two methods may be used to confirm each other. A metaphysical theory might be vindicated *both* as an explanation of our experience and also as rendered probable by various *a priori* lines of argument emanating from our experience.

There remains the claim that in some way men can have intuitive knowledge of God, intuitive at least in the sense of not being the result wholly of an inference of any kind. It has been argued that this is impossible because immediate awareness can only tell us that we have a certain experience, not that anything objective exists beyond our experience. But this surely begs the question. How can we know that it is not possible to be aware of the existence of God otherwise than by inference or by sense-experience? The claim is not that people have some peculiar kind of sensation or emotion when they are aware of God or that they are entitled to infer the existence of God from this peculiar feeling, which would surely be a very weak inference, but that they have some kind of experience not adequately describable as mere sensation or emotion which makes them realize the presence of God. This may not be so, but how can we be entitled to exclude it *a priori* as a possibility? It is argued that 'an experience of a distinctively mental kind cannot of itself yield us any information about anything other than the experience',[1] but if we are going to argue in that way should we not have to argue equally that no experience of knowing, being an experience of ours, could ever tell us anything about what is not an experience of ours? It is from the nature of the case not possible to give an argument to show that people have knowledge or veridical cognition of God not based on argument, but how can we possibly prove that they have not?

In general all arguments from the theory of knowledge against

---

[1] A. MacIntyre in *New Essays in Philosophical Theology*, ed. Flew and MacIntyre, p. 256.

the objective validity of religious belief seem to me to suffer from the following weakness. We have no way of proving *a priori* what sort of things we can and what we cannot know. And the same applies to 'rational belief'. We can then only arrive at such episte-mological generalizations by induction. But if we say: All instances of knowledge and rational belief have characteristic *c*, knowledge of or rational belief in God would not have characteristic *c*, there-fore there can be no knowledge of or rational belief in God—this begs the question. For unless the propositions in question have already been shown to be objects neither of knowledge nor of rational belief, we do not know that the characteristic *c* is possessed by all knowledge and rational belief. It may now be urged—and this is the only argument left—that at any rate all other kinds of knowledge and rational belief have characteristic *c* and therefore probably all do, but this is a very weak argument. It is not in the least to be expected that knowledge of, or rational belief in, God if it occurs will be very like other kinds of knowledge or rational belief. There are enormous differences between different kinds of non-theological knowledge, e.g. between mathematics and know-ledge by sense-perception, and God is *ex hypothesi* so very different from all finite existents that we should antecedently expect that the way in which men know of God is very different also. And in fact it is not only admitted, but very much emphasized by religious people that the knowledge of God is quite different from all other kinds of knowledge, though of course there are analogies between it and some of them.

Religious assertions have been denied objectivity on the ground that, if they had it, they would have to be knowable and testable in certain ways, i.e. they must either be verifiable by sense-experience directly or they must be scientific propositions or they must depend on language. But the proposition that these are the only ways of knowing or testing propositions is one that itself can certainly not be established either by sense-experience or as a scientific hypothesis or by appeal to linguistic usage. (Theological propositions certainly function verbally like other propositions, and it is perfectly in accord with ordinary linguistic usage to speak of them as true or false.) It has been urged in reply to this that a proposition which lays down the rules about testing propositions is not itself subject to the same rules as the propositions tested, but still a philosopher cannot assert propositions without justifica-tion and it remains a question how on earth this proposition is to be justified. Religious believers are commonly accused of dogmatism by their opponents, but here the boot is on the other foot, it is the assailant of the objectivity of religion who seems to be the dogmatist because he asserts *a priori* that propositions can only be known in certain ways and denies that religious statements express propositions because they cannot be known in these ways.

There remains the most plausible or the least unplausible argument used by the type of critic I have been discussing against the meaningfulness of religious assertions in so far as they are metaphysical. It is urged that such assertions can have no factual meaning because the terms they use are either themselves drawn from, or are at least defined in terms drawn from, contexts of ordinary life and therefore lose their meaning in the very different context in which they are placed by the metaphysician. Thus it is said that the term 'intelligence' has in ordinary life a precise meaning which can be understood in terms of human action and conversation but that it loses its meaning when applied to a disembodied spirit or to a being so much above us as God. But such an argument does not show that we can attach no meaning to 'God', only that we cannot attach such a clear and definite meaning as we can to the terms applicable to human beings. And what theologians would deny that we have a much less adequate idea of God than of a human being!

We may thus confidently reject the arguments which have been recently brought to show that theological assertions can have no objective meaning. It is another and more difficult question whether or how far we can justify them as true.

XIII

AWARENESS OF GOD

'Proofs of God' are under a cloud today, and whether the cloud can be dissipated or not, I am not going to try to dissipate it in this article. Modern thinkers have created a mental climate very unfavourable to metaphysics, but they have certainly not succeeded in disproving on principle the possibility of valid and fruitful metaphysical arguments even in the old transcendent sense of 'metaphysics'. However, I must admit that in my opinion the best that can be said of *arguments* for the existence of God is that they give some intellectual support to the belief, not that they are really decisive. If this is so, it becomes of very special importance to consider whether those may be right who maintain that we can come to knowledge of or at least justified belief in God otherwise than by inference. I am not considering the views of those who base the belief solely on authority: argument would be required to decide whether we ought to accept an authority, and if so which. What I am referring to is the claim that there are certain 'mystical' and other religious experiences which can without argument adequately and rationally assure one of God's existence. Obviously from the nature of the case a man who makes this claim for himself cannot *prove* to others that he is right, but can any good reason be given to support the view that he is wrong? If not, the possibility remains that those who dispute with him are in a similar position to that of a tone-deaf man disagreeing with Beethoven about the value of music.

A good deal is said about religious emotion, but if the experience is to do what is wanted it cannot be a mere emotion. To have an emotion is not the same thing as to know or believe anything, and a person who makes the above claim is not usually intending to base his belief on an argument to the effect that the emotions he has can only be explained causally by reference to God. His claim is on the contrary a claim to what has commonly been called 'intuition'. It is a cognitive phenomenon, not a mere feeling, though it may be connected very closely with certain emotional feelings. On the other hand it is neither an apprehension of the validity of an argument

nor an empirical perception. To intuit God is not to see a vision or
hear a voice.

Let us then consider the various objections that may be brought
against the view that men can have valid cognition of God otherwise than by inference. I shall speak of 'cognition' and not of
'knowledge' because the latter term connotes an absolute objective
certainty which it at the best seems hardly sensible to claim, however subjectively certain the believer may feel. One objection was
based on the theory that an ostensible statement can have factual
meaning only if it is capable on principle of verification by
sense-experience, for it is plain that the statement that God exists
could not be verified in any such way. But it would be generally
admitted today that the theory of meaning in question has not
been proved and can only be treated as a methodological postulate.
If so, it cannot be used to show that theological statements are
meaningless.

But, while denying the possibility of such a short-cut to naturalism, I do not deny that there are difficulties about the meaning of
religious language. The main one, I think, is this. Admittedly any
words used in such language (or at any rate any that are under-
standable by non-mystics) must either themselves be words which
originally represent what occurs in the ordinary contexts of life or
be definable in terms of such words, and it has been objected that
in theology (and in metaphysics generally) the context is so different that the original meaning of the words is destroyed and there is
no meaning to replace it. For example, it is argued that the meaning
of the word 'mind' or 'intelligence' is so essentially linked up with
the physical organisms through which alone mind is manifested
to us in ordinary life that it is meaningless to apply it to a discarnate being, especially one whose mental processes are held to
be so totally different from ours as to involve knowledge of
everything. It seems to me that a reply can be given to this in
terms of degrees of clarity or obscurity. I am not a mathematician
and cannot understand the ways in which Einstein manifested his
intelligence, so the statement that he was extremely intelligent
means much less to me than it does to a person acquainted with all
the ramifications of the relativity theory. But it would be very odd
therefore to conclude that it has no meaning for me. And it would
still have meaning for me even if I were a child who had not done
any sort of mathematics at all but had encountered intelligence in
other forms, Similarly we can surely attach some meaning to the

statement that God is an intelligence even though we realize that the distance between Einstein's intelligence and that of God is still greater than that between the intelligence of the child and that of Einstein. To understand in some measure the proposition that God is an intelligence it is not necessary to have any concrete idea how God's intelligence works. I do not know the kind of way in which Einstein reasoned in his exalted sphere of mathematics, still less does the child. No theologian of repute will maintain that one can know what God's intelligence is really like as we can know in regard to a man; on the contrary, theologians themselves most strongly emphasize the extreme imperfection and obscurity of any ideas of God. But this is not to say that they mean nothing when they talk of God. They mean that the world owes its existence and nature to a being who is immensely better and wiser than we are and has no imperfections. I cannot see how that statement, whether true or not, can be regarded as quite unintelligible. Perhaps some metaphysical statements made about God, e.g. that 'His existence and His essence are identical', are really meaningless, but this need not apply to all, though something more or less like St Thomas's doctrine that we can make affirmative statements about God only in an analogical sense may well be needed.

Nor does it seem to me that the conception of a disembodied intelligence can possibly be dismissed as self-contradictory or meaningless. I think the best way of dealing with anybody who says that it should be is to ask him whether he claims to see a *logical* connexion between experiences and bodily processes. If he does not, I do not see how he can possibly maintain his position. He cannot say that there is any *a priori* objection to the notion that there may be beings who have conscious life without having bodies. Even if in fact the experiences which we have should be just attributes of the body or even if they should turn out to be (a supposition I myself think absurd) strictly identical with physiological processes,[1] it would always remain conceivable that this might not have turned out to be the case, which shows that the question of the possibility or impossibility of disembodied mind cannot be settled *a priori*. The pain I feel or the thought that I think at least appears as something different from the brain-process or behaviour-processes connected with it as they appear to the physiologist, and therefore the latter must admit that it is at least conceivable, even if not in fact the case, that they might really be

---

[1] v. Smart, *Philosophy and Scientific Realism*, Ch. V.

different. If discarnate beings have no sensory experiences—
though we cannot indeed deny *a priori* the possibility of their
having experiences qualitatively like those in us which are caused
by our sense-organs, because we cannot see any connexion *a priori*
between an experience and a sense-organ—we cannot have any
idea of what they feel like, but neither can we if they have sensory
experiences quite different from ours, and who can deny or find
meaningless the statement that there may be beings who have
quite different sensations from ours? It has been argued that no
thinking is conceivable without words or other imagery, but this
falls under my previous argument that we can understand (partially
and formally) what can be meant by calling some being intelligent
without having any idea as to the way in which the intellect
concerned works concretely.

I do not accept as a necessary condition of the meaningfulness
of a hypothesis that a number of specific verifiable propositions
should be deducible from it, but I may point out that even from
the forbidding metaphysical proposition 'God is omniscient'[1] we
could deduce a great number of specific propositions telling us
what God does know, e.g. God knows that $2 + 2 = 4$, and that if
there is a conscious being, God, He must himself verify that He
knows them. And if we survive bodily death as discarnate spirits,
we shall surely be able to verify that we survive. On the other
hand the negative propositions that there is no omniscient being
and that we do not survive death it is *a priori* impossible to
verify.

One effect of the recent linguistic developments in philosophy
has been to lay great emphasis on the fact that language can perform many other functions besides that of making statements.
There is no doubt that, even if theological sentences do make
factual statements about reality, this is not all they do. They also
express and communicate emotion, incite and commit to action.
But it seems as if they do these things only on the basis of factual
claims, especially about God. While it is important to dwell on
the former functions of religious language, we need not exclude
the latter. In my view no good reason has been produced for
saying it is senseless to make such factual claims. Whether they
are true is another matter. Why should 'facts' be necessarily
limited to those potentially present to sense-perception? If God

[1] I do not mean by taking this example to suggest that 'God is omniscient' is a
proposition we directly know to be true.

does exist, then this is assuredly by far the most important fact about the universe.

Leaving the question of meaningfulness, let us now ask whether the possibility of veridical religious insight can be refuted by an epistemological argument of any other kind. It seems plain that we cannot prove or otherwise know any *a priori* proposition which excludes the validity of all alleged cognitions of a certain kind (unless we include under this heading such a proposition as that we cannot know what is self-contradictory or what is false). Those who today exclude religious insight on principle would be the last to deal so freely in the *a priori*. Can their negative proposition then be empirically grounded? Let us put it in quite general terms. To refute the possibility of religious cognition on epistemological grounds we must have good empirical reasons for holding to be true a proposition which ascribes a general property x—it does not matter for my purpose what x is—to all kinds of well-accredited cognitions, and we must find that this property is not possessed by alleged religious cognitions. How could this be? A universal proposition about a genus can be based empirically if we establish the proposition by adequate observation for all its species. I shall for the sake of argument waive the difficulty of establishing such a proposition *empirically* for *any* particular kind of cognition. But in any case we are now confronted with a vicious circle. The general property must not belong to alleged religious cognitions, for otherwise we cannot use the argument to discredit religious cognition. Therefore we can establish the truth of the general proposition by empirical generalization only if we already assume that alleged religious cognitions are not well-accredited cognitions, thus begging the question. If religious cognition is well accredited, it follows that this property is not possessed by all well accredited cognitions. The argument cannot run: No cognition of type A is veridical. Religious cognition belongs to type A. Therefore religious cognition is not veridical. For the first premiss cannot be established as a universal generalization without assuming the conclusion. If we are to discredit religious cognition by an empirically based epistemological argument, we shall then have to adopt a less conclusive form of induction and argue that, because all other kinds of cognition which are well accredited have a certain property, religious cognition is unlikely to be veridical since it does not possess this property. But this only follows if we are entitled to assume that religious cognition, if veridical, will be like other forms of veridical cognition. *Prima facie*, we should however expect it to be very different, since its object is so different. On any rational concept of God, God is immensely different from any other kind of being, and therefore we should expect cognition of God to be vastly different from other kinds of cognition. This very difference is emphasised strongly by most philosophers of religion and theologians. This makes the argument from the analogy of other well accredited kinds of cognition to the conclusion that religious cognition is not well accredited if it does not possess similar properties a very weak one. (Not that we should go so far as to exclude all analogies from the knowledge of finite things as being of no help at all in describing religious cognition of God.) I think I have now shown that we can dismiss on principle any epistemological argument to the effect that there cannot be any veridical or reliable cognition of God.

It may be contended, however, that, though such cognition cannot be shown impossible, we have no right ever to admit it because psychologists have given an adequate causal explanation of our religious beliefs. In discussing this question we must make certain distinctions. It is plain that the mere fact that a belief can be explained psychologically does not show it untrue or unjustified. My belief that the Prime Minister is mortal can be explained psychologically. I believe that all men are mortal and that the Prime Minister is a man, and these two beliefs together lead me to believe that the Prime Minister is mortal. But this explanation does not cast any doubt on but rather validates the belief. There are however some modes of causal explanation which, if they could be validated, would show that a person was unjustified in holding the belief the occurrence of which they explained, and this would apply to Freudian explanations of religion. What would invalidate a belief was not that it was caused but that it was caused in a particular way. Suppose my belief were caused not by belief in the propositions I have mentioned but by a desire that the Prime Minister should die. In that case it would follow that I was unjustified in holding the belief, although it happened in fact to be true. But it would not in the least follow that, because my belief that he will die sometime was in that case unjustified, the same belief would be unjustified for somebody else who inferred it from the premisses I have given. Similarly if it could be proved that a man believed in God simply because he wanted to, it would follow that the particular man's belief in God was unjustified for him, but it would not follow that nobody's belief in God was justified unless it could be proved that belief in God was always due to such a desire, and this would be hard indeed to establish.

Now the psychologist can point to certain desires and 'complexes' which might give a psychological explanation of a kind that, if it fitted, would make religious belief unjustified. But how could he show that the alleged causes accounted for all belief in God? The most the psychologist can establish is not that religious beliefs are due to the factors he mentions, but that there are certain factors which *might* lead a person to hold a religious belief even if it were unwarranted. It is well known that a strong desire can lead a man to believe something for which there is precious little evidence. The psychologist may point to certain desires, conscious or unconscious, and perhaps other factors, which may lead to a religious man being prejudiced, but he cannot prove that all religious men are in fact prejudiced by them. The risk of being thus prejudiced is present in the case of any argument which leads to attractive conclusions, but we are not therefore obliged to abandon all arguments which lead to such conclusions because of this risk, although of course when considering such an argument we ought to do our best not to be prejudiced. The same should surely apply to ostensible intuitions.

Further, the religious man can retort that, if there are some factors which may make a man likely to hold a belief in God even if it is false, there are others which may make him likely to reject the belief even if it is true. For *prima facie* appearances, at least superficially considered, are very much against it. Even if the problem of evil turns out, as it has done for so many thinkers, on careful reflection not to constitute an adequate refutation of the belief in God, it must be admitted that this world with all the suffering and other evils it contains looks *prima facie* most unlike the work of a perfectly good, omnipotent being, and this can well go very far towards explaining the difficulty people have in envisaging a God.[1] There is, further, the total absence of suggestions of God in any ordinary everyday experience. The things which occupy our life for the vastly greater part of our time (at least in the case of most of us) carry with them no suggestion of God for the natural man, at least

[1] This argument of course assumes that it is possible to deal with the problem of evil in such a way as at least to mitigate the *prima facie* objection which it constitutes to belief in God, a topic I have no space to discuss here. If not, *cadit quaestio.*

unless he goes out of his way to reflect. It is certainly most difficult for us to get away from the material practical world sufficiently to concentrate our full energies even for a very short time on the attempt to find God, if God is to be found, and relatively few people have the zeal to do this. (Probably we should add that of those who have done it very few have failed to attain a genuine religious conviction.) The circumstances I have mentioned can very adequately explain why so many people have no religious belief or a very weak one or one based simply on the authority of others. If the proposed psychological explanation is on Freudian lines, we can indeed retort too with the *argumentum ad hominem* that, if Freud explains religious belief by the father image, we could equally well explain its opposite by the unconscious aversion to one's father, which according to Freud plays such an important part in human psychology, so that this game will not show which side is more rational.[1] So, if the atheist or agnostic can explain how people may be theists even if theism is false, the theist can explain at least as easily how people may be atheists or agnostics even if theism is true. Thus at the level of psychological explanation the battle is a drawn one. Each side can suggest ways in which the belief or absence of belief of the other may be caused by irrelevant factors but cannot prove that it is so caused. So the religious man who has faced his difficulties and retains his intuitive conviction after having asked himself if it may not be due to his desires need not be much worried by the psychologist, unless he indeed insists on claiming *certainty* for his religious views, which is in any case very unreasonable. For himself the experience may carry its own evidence which he cannot, even if he will, reject except perhaps by diverting his attention from what he is contemplating. A strong point in his favour—and I want to emphasize this—is that it seems to be what is best in us rather than what is worse in us which inclines us to and is associated with the belief in God. People who have offered facile psychological explanations of religion do not seem to have realized at all the immense difficulty of the enterprise of establishing the conclusion that religious belief in general, as opposed to the beliefs of some particular people, is due to the causes to which they assign it.

The alleged cognition is intuitive in character, and this is of course made the ground of various objections to it. The mere fact that it is intuitive cannot however entitle us to reject it as worth-

[1] v. Klausner & Kuntz, *Philosophy: Alternative Beliefs*, p. 262.

less. If we mean by 'intuition' a cognition not based either on mediate inference or on sense-perception, introspection or memory, we cannot reject all intuition without also rejecting all inference. For to argue A, therefore B, therefore C, we must see the connexion between A and B and B and C and we cannot see this by mediate inference. Or at least if we do, it can only be through interpolating other stages in the inference, a process which must come to an end sometime. Of course we might well admit intuitions of this kind without admitting intuitions of God, but the argument I have given shows at any rate that 'intuition' is not necessarily something discreditable never to be admitted by a respectable philosopher.

Some seem to think it a fatal objection to the claim to intuition of God that an intuition is something in one's mind and therefore cannot establish a reality beyond us. But the former proposition must be true of every cognitive process. In any sense in which intuition is just in our mind so are mediate inference and sense-perception. For me to have knowledge or justified belief of any sort something must happen in me, but it does not follow that I am aware only of a happening in my mind when I acquire the knowledge or belief and see or think I see it to be true.

It has also been objected that to appeal to intuition gives no explanation but is just an example of faculty psychology in the old bad sense, a pseudo-explanation by faculties or dispositions. My reply is that what the intuitionist is giving is not a supposed explanation but an assertion that the cognition to which he is referring needs no further explanation or justification. For us to have a reason for believing anything there must be some things which we are entitled to believe without a reason, and the question about intuitions is the question which these are. That surely is a sensible and important question. It is common among the most 'modern' philosophers to admit that there are kinds of thought which do not fall under the rubric of either deductive or inductive argument, and I do not quite know how to distinguish this view from an appeal to intuition.

It has also been said[1] that any claim to intuition is useless as evidence because it can prove nothing to one who does not already possess the intuition. But suppose this common situation. A man has an intuitive conviction of God. He is aware that what seems to him a veridical intuition might still not be so, and it

_____
[1] MacTaggart, *Some Dogmas of Religion*, pp. 38–40.

would be very rash of him to place much confidence in it if he
thought himself the only person who had it. But if he finds the
intuitive conviction is very widespread and possessed by a vast
number of men who in other respects deserve the titles in a special
degree of 'good' and 'wise', his attitude may well be transformed.
It seems to me quite obvious, without this being derived from
another premiss or requiring derivation, that it is wrong to hurt
another man merely to give oneself the pleasure which some people
feel in watching others suffer. But suppose I never met anybody
else who had this intuitive conviction. Then it would surely be
only reasonable for me to be very doubtful about even an intuition
that is subjectively as clear and convincing as this one. It would not
disprove the possibility that I was right—I *might* have been the
first person to see a fundamental ethical truth—but unless I
thought myself a heaven-sent prophet I could hardly regard this as
anything else but most unlikely, and if I was reasonable I should
have to admit—Well, I cannot help instinctively thinking like this,
but I cannot suppose it in the least likely that everybody else
should be wrong and I myself right, so I had better dismiss it as a
psychological kink on my part. But the situation is totally transformed by the fact that I do find that most people agree with me
here, thus confirming my intuitive conviction by theirs. This is the
role of authority in religion. No doubt if we take the case of a
man who has no vestige of intuitive religious conviction, it is
unlikely that an appeal to the intuitive conviction of others will
convince him, but even he will be unreasonable if he takes it for
granted, because he has not got it himself, that those who have it
are necessarily wrong. And, if a man has such a conviction in a
weak degree, he is justified in attaching incomparably more weight
to it when he realizes its prevalence in a stronger and more
developed form among others whom he highly respects. We must
not think of religious intuition as necessarily limited to a few
great mystics. It may well be in some (though a much lesser)
degree possessed by the plain man who says 'I cannot prove but
I feel that there is a God'. 'Feel' here does not mean 'have emotional feelings'—if so, it would not be followed by a that-clause—
it means 'believe intuitively'. Religious belief has often been
claimed by those who hold it to rest on argument or supposed
supernatural authority, but an examination of the arguments makes
one strongly suspect that they mostly either owe what plausibility
they have to some intuitively believed premiss of a religious kind

or are ways not of proving God but of helping people to come to see for themselves non-inferentially that there is a God.

To say that a cognition is intuitive is not necessarily to deny that it is mediated in some way. Thus the cognition of God might be called 'intuitive' because it was not based on argument, and yet it might be mediated by certain experiences which could help one to 'see God'. The apprehension of something may well lead to the realization of something else without the former being a premiss from which the latter is deduced. There is a distinction between seeing some truth as the result of seeing others and inferring it from these others. To say that some being mediates God is to say that a man may by considering that being be put in a state of mind in which he can catch a glimpse of God. The awareness of God is commonly held to be mediated by nature, the goodness in other people, many kinds of symbols and many specially vivid experiences of life, moral, aesthetic and practical. For Christians Christ can in a special degree be said to mediate God, whether the orthodox doctrine of the incarnation be true or false. The relation of mediation has some analogy to inference and may even be mistaken for it, but it may carry one beyond what we could infer. The concept of mediated cognition that is yet not inferential is not one which has to be specially invented to fit the case of religion. It may be argued that it is also needed for the solution of problems such as that of the knowledge of physical objects and perhaps of other minds, where our cognition is plainly *mediated* by sense-perceptions and by the bodily behaviour of others but its objects cannot be either identified with or perhaps satisfactorily inferred from the mediating factor, and it may even turn out that in a comprehensive epistemology we need to give this concept a place in dealing with every or almost every form of human cognition. But, even if I had yet adequately developed this theory, there would not be space to work it out here.

Religious conviction has been so widespread, so dominating a factor in very many, indeed in most who were in other respects among the greatest and best of men and so much the basis throughout history of a whole, most fundamental side of life and thought as to make a very strong *prima facie* case for the view that there is at least 'a great deal in it'. But at this point we are brought up sharply by objections based on the divergences between the adherents of different religious beliefs. A very large part of the divergences are admittedly divergences regarding arguments, e.g. about the best authority, and not divergences about intuitions, but in so far as there is a conflict of intuitions, what are we to say? There is no doubt a tendency to have an intuitive conviction that the beliefs of one's particular religion or even particular sect are true. In dealing with this objection we must recognize that intuition is not infallible, unless we choose to make it so by a verbal trick as we do 'knowledge', i.e. by declining to give the name of 'intuition' to what we have decided is mistaken, and even then we must admit that at any rate a person may well be mistaken as to whether he has an 'intuition', though not in that case as to whether the intuition is right if he has one at all. Obviously a person may think he is seeing intuitively what is really the result of an inference, perhaps a bad one, or the dictum of an authority that he accepts, especially if the belief which primarily strikes him as intuitive is for him strongly linked by emotion and habit with other teachings of that authority. A man might well really see intuitively that A was B but think that he thus saw that A was C because he implicitly inferred C from B or took for granted that B involved C or because he simply confused B and C. It is only reasonable to expect that people will tend to interpret their religious intuitions, if they have any, in terms of the religion in which they have been brought up. On the other hand the fact that a person is already familiar with a certain view need not exclude the possibility of his being able later to verify it by an intuitive insight which he did not possess when he was first taught it, and in very many cases his most distinctive religious experience has led someone to embrace views which he did not hold earlier and so change his religion. The fact that a belief is intuitive and cannot be proved does not exclude its being subjected also to other tests, which can mostly be summed up under the heading of coherence, whether internal or with other beliefs, and these tests are available in helping one to decide between conflicting intuitions. Nor is it just a question of accepting an intuitive conviction as a whole as it stands. Intuitions, or, if you prefer this phraseology, 'ostensible intuitions' are subject to correction. It may indeed happen that intuitions which conflict as they stand can be reconciled if one is slightly amended, and this may be a strong reason for the amendment. We must not suppose, especially in the field of religion, that the only alternatives are clear intuitive insight into a definite proposition and no intuition at all. An intuition may be confused and yet give some truth even if we cannot be sure that we have sorted out what is true in it from what is false, and in that case we require help by careful analysis and inferential thought.

We must not, however, overestimate the extent to which religious intuitions diverge. It would obviously be impossible to establish the creed of any particular sect *in toto* by just appealing to the intuitive conviction of members of the sect. But it does not follow that one could not legitimately appeal to intuition to establish the most fundamental principles of religion in general. Actually on major points the nucleus of agreement between mystics of different religions and different civilizations is in fact surprising. Younghusband says 'All the world-religions affirm the love of God for his creatures,'[1] and though this is not true of all mystics, since they do not all believe in a personal God, I should think they would practically all agree at least in finding a supreme value in a being over and above the natural world with which being they claimed to be united. The mystic has actually been defined as 'the person who in the course of his own experience has in some moment become aware of the nature of things as supreme good'.[2] The difference between those mystics who say they believe in a personal God and those who do not I shall contend later is largely a question of degree.

I think in view of all I have said that it is only philosophical to keep at least an open mind as regards the possibility that religious cognition may be veridical, and if so it is a question of great importance what, if anything, it could be regarded as establishing. The best way to approach this subject is, I think, to ask for the fundamental presupposition (or presuppositions) without which a religious attitude could not be justifiable at all. Obviously it is reasonable to give much more weight to an intuition of this than to intuitions or ostensible intuitions of doctrines peculiar to particular religions. There is a definite presumption in favour of the substantial validity of what is a necessary presupposition of a whole major department of human thought. This is not just an appeal to the mystic but an attempt to find the presuppositions of man's religious experience in general. Mysticism is not the only form of religious experience nor even the only intense form. Christ and St Paul are rarely, if ever, called 'mystics'. Now the most fundamental presupposition of religion, you may expect me to say, is the existence of God. But I shall not say this. More important than the

---

[1] *A Venture of Faith*, p. 155.
[2] W. E. Hocking, *The Coming World Civilization*, p. 138.

existence of God is God's goodness, and the corollary from this that the universe is governed in accordance with a supremely good purpose and is possessed of supreme and overwhelming positive value if we could only see it as a whole, a corollary which is sometimes held in its own right on the strength of religious experience without believing in God as the term is ordinarily understood. So I should agree with Whitehead in making the basic presupposition of religion 'the fundamental rightness of things', meaning by this not that there are no bad things but that the good somehow preponderates.

I do not wish to gloss over the tremendous character of the assumption proposed as I understand it, but I have certainly not space here to deal with the problem of evil. The question is left open here whether the only intelligible way of interpreting the postulate I have mentioned will not turn out to be in terms of God conceived as personal at least in some analogical sense of the term. It has been contended that religion can retain an emotional and practical value without committing one to any beliefs about objective reality, and if all metaphysical beliefs of a religious kind should have to be dismissed as unjustifiable, this is a salvage operation worth undertaking. But it would be a salvage operation of a pretty desperate kind. One may be helped morally by stories which are never even believed to be true, but most of the specific ways in which religion helps and comforts a man depend on the holding of objective beliefs. It is no comfort to be told to be of good cheer because God's purpose will never be thwarted, nor is it any moral help to be told that God will aid you in your moral struggles, if you do not believe that there is any being in the least like what we mean by God.

What seems to me plain is that a certain view as to the value of Reality or the being on which reality is based is the most essential religious doctrine. For the ordinary person this belief is much more intelligible and helpful if put in terms of a personal God, but it may be held that this is only a symbol or metaphor. Even so the value of religion, as ordinarily understood, will be largely destroyed if it does not at least stand for some objective truth not too unlike the plain meaning of the symbols for the latter to be regarded as some approximation to the truth. And by far the most central conception here is that of value. Religion adjures one to adore and enter into communion with its object, but it certainly would not be good— much less the supreme good—to adore and enter into communion with what was not good. Worship of what is indifferent or bad or even less than the highest, though good as far as it goes, is commonly called by the religious man 'idolatry' or 'blasphemy', very severe terms of abuse. The value claimed for communion with God in religious experience is obviously inseparably bound up with the idea of the perfect goodness of God. And the experience of 'peace' which plays such an important part in religious experience surely implies the supreme goodness of that on which the mind rests and the confidence that this goodness will prevail or perhaps has in essence in some sense already, or rather timelessly, prevailed. In characterizing God very much commonly is said of His power and His mysterious nature. Now the doctrine of the omnipotence of God is of great religious importance because in its usual context this alone will give us a guarantee that His good will prevails; and God must be mysterious to us. But we cannot or at least ought not to worship power and mystery as such. All that matters ultimately is value, and religion in so far as it is of value in itself can only lie in an appreciation of the value of its object. It was a grievous perversion when some theologians (fortunately only a small minority, I think), because they considered it a limitation of God's power that He should be governed by the moral law, made the moral law the mere outcome of God's will thus reducing His goodness to a tautology. To worship power as such is like fawning on a dictator just because he is a dictator.

The central emphasis I have laid on value in the interpretation of religion is not necessarily contradicted by religions which stress the badness of the world, because they assert the supreme goodness of a more ultimate reality behind this evil world. Buddhism may seem an exception, but despite its pessimism about the world and alleged atheism it regards the world as at least governed morally.[1] The law of Karma is a principle of justice decreeing that all shall be rewarded and punished in proportion to their good and bad deeds, and even if one does not think the concept of punishment as retributive the highest, the doctrine of Karma was certainly accepted as the expression of a strong moral conviction natural to men. Further, the punishment is not treated merely as end-in-itself, but as a means of purifying and training men to lead a better life. Also, the Nirvana of Buddhism has been regarded by most Buddhists not as annihilation but as a heaven describable

[1] In so far as it is not a mere system of moral training without any sort of metaphysical outlook, as I suppose it is for some Buddhists.

by us in negative terms only because it is so much above our ordinary experience. To this heavenly goal Karma operating through the world process was held eventually to lead. We cannot therefore say that Buddhism does not make the world order fundamentally ethical, and it is optimistic and not pessimistic as regards the ultimate destiny of man. What it does not usually give in its more rationalized form is the conception of a personal God. But it is an objection to making the personality of God a completely essential concept for religion that we should then have to deny the title of religion to most varieties of Buddhism and some of Hinduism.

To say that a certain principle is presupposed if the religious attitude is to be justifiable is not to say that all religions carry out the principle consistently. A religion can very well be inconsistent with its own fundamental principles in certain subsidiary dogmas maintained by it or by some of its adherents. People can have all sorts of inconsistent attitudes without being in fact worried by the inconsistency. My point is rather that it would not be good or rational to take a religious attitude if the postulate I have mentioned did not express a truth. If reality is not essentially good or dominated by a righteous purpose, the characteristic religious attitude would be irrational in a sense like that in which it is irrational to be afraid of the dark or feel sympathy with an inanimate thing because it is burnt.

' I have not made the belief in a personal God a necessary condition of consistently maintaininting the religious attitude, but this does not necessarily debar one from appealing to religious experience to justify the belief in question. The argument could now take the form that, although some may think they have a genuinely religious attitude to a non-personal being, they are really implicitly personifying the latter. For the religious attitude involves love, adoration, and other emotional attitudes which are only intelligible as attitudes towards a being viewed as a person, or if this is too much to say about religious attitudes in general, one might contend that the most desirable, characteristic and developed types of religious experience involve just this.

It may be objected on the other side that some mystics, who possess an obvious genius for religion, have quite an extraordinarily intense religious experience and have spent most of their energy developing it, yet decline to accept the belief in a personal God. But it is not impossible to suggest a synthesis of the two rival views.

For, on the one hand, even orthodox Christianity does not claim without qualification that God is personal. One could hardly be more orthodox than Thomas Aquinas, yet he denied that any positive attributes are to be ascribed to God except in an analogical sense. The doctrine of the Trinity itself has commmonly been interpreted by theologians as implying that God is not personal in quite the ordinary sense. At the same time of course Christianity would assert that God contains in His nature all that is of positive value in personality, only excluding the limitations which for a finite person are involved in the notion. Now, on the other hand, the mystics who believe in an impersonal God will mostly admit that at least the analogy to personality has some application, though it must not be taken literally. At any rate they themselves apply it. Even if it is intended only for relatively inferior minds who have not attained the mystic height of religious experience, these constitute by far the greater part of the human race. And an analogy cannot help without some degree of similarity in some respect. Further, mystics in describing their experience constantly use terms drawn from personal intercourse, and it is impossible to see how they could describe their experience intelligibly without these. The extent to which the word 'love' figures in accounts of mystical experience is very remarkable, and the term would be completely pointless if there were no analogy here to our relation with human persons. This suggests that the difference between regarding God as personal and impersonal may be regarded as one of degree. On the one hand if we conceive God as personal, we have to admit that he cannot be personal in the sense in which human beings are and which is intrinsically bound up with our limitations; on the other hand those who insist that God must be regarded as impersonal still have to talk in personal terms if they are to convey any meaning. Certainly the main attitudes inculcated by religion towards God are only appropriate to a being who is in some real sense personal in at least some aspects of his nature. We may say that God is 'super-personal', but the trouble is that, if we try to think of God as other than personal, we are in fact thinking of God as sub-personal, as some kind of unconscious vital force, intrinsically lower, not higher, than ourselves. For, although we may very well say that God has properties higher than personality and not involving personality, we have no conception at all of what these properties are. The only non-personal beings of which we have any idea are either animal or inanimate, and we cannot liken God to these rather than to human beings. Hence the necessity of using the conception of personality in thinking of God. If we use personal terms or terms signifying personal relations at all, it is then a question of degree how much we insist on their analogical or metaphorical character, so that there is no clear dividing line between a personal and an impersonal view of God.

But there is another very interesting possibility. It may be that the religious experience of one who affirms belief in a personal God and one, perhaps equally religious, who denies God's personality both have an appropriate real object, but that the objects of the two are different. Philosophical theologians have again and again been involved in difficulties and controversies because of the tendency to identify God with Reality as a whole, since to make God anything less seemed to make Him less than the greatest possible and so to contradict God's metaphysical (though not necessarily His ethical) perfection, and because of that side of religious experience which points to immanence rather than transcendence. Yet this identification has been even more strongly opposed because it seemed incompatible with the notion of God's personality and raised the metaphysical difficulties involved in including human minds in God. Perhaps the solution may be that we have here a conflict between two different modes of religious experience each with a different object. There might be a certain religious experience of the Whole such as the more characteristically mystical mystics have in high degree and also a religious experience of a personal or at least quasi-personal God who is part but not all of the Whole, and both experiences might be veridical without being incompatible with each other. They would then only seem incompatible because they were conceived wrongly as referring to the same object. And perhaps religion could not attain its full value without both. This suggestion opens up very interesting possibilities for discussion and may by separating the two concepts help to solve some antinomies about God.

I am not of course claiming to give any conclusive reason for accepting the religious point of view. But, even if the philosopher cannot prove it justified, it is a very important task of philosophy to analyze what it involves, since very many people even today feel themselves ultimately bound to accept it and it cannot be shown wrong.

XIV

TWO 'PROOFS' OF GOD'S EXISTENCE

I do not think that the existence of God can be proved or even that the main justification for the belief can be found in argument in the ordinary sense of that term, but I think two of the three which have, since Kant at least, been classified as the traditional arguments of natural theology have some force and are worthy of serious consideration. This consideration I shall now proceed to give. I cannot say this of the remaining one of the arguments, the 'ontological proof', which I shall therefore not discuss here.

Let us then turn to the 'cosmological proof' or 'the first cause argument'. In dealing with it I had better say at the start that I am not conscious of any intuitive awareness that the contingent entails a necessary being. If this is indeed intuitively known, as has been claimed by some philosophers, the existence of God can be regarded as established *a priori* from the single empirical premiss that some man exists, but I am afraid it is not so simple as this. I am far from wishing to deny that there may be intuitive awareness of God in the sense of a trustworthy cognition other-wise than by sense-experience or inference,[1] and I do not think this claim incompatible with the cognition yet being mediated in some way by the natural world. But the religious consciousness has not usually been claimed to consist of insight into a logical connexion, and unless it is this I do not see how it can provide the link without which the cosmological argument must collapse. Can we then get an adequate argument by appealing to the notion of cause without any intuitively accepted premiss except the principle of causality itself?

The principle that everything is caused has no agreed demon-stration and may be held to conflict with human freedom, but it can be replied that, even if a being once in existence may act in a way not completely determined by antecedent causes, surely even the staunchest indeterminist would find it hard to believe that the world came into being simply from nothing without any cause.

[1] See my article on 'Awareness of God' above (No. 13)

(The scientists who talk of the perpetual creation of matter regard matter as made from 'energy' and therefore presumably as caused. The concept of energy itself surely has to be analysed in a way which involves causal laws.) But this assumption about causality may be said not to exclude the possibility of the world always having existed, if 'world' is used sufficiently widely to cover the whole spatio-temporal process throughout time. This is indeed still logically compatible with the world being dependent on God but does not as yet provide a starting point for an argument to the effect that it is dependent on God. One way of providing such an argument would be to contend that the world must have had a beginning on the ground that there would otherwise be a vicious infinite regress of past events and that, since a first event can have no cause in the natural order, its cause must be found in a being outside the natural order. But it would be risky to stake very much on this argument. The notion that the world, i.e. the whole temporal series of changing things, had no beginning seems to me a very difficult one, but I must admit that the philosophers most skilled in investigating the antinomies of infinity do not now feel this difficulty and that Kant's attempt in the first antinomy to prove that it is on a realist view insuperable was unsuccessful.

But the main force of the cosmological argument depends on the inclusion in the notion of causation of a concept which, since Hume's influence became important, has been much under suspicion, the concept of the cause as giving an *explanation* of the effect. If we think of causation in terms of explanation, there is certainly much force in the first cause argument. If one explains *A* by its cause *B*, *B* by another cause *C*, *C* by *D*, *D* by *E*, and so on *ad infinitum*, nothing is ultimately explained at all. To give a final explanation we must go back to something that is evident in its own right, and if causation is to be interpreted as *explaining* the effect, the explanation could not be satisfactory without the introduction of a being that could be said not to need a cause beyond itself. Nor would it be an explanation in any ultimate sense if the existence of this being were merely a fact without a reason for it. Yet the reason cannot lie in anything else, it would have to lie in the ultimate cause itself. Otherwise nothing is really explained at all for the same reason as that which makes it impossible to justify or give a valid ground for any statement I make unless I come back to some premiss which has to be accepted in

I

its own right. This view of causation was practically universal till Hume's influence became important, but it is very widely questioned and denied today. On the alternative view now more generally held, at least in this country, to state a causal law is simply to mention a kind of events *A* which are commonly followed by events of another kind *B*, or at least we have no right to assert any objective connexion between cause and effect beyond this. Such a view of causation I call the 'regularity view'. It is plain that it would not give much support to the first cause argument. I think, however, it is liable to severe criticism on its own ground without any reference to the problems of theism. By this I do not mean merely that it is not the common-sense view of causation: it is quite obvious that it is not. It is a highly sophisticated doctrine which eviscerates causation by eliminating most of the content we have in mind when we use the term in daily life. We do not think of the cause as only followed regularly by the effect, we think of it as in some way necessitating and so explaining the effect. If *A* is simply followed by *B* however often, this does not explain *B*, but if *B* follows from the nature of *A* it does up to a point give an explanation of *B*. If we thought of causation as only regular sequence, we should suppose that there was no more special intrinsic connexion between the striking of a match and the flame it caused than between the former and any other event. But it may be said that, although the concept of explanation is part of the common-sense notion of cause, it has no business there, i.e. that we have no right to suppose there is anything in causation in the world beyond regular sequence. Are there any grounds for supposing that there is more in causation than that and indeed something which would justify the explanatory view on which the first cause argument depends? I think there are two at least of very great force and very considerable philosophical importance.

(1) As Hume himself realized, it is very difficult to defend any inductive arguments if we do not suppose a necessary connexion between cause and effect. The fundamental principle of induction is that similar events occur under similar conditions. If there is a necessary connexion between causal conditions and consequences so that the former necessarily determine and thus explain the nature of the latter, there will be an adequate ground for thinking that this will happen, but if there is no necessary connexion there will be no such ground.

(2) In the absence of any explanation it would be a fantastically improbable coincidence that some event of a certain kind A should in all or almost all observed instances be followed by an event of another kind B. It would be like having all the trumps in whist in one hand many times running or more improbable even than that, since the number of kinds of events which might in the absence of such a law follow are infinite.[1] But how could the improbability be removed? It certainly could not be removed just by positing a causal law in the regularity sense. To posit such a law connecting A and B is just to say that A in fact is always or usually followed by B, and you could not possibly remove the objection that it was an incredible coincidence that B should frequently follow A by saying merely that it always or usually happened. To say just that in fact it always happened or happened mostly in unobserved instances as well as observed would not be to remove the improbability but to increase it. There are only two alternatives, I think, to making the regularities which are actually given in experience the most incredible of coincidences. One is to suppose that the occurrence of all physical events has been directly determined by a purposing mind, as Berkeley supposed, the other is to suppose that there is something in the natural cause which in the context of the natural order as a whole necessitates and so explains the effect. The former course of argument introduces God straightway, although in a fashion which most philosophers would not accept; the latter gives a conception of cause which could provide a basis for the first cause argument for God.

Whether these are valid arguments against the regularity view of causation or not is a very contentious question with which it is not possible to deal adequately here.[2] I myself believe that they are valid, and it must surely be admitted at least that they give some *prima facie* reason for thinking that the view of causation according to which it does provide a genuine explanation of events is not to be lightly dismissed. There is the point often cited against it that we do not see the connexion between cause and effect *a priori*, but this is far from conclusive. There may be many necessary connexions which it is quite beyond present human power to discern. Further, supposing the view I suggested

---

[1] Some of the objections to this argument also appear as objections to the argument from design which I discuss later in this article. I reply to them below.

[2] For a fuller discussion of this, see article VI above.

is true, we could not possibly expect to see the necessary connexions (at least on a realist view of the physical world) because we do not know the internal nature of matter and so could not possibly have insight as to what it could or could not entail. It can hardly be a strong argument against my view that something is the case which, even if the view were true, you would be bound to expect would be the case.

But apart from the question of the correct analysis of the concept of causation, the question forces itself on me—What is the reason why things are as they are? After all, it does seem incredible that the physical universe should just have 'happened', even if it be reduced to the juxtaposition of some trillions of electrons and other minute particles. Does it not cry out for a further explanation of some kind? Even if causal talk in science is regarded simply as talk about regular sequences, this question remains. It has often been said to be meaningless, but I cannot see any ground for thinking it so. The verification principle from which the meaninglessness of such enquiries was originally deduced has admittedly not been proved but is merely methodological even according to most of those who assume it in their reasonings. If the question is once asked, is there any possibility of its being answered, and would the answer have to be in terms of theism? This turns on the concept of a 'necessary being' or 'causa sui'. God could not of course be cause of Himself in the sense in which a physical thing or event could be cause of something happening in the world, but this does not necessarily vitiate the argument. The contention is that ordinary causation could not give an adequate ultimate explanation unless it were supplemented by this other kind. According to the first cause argument no explanation of the world is possible unless there is a being that is its own explanation. But how can such a being exist? A being would be 'necessary' in terms of this argument as usually understood if it was an a priori necessary proposition that the being existed. But there are grave difficulties about supposing that any proposition that something exists could be logically a priori. It is not merely that we do not see how such a proposition could be a priori, it seems as if we see that it could not be a priori. The form of the objection to a necessary being in which it appeals to me most is that given by Kant when he says that there could be no contradiction in the supposition that something does not exist because, in supposing that it does not exist, you have already removed any attributes that could contradict each other.[1] (No doubt if two different beings were logically connected, there might be a contradiction in asserting the existence of one and denying that of the other, e.g. if it were held that our existence entailed God's, but by a 'necessary being' is meant not merely a being that is necessarily presupposed if the world is to exist but a being necessary in its own right so that there would be an internal contradiction in denying it to exist, at least if the necessity is understood as logical). I am thus inclined to agree with the great number of philosophers who have denounced the notion of a necessary being as absurd, if by 'necessary' is meant logically necessary.

Professor Findlay[2] has gone a step further and treated the argument against a necessary being as a proof of atheism on the ground that the notion of God includes necessity and yet such necessity is impossible. It has also been asserted that it would be blasphemy to worship a God who was not regarded as necessary. I do not see myself why this should be so. We ought, I should have imagined, to worship God for His supreme goodness and not for the alleged characteristic of being 'necessary', and it is surely plain that logical characteristics are not suitable objects of worship at all. I further think that even without this necessity there would be sufficient left of the concept of God to escape the charge of atheism. Still it must be admitted that the concept does for most religious men involve necessity as an ingredient regarded as of vital importance. The existence of God, it is felt, could not be merely a contingent fact, and if it were God could not be regarded as the completely supreme being but only the being that happened to be strongest. But, I ask, need the necessity be logical necessity? Might not God be necessary in some sense other than that in which his necessity would mean that there was an internal contradiction in denying His existence? After all, it is not claimed by religious people that they see the logcal necessity of God, unless

[1] In using this argument I am assuming that it is self-contradictory to deny a true *a priori* proposition, but it is very important to realize that this does not commit one to the view that all *a priori* propositions are 'analytic' in a sense which makes them verbal, a view which I strongly oppose (v. *Clarity is not Enough*, ed. H. D. Lewis, chap. VI esp. p. 160). All it commits one to is the indisputable logical principle that, if p entails q, not-q entails not-p, which is equivalent to saying that q contradicts p.

[2] *Mind*, 1948, reprinted in Flew and MacIntyre, *New Essays in Philosophical Theology*. Professor Findlay no longer holds all the views expressed there.

they accept the ontological proof and if they do that they are relying on a (bad) argument and not on religious intuition.

But before we discuss this topic further let us consider another even more vital point. Suppose that there is a first cause and necessary being. How do we know that this being is to be identified with God as ordinarily conceived? How do we know or even have reason to surmise that this first cause and necessary being is a supremely good, wise, loving spirit possessed of all perfections in the fullest conceivable sense? The line of argument which may be popularly expressed by saying that the cause must be at least as great as the effect could not establish more than that God is at least as good as the best man which, although comforting as far as it goes, is certainly not enough for the theologian (even apart from any doubts there may be about the axiom concerning causation used in the argument). Descartes' attempt by reference to the idea of God to prove the existence of a perfect cause of this idea is rarely defended nowadays and invokes premises which certainly do not seem self-evident. As far as I can see there is only one line of argument which could possibly establish the desired conclusion when combined with the first cause argument. This would be the argument, if such an argument be possible, that for a being to be necessary that being would also have to be perfect. Such a proposition is not disproved by the fact that the ontological argument has failed to prove its converse, but I am not at all clear as to what I suppose is the orthodox argument for it, namely, that any being that was not perfect could not be a necessary existent because its existence might be prevented by that of another being. We must not be misled by the metaphor of a number of unrealized essences trying to jostle their way into existence and the strongest prevailing in the struggle, a metaphor which is certainly suggested by the classical formulations of the argument with which I am familiar. But I find it very difficult to understand the argument when we have eliminated metaphors like this. If there is a necessary being at all, it seems to me antecedently more plausible to suppose that the most perfect being conceivable should be necessary than that any imperfect being should have this unique position, but I should be very grateful to any philosopher who attempted to state the argument that this was so in a more acceptable form than, as far as I know, it has yet assumed. However, I myself feel more at ease in approaching the problem from the other end.

So I shall now ask this question: If the universe as a whole is to be rationally explicable, as is claimed in the first cause argument, what sort of explanation could it have? It is no ultimate explanation to refer it to God unless the existence of God is self-explanatory in a way in which the existence of no other being could be. Otherwise either the principle on which the first cause argument depends, namely the principle that there must be an ultimate reason for the existence of anything, has to be abandoned, or another cause has to be posited beyond God. Without an answer on this point the child's question: What is the cause of God? is sufficient to make the argument collapse. And if we hold to the position, as I think we must, that an affirmative existential proposition cannot be logically necessary, an explanation in terms of logical argument is not possible. What ultimate explanation then could there be for the world? If we are to meet the demand of the human intellect that there should be a reason for the world, we seem to need a reason of such a kind as will give an explanation of existence without making the non-existence of anything logically self-contradictory. There remains only one alternative, as far as I can see, which might do this, namely an explanation in terms of values. In that case God's existence will be necessary not because there would be any internal self-contradiction in denying it but because it was supremely good that God should exist. It is not indeed evident to us *a priori* that the best possible being must exist, but a universe determined by values would certainly be rational in a very important sense in which a universe not determined by values would quite fail to be so and the hypothesis that complete perfection does constitute an adequate ground for existence seems to be the only one which could make the universe intelligible and give an ultimate explanation of anything. If God's existence is determined by values, the existence of everything is, since a good God would only create the world because it was good in the long run that it should exist. The problem of evil indeed starkly confronts us here, but so it does all theism. The suggestion of course is not that the universe as a whole is completely perfect but that God is. No doubt the theist can say that the attainment of one good is often incompatible with that of another, that some goods necessarily require for their realization real evils—you cannot have the great good of conquering evil if there is no real evil to conquer, that we are very far from seeing the whole pattern, and on an indeterminist view that in us the good of moral virtue requires free will and therefore the possibility of evil. Whether the problem can be dealt with tolerably along these lines I have not space to discuss here.

We must indeed admit that we do not see *a priori* that the being who has the highest degree of value must exist, but on the other hand there is no doubt that a world in which existence was ultimately explained in terms of values would be in a very important sense more rational then one in which it was not. To quote Archbishop Temple, ' . . . the chain of causes is not self-explanatory. . . . There is in fact only one principle which is self-explanatory; it is Purpose. . . . If there is a principle which is in fact accepted by the mind as self-explanatory, it is justifiable to adopt it provisionally and see what happens. Now there is one such principle—Purpose. When in tracing any causal nexus we reach the activity of a will fulfilling a Purpose with which we ourselves sympathize, we are in fact satisfied.'[1] No doubt the last word means 'intellectually satisfied', otherwise the sentence would be a tautology.

The suggestion that the explanation of the world is in terms of value has these advantages over the suggestion that it is in terms of logical necessity. (1) It can provide a reason why something should exist rather than not exist, which a logically necessary principle cannot do. There is no self-contradiction in anything not existing, but it is clearly better that something good should exist than that it should not. (2) It overcomes one of the chief difficulties of the rationalist, i.e. how to pass from the universal to the particular. Universals must be exemplified in particulars for there to be anything of value at all, and as anybody who loves another person knows, a special value attaches to their particularity. (3) It would clearly establish the perfect goodness of the supreme being, which I do not see how an explanation in terms of the logically necessary could do. If any being exists on account of its value God must so exist.

It has been common enough in the writings of theologians and philosophers of religion to derive the necessity of God's existence from his perfection, but perfection has commonly been conceived in a metaphysical way which seems to me to present great difficulties. It has been regarded as involving the inclusion in God's nature of all 'positive attributes', but in that case we can only avoid assigning to God evil as well as good attributes by taking the view that evil attributes are negative. I do not myself regard

[1] *Contemporary British Philosophy*, ed. J. H. Muirhead, First Series, p. 418.

this view as a tolerable one. Perhaps evil is always the *consequence* either of the lack of something good or as in moral evil of the mal-arrangement of intrinsically good or at least indifferent elements in the nature of certain finite beings, but this consequence is surely itself very often something evil in a very positive sense. Bereavement or blindness is just a lack of something that the subject might have, but the misery caused is positive enough. I do not see how all evil can be called negative in any reasonable sense unless pain can be regarded as just the absence of pleasure, which it is obviously not. And can malice be regarded as a desire in itself indifferent in respect of value but just out of place or excessive in its quantity in relation to other elements in a man's nature? I think not. But if God is the bearer of all positive attributes and we cannot maintain that the evil attributes are only negative, God will have to be conceived as hating men as well as loving them, as being unjust as well as just and that in an infinite degree, thus carrying in his being a logical self-contradiction of the most flagrant character. This illustrates a possibility which cannot in any sense be eliminated even if my objections against the notion of evil attributes as negative should rest on a misunderstanding. How can one in any case possibly know that different positive attributes might not be incompatible with each other, thus making the notion of a being with all positive attributes self-contradictory? Qualities which present themselves to us in experience as positive, e.g. different shapes and colours, certainly can conflict. Of course these would never be admitted to be attributes of God, but our experience does seem to make it quite clear that on principle attributes can conflict in respect of their positive nature since one can exclude another of the same kind, and if so how do we know that this might not apply to attributes which would have to be included in the nature of a being that comprised all 'perfections'? Indeed, going further, is it even thinkable that a being could have some positive attribute without excluding another except as regards attributes so abstract and general as to apply to everything? Further, it is not at all clear in what sense God could be said to have all the positive attributes there are if God is not, for example, coloured and triangular, as of course nobody would say He was. Triangularity and even colour are surely given in experience as attributes of something, if only of sense-data, and they are surely positive qualities and not the mere absence of something. I dare say I have missed here the precise sense in which the philosophers

I have been criticizing used the terms, positive and negative attributes, but at any rate they need to make it a great deal clearer than, as far as I know, they have yet done, if they are to escape these objections.

In traditional philosophical arguments about God too much stress, I think, has been laid on the metaphysical and too little on the ethical attributes of God. However value is analysed, the thing that matters in religion and makes religion worth having is that it tells us that the being on whom everything depends is absolutely and supremely good. The doctrines of the omnipotence and omniscience of God are of importance here because it matters very much whether we can regard the supremely good being as in control of everything and not merely as fighting a war in which He might quite well be defeated, but I do not see how anything could give a title to worship except supreme goodness. The power and awesome mystery of God have often assumed the centre of the stage, but while a fully satisfying religious view does require the omnipotence of God and a being so much above us as God must be deeply mysterious to us, the worship of power as such is not good but evil and to worship mystery as such is to worship something simply because we know not what it is like. I sound rather Kantian in this, but I do not, like Kant, wish to make religion of value only as a means to morality. If God exists, the experience of communion with God must have value in its own right and not only because it makes those who enjoy it better morally. But this can only be because of the supreme goodness of God.

I may still be blamed for having, after all, admitted an *a priori* affirmative existential proposition when I suggested that it might be the case that because He was supremely good God must exist. The proposition would plainly not be empirical and it would equally plainly be affirmative existential. But it escapes what seems to me the main objection to the admission of logically necessary affirmative existential propositions in that it is not claimed that there would be any contradiction in denying it. It remains the case that we cannot positively see it to be true—perhaps to see that we must, as St Thomas held, wait for 'the beatific vision'— and all I can say in its defence is that it is the view which comes nearest to providing a rational explanation of things. I do not think this is a negligible argument in its support, although a great host of theologians who have attempted to tie religion to irrationalism will look upon it as a positive objection.

There remains the question which not only Barthian theologians but positivistically inclined philosophers will press: Have we a right to demand a reason for things? Have we a right to assume that the view which seems to come nearest to providing us with a rational explanation of the world is likely to be any nearer the ultimate truth than a view which does not? The most plausible alternative to theism is not any rival metaphysic but agnosticism. It may be old-fashioned, but I cannot eliminate from my own mind the conviction that there must be a reason for the world and why the world is what it is. And I should further argue in support that, if we had not asked such questions and had not made such assumptions, we should not have developed science. I do not think we can make a rigid distinction of principle between the questions and assumptions of science or even commonsense knowledge and those of metaphysics in so far as metaphysics is by its own standards legitimate. At least I do not think we can do so to such an extent as to regard it as a good argument for a scientific theory that it provides a rational explanation of certain facts in a coherent system and yet deny that fulfilment of the same criterion can count as a ground for regarding a metaphysical theory as some approximation to the truth. No scientific propositions which would be generally regarded as deserving the name of such can be established by observation alone or by observation plus mathematical demonstration. A further criterion which might be described as ability to explain phenomena coherently is needed, and a universe in which everything could on principle be explained must come much nearer to that ideal than one in which no event ultimately can. It is said today that scientists do not give anything of the nature of an explanation when they refer to causal laws but merely describe what actually happens, but I hope I have said sufficient earlier in this article at least to cast doubt on such a view of causality. We may add that in historical origin the scientific demand for causes was certainly a demand for reasons and owed its inspiration largely to this, though scientists under the influence of philosophical scepticism have now moderated their claims as to what they are doing. But the goal to which all explanation points and which must be attainable if there is ever to be an ultimate explanation is to be found in the conclusion of the cosmological proof. This at any rate is the best defence I can give of the argument and I must leave it at that.

Let us now turn to the third argument of natural theology, usually called *the argument from design*. We must grant at once, as Kant insisted, that this argument cannot prove an omnipotent, omniscient or perfectly good God or even a creator as opposed to an architect who made the world out of given material, or for that matter a single God, as opposed to a plurality of gods (provided at least the latter, unlike the Greek gods, were sufficiently in agreement to produce a unified plan). But to know that mind was at the basis of the material world even without a conclusive proof of these additional doctrines of orthodox theism would be something of value in itself and would give additional confirmatory support to other arguments or claims to intuition which themselves went further. It is significant that Kant and even Hume were greatly impressed with the force of the argument, although according to either of their epistemological doctrines it as metaphysical ought not really to have had any force whatever. To avoid complications my discussion of the argument will assume realism about physical objects.

There is a general misapprehension of the argument from design which must be corrected before its force can be properly assessed. This misapprehension was shared, for instance, by Hume and is the main basis of the criticism of it in the famous *Dialogues Concerning Natural Religion*. It is commonly regarded as an argument from analogy, and I must agree with critics that regarded merely as such it is distinctly weak. It would then take the form: living organisms are like machines, in our experience machines are always designed by a mind with an end in view, therefore living organisms (and so the whole world on which they depend for their development) are probably designed by a mind. But it is objected that the two likenesses on which the argument thus stated depends are neither of them at all marked. Organisms are not very like machines, and the mind posited must admittedly be conceived as very different indeed from human minds. Although the first analogy criticized has been somewhat strengthened recently by a comparison of the brain to computers, this criticism of the analogy argument must be regarded as serious. As Professor C. D. Broad has pointed out, there is the further objection that in the realm of our experience all machines have been made not only by a mind but by an embodied mind, and therefore if the analogy is to be used to establish a mind who created the world it will also have to be used to give that mind a body, and then by the same analogy another mind with a body will be required to create that body and so on *ad infinitum*.

But I think the force of the argument from design depends mainly on its being an argument from inverse probability and not from analogy. Although on any theistic view the analogy of the human mind must be used in thinking of God, the argument from design is itself not primarily an argument from analogy, i.e. an argument from likeness in some respects to likeness in others. It is an argument to the effect that to posit a purpose is the only way of accounting for certain phenomena which will remove the stupendously unlikely coincidence that they should show all the features of the results of purposes without there being a purpose. Whatever the defects of Paley's work, this is at least brought out well by his illustration of the watch. It does seem fantastically improbable that living bodies should show such extraordinarily detailed adjustments to ends as they do unless some explanation of this can be given, and it cannot be explained by ascribing the adjustments to purposes of minds inhabiting the living bodies in question. If we held that these empirical facts do not require any special explanation, should we not be acting like somebody who on finding a number of fallen leaves in autumn arranged in such a way as to make an intelligible discourse was quite content to say that they had been blown into their positions by the wind and did not accept the phenomenon as any ground for supposing that an intelligent being had arranged them thus? Since they must fall in some order or other, it is logically and scientifically possible that the wind might have blown them to the positions they occupied, but still no one would for a moment accept this supposition as reasonable.

A number of criticisms have been directed against this argument on general grounds besides the more specific and perhaps most serious one that the theory of evolution has now rendered the argument from design futile by providing an alternative explanation, which objection I shall discuss last. First, an attempt has been made to rule out the argument on the ground that any particular arrangement of matter whatever is bound to be immensely improbable, as with, say, any particular distribution of properly shuffled cards. But the improbability on which the argument from design is based is not the improbability of the existing arrangement of matter in itself, but the improbability of a chance arrangement which fitted in so well with certain purposes. It would be irrational to accuse me of cheating at cards merely because the odds were many millions to one against my getting the cards I did get, since this would apply to any distribution of cards whatever, but apart from any defence which I hope might be based on my moral character the accusation would take a very different guise if the distribution involved all the trumps being in my hand and this repeated itself several times running. Yet the odds against this happening by chance, fantastically high as they are, can be shown to be less than the odds against the existence of such a vast number of bodies apparently purposive in such intricate detail being due to mere chance. If an observed distribution fits in with what a mind could have contrived in order to fulfil a certain purpose and the odds are immensely against this having occurred by chance, surely it does make it very probable that the distribution was the result of purpose unless there is some conclusive objection to this? The monstrous unlikelihood of what otherwise would be a fantastically improbable coincidence can be removed by the simple assumption that the apparently purposive arrangements are really brought about for a purpose.

Secondly, it is objected that, while we can use an argument from inverse probability in favour of a particular hypothesis about something in the world, we cannot use it about the world as a whole. But to say that the circumstances are different from those in which an argument is generally used does not vitiate the argument unless it can be shown quite specifically that the circumstances are different in a particular way relevant to the logic of the argument. As far as I know, this has not been done in the case in question. It has not been shown specifically how any steps of the argument are vitiated because it refers to the world as a whole. Further, it is not true that it is an argument from the world as a whole: it is an argument from particular features of certain beings in it. The world as a whole is involved only because the purposiveness of these particular features cannot be adequately explained on the lines suggested without adding a metaphysical hypothesis about the whole universe, since the organic depends closely on its inorganic environment and it does not seem reasonable to think of part of the universe and not the whole as created by God.

Thirdly, it has been objected that in an infinite time (and space, if space be infinite) there is room for an infinite number of possible combinations, and that therefore it is not, even apart from a designing mind, improbable that there should be worlds or stages in the development of a world which display great apparent purposiveness. Given sufficient time an army of monkeys strumming on typewriters at random would according to the laws of probability be likely to produce all the books in the British Museum. There is, I think, no scientific evidence that matter has been changing for an infinite time or extends infinitely in space, rather the contrary, and I doubt very much whether even the generous time allowance given by current astronomy would be sufficient to remove the improbability of there being so many such purposively organized bodies in the world. But in any case doubt is cast on the objection by reflecting what our attitude would be towards somebody who when playing bridge had thirteen spades in his hand several times running, and then used such an argument to meet the charge of cheating. Our attitude to him would, I think, hardly be changed even if we believed that people had been playing bridge for an infinite time. If we were satisfied that matter had existed and gone on changing for ever, would we conclude that the presence of leaves on the ground in such positions as to make an intelligible book no longer provided evidence in favour of the supposition that somebody had deliberately arranged them? If not, why should this assumption upset the argument from design? Granted this universe, it is still a much less improbable hypothesis that it should really have been designed than that it should constitute one of the infinitely rare stages which showed design in an infinite series of chance universes. Similarly about space. It may be replied that we could not have lived at all except at such a stage, but the point just is that it is antecedently extremely unlikely that there should have been conditions under which we or any other beings similar to us could have lived.

I do not think that we can do justice to the empirical facts which users of the argument from design adduce by talking of 'unconscious purpose'. This notion seems to me unintelligible or outright self-contradictory, unless it either means that things go on as if there were a conscious purpose without there really being one or refers to the presence in a conscious mind of a purpose the presence of which in himself that mind has not introspectively discriminated (or perhaps for reasons such as psychoanalysts dwell on could not discriminate). In the former sense it does not solve but merely restates the problem, in the latter it would already presuppose a conscious mind. To explain the purposive character of organisms and remove the unlikelihood to which I have referred, one requires purposeful design, and I do not see how this could occur without consciousness. The coincidence between organs of animal bodies and the interests of the animals, if it is to be explained by purpose at all, requires that the purpose should consist in foreseeing the results of a certain structure and deciding accordingly to develop that structure, and this implies a conscious mind. No other explanation is an explanation by purpose at all, and to talk of a purpose which is not present in any mind seems to me as unintelligible as it would be to talk of triangles which had no extension. Spinoza sought to explain the appearance of design by reference to necessary laws without a designing mind, but it would be a very improbable coincidence that the laws happened to fit in with the results that would have been expected if purposes had been at work. This would still be an unlikely coincidence if, as I suppose Spinoza held, the laws could be deduced by some kind of superhuman logic. There is nothing, I think, in the nature of logic as such that makes it any more likely to lead to results which fulfil purposes, other than the purpose to reason logically, than would the mechanical alogical laws postulated by a modern physicist. As Stout said:

Teleological order belongs to mind by its own intrinsic nature, and it does not belong to mere matter by its own intrinsic nature. . . . The constituent particles of the material world might conceivably have been grouped in an endless multiplicity of alternative ways without positing such teleological order as we find . . . It is accidental to the nature of matter as such however completely it may obey causal law, that its parts should be combined and inter-related in this way; and as a mere question of chance the odds are immeasurably against it. There is, therefore, at least a strong presumption in favour of the first alternative, that the teleological order of nature in general has its source in mind.[1]

It is objected against the philosophical use of arguments from inverse probability that the probability of a hypothesis based on an argument is always some multiple of its probability antecedent to the argument and that such an argument is therefore invalid

[1] *God and Nature*, p. 262.

unless we can first show that the antecedent probability of its conclusion is not zero or infinitesimal. For a finite result can never be reached by the multiplication of zero or 1/infinity. It might be retorted, however, that even apart from other arguments for God, the force of which might be disputed, the widespread and deep intuitive conviction in God and the enormous part such a belief has played in the life of man, even though they do not prove its truth, give it at least a finite probability antecedent to any specific argument from design, and even if this antecedent probability were held to be very small, it would, if other objections against the argument from design can be overthrown, be quickly multiplied into an overwhelming probability in favour by the odds against such a purposive world as we know resulting from a chance conglomeration of atoms. This would directly follow from accepted formulae in probability theory. So to reply in this way it is not necessary to argue, even if it is true, that the belief in a mind behind the world is made very probable by other considerations, all that is needed is that its probability should not be zero or quite negligible, i.e. of the order of one in thousands of millions, which would amount to saying that something could be said for it and it is not known to be impossible that there should be such a mind. It might be thought that an argument like this would require the fulfilment of the impossible task of measuring these probabilities in numerical terms, but even though an exact numerical probability or improbability cannot here be specified, it is clear that in the absence of some explanation or counter-argument the occurrence of such a degree of purposiveness as we observe in nature would be more improbable than phenomena, such as the throwing of a die with the six uppermost a hundred times in succession, to the probability of which a definite numerical value had to be assigned so low as to disprove the theory of coincidence decisively for any reasonable man.

But I think the objection about antecedent probability can be met in a more radical way, namely by denying its fundamental assumption. It is true that before evaluating the probability of the conclusion supported by a particular argument we ought to consider its antecedent probability in the sense that we ought to take account not only of any probability given to it by the argument before us but of the probability it would have prior to this argument. But this antecedent probability should mean the probability given it by other arguments which have been or could

K

have been brought, and it does not follow that we must take into account the probability that the hypothesis would have prior to any argument whatever. This would be absurd, I should say, because probability is essentially relative to some data, and in that case it is no more reasonable to say that a supposition could be probable prior to any argument for it than to say something was inferior if there were nothing to which to compare it that could be called superior. Therefore inability to establish such absolute antecedent probability is no ground for rejecting an argument. We cannot reject it just because it does not fulfil a meaningless condition. And if applied in practice the requirement would lead to the conclusion that nothing that was not directly observed could ever be made probable because any argument establishing its probability would have to be supplemented by another argument that it was probable prior to the first argument and so on *ad infinitum*.

We have now considered a number of objections to the argument from design, but two of the most difficult problems remain, the problem raised by the occurrence of dysteleology and the question as to whether the acceptance of the theory of evolution does not largely destroy the force of the argument from design. Of the former I shall say very little; it is part of the general problem of evil, which there is not space to discuss here, and which must in any case be a problem for theism. It is not a special objection to the argument from design as an argument but to its conclusion, except in so far as it is thought that the methods apparently adopted by Nature are not worthy of a mind of great goodness and intelligence. I shall just make a remark which may seem unfair but which I think is highly apposite, namely that apparent design is a much stronger argument for the presence of a superhuman mind than is apparent absence of design or even apparent presence of poor design as an argument against it. For it is antecedently highly probable that, if there is a God, a large part of His doings will be quite incomprehensible to us and so appear without purpose or even perhaps to have a bad purpose. What view should we take of the logic of a dog who argued that I was a being without any intelligence because he could see no purpose in my present activity of writing this article? Yet the wisdom of God presumably exceeds ours in a much greater degree than ours exceeds the intelligence of a dog.

I thus hold that at least prior to the establishment of the

theory of evolution by natural selection the argument from design
was a very powerful one, but I am not sure how much its force
has been diminished by the establishment of this theory. For an
alternative explanation of the appearance of design is now provided of a kind which would not involve the supposition of a
designing mind. Evolution is of course perfectly compatible with
the ultimate creation of the world by God and may indeed be
regarded by a theist as just the way in which God created living
beings. But the question is raised whether the evolution theory
does not explain the appearance of design sufficiently to leave no
further ground for posulating a designer to explain it. Whether
there are held to be other grounds for the belief in God or not,
at any rate it may be thought that the argument from design
disappears. To this various replies have been made. It has been
said that for the evolutionary process of natural selection to start
at all there must be organisms capable of reproduction, but even
the simplest such are far more complex than a motor-car, and
it would certainly be ridiculous to suppose inorganic matter
coming together of itself fortuitously to form a motor-car. It has
also been urged against the probability of an explanation of the
appearance of design simply by natural selection that, since one
may go wrong in a vast number of ways for any one in which one
may go right, the probability of a random variation being unfavourable is much greater than that of its being favourable; that
in order to produce the required effect on survival a variation
would have to be large, but if it were large it would usually lessen
rather than increase the chance of survival, unless balanced by
other variations the occurrence of which simultaneously with the
first would be much more improbable still; and that the odds are
very great against either a large number of individuals in a species
having the variations together by chance or their spreading from
a single animal through the species by natural selection. It has
further been contended that, since any organic life depends on
extremely complex inorganic conditions, the necessity for supposing design reappears in the inorganic world, where evolution
by natural selection cannot be adduced as a possible explanation.
I am afraid I have not the biological knowledge required to discuss
these arguments adequately, but at any rate when we reflect that
the human brain contains ten thousand million cells organized
into a working system, it should surely appear by no means clear
that it is not wiser to suppose that this was the result ultimately

of design by a mind than to suppose even with the help of natural selection that a universe in which such systems are so common resulted ultimately from a fortuitous concourse of atoms. The argument from design I hope I have shown by no means deserves the contempt which in some quarters is poured on it.

But apart from the specific argument from design I am still more impressed by the fact that, when I consider the physical world, its order, its system, its beauty strongly suggest that it is a product of mind or at any rate that the least inadequate category for interpreting it is mind.

INDEX

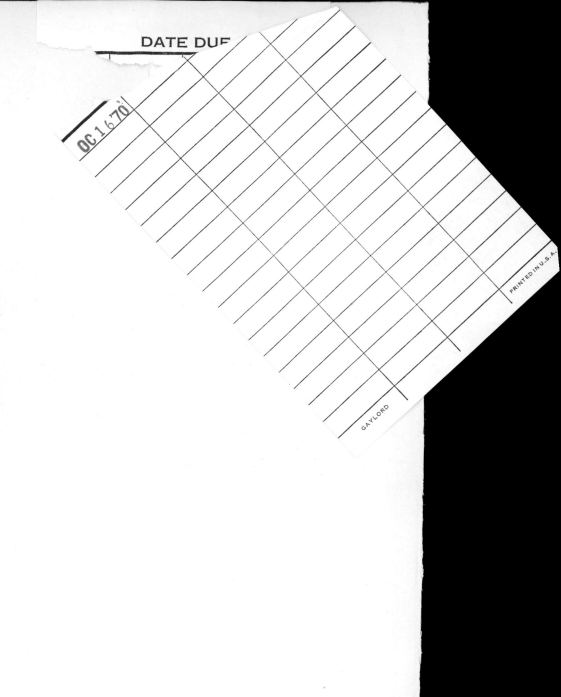